Debbie Piner

Entering
child's world

A PLAY THERAPY APPROACH

Entering the child's world
A PLAY THERAPY APPROACH

J P Schoeman
M van der Merwe

ENTERING THE CHILD'S WORLD
A PLAY THERAPY APPROACH

Copyright © Kagiso Publishers 1996
Masada Building, cor. Proes & Paul Kruger Streets, Pretoria 0002
PO Box 629, Pretoria 0001

Bloemfontein • Cape Town • Durban • King William's Town •
Mmabatho • Pietersburg • Port Elizabeth • Pretoria • Umtata

First edition, first impression 1996/01

Typeset by Kagiso Publishers DTP
Artwork by Willem Loots, Designaline, Kempton Park
Cover artwork courtesy Santam Child Art Collection: "Happiness is being friends"
by Nicolellette Garrett, Cresta Nursery School, Randburg
Printed and bound by Sigma Press (Pty) Ltd, 43 Eland Street, Koedoespoort, Pretoria

ISBN 0-7986-3558-4

© All rights reserved. Apart from any fair dealing for the purposes of research, criticism or review as permitted under the Copyright Act, no part of this book may be reproduced or transmitted in any form or by any means, electronic or mechanical, including photocopying and recording, without permission in writing from the publisher.

About the authors

Dr Hannie Schoeman is a senior lecturer in the Department of Social Work at the University of Pretoria. She also has a private practice, in which play therapy informs her work with children.

Mariëtte van der Merwe is editor of *Social Work Practice* which is associated with the Department of Welfare. In her private practice, she concentrates on crisis intervention and short-term therapy with traumatised children, emphasising a play therapy approach.

Siphiwe Matsemela is a senior social worker at the Jubvlani Place of Safety. She has postgraduate training in the play therapy approach, which she applies to her work in the welfare field.

Preface

The very relevant issue of direct work with children is the subject of this book. However, to students (whether formal or informal), a background knowledge of the theory of play therapy must precede practical work. Furthermore the building of theory in any discipline is an on-going process. *Entering the child's world: A play therapy approach* must therefore be viewed as a starting point in the study of play therapy in South Africa, and as an instrument to stimulate discussion and share views.

An important aspect to be noted here is the necessity of placing play therapy within a firmly South African context. South Africa is typified by a diversity of languages and cultures. Consequently, it is logical to ask if the approach described in this book is applicable to children from all cultural groups, as in many cases techniques have been thus far mostly used with white, middle class children. Therefore, the reader is asked to test the techniques on children from other cultural and socio-economic groups, to adapt them as necessary, and to write about them in social work journals. This is the only way in which the knowledge base on work with children can be expanded and can be made relevant to the South African situation.

On the other hand, the important common characteristic of the target group, namely, that they are all children, means that they share some of the common features that were incorporated in the development of this approach. When working with children, techniques that are simple and pleasurable and that make provision for a short attention span should be effective. This is true of most of the techniques described here. Keeping in mind that the forms of play should be practical enough to use in even the most deprived communities, most of them do not require expensive material. For instance, the hand puppet which is the most effective in therapy is a cheap, simple doll made from an empty soup packet or jelly box cut open on one side with a child's drawing of a monkey face stuck to the open side, making provision for the opening to serve as a mouth. This is made of waste material and should be possible to obtain even in the poorest community. The more expensive stuff is often so elaborate that it tends to divert children's attention to the detail and colour.

As far as possible, the authors have tried to make suggestions for adaptations to the techniques described and to make them affordable for everyone. Regarding cultural differences, only testing and retesting will show in the end which techniques are suitable for the broadest range of children.

As the development of cross-cultural competence is not the focus of this book, it seems fitting to provide readers only with a basic philosophy, described by Lynch and Hanson (1992:xviii), to serve as a fundamental guideline for cross-cultural intervention. The philosophy is based on three primary emphases, namely:

- A prerequisite to successful intervention is that therapists should have an understanding of their own cultural, ethnic and language background and their values and beliefs about individuals who are different from themselves. This points to the importance of self-awareness.

- All families/children/clients are unique. Although they are influenced by their ethnic, cultural and language backgrounds, they are not fully defined by them. Differences in these areas should therefore be used to enhance interactions rather than to stereotype or to function as the only determinant in the approach to intervention.
- The interventionist's role is twofold. First, it is his or her obligation to work together with the family to develop culturally sensitive intervention techniques. Second, the new (or mainstream) culture should be interpreted to the family and family members should be assisted in finding ways to negotiate it.

Lynch and Hanson (1992:xix) state that the current match between many professionals and the families whom they serve is not perfect. However, this should not impede the rendering of a high quality service. Child therapists need to expand their cross-cultural competence and learn to respond sensitively and appropriately to clients from cultural groups different to their own.

Acquiring cross-cultural competence is essential for the child therapist following a goal-directed, individualised approach. Each child's cultural heritage, language and ethnicity should be taken into account during the assessment, planning and implementation of a helping strategy.

The use of the male pronoun (he, etc.) for the child client and the female pronoun (she, etc.) for the therapist is for the sake of convenience only and no gender discrimination is intended.

The authors

Bibliography

Lynch, E.W. & Hanson, M.J. (Eds.). 1992. *Developing cross-cultural competence: A guide for working with young children and their families.* Baltimore: Paul H.

Foreword

Play is part of every child's world. Through play, the child gives meaning to the world by exploring it, by discovering it and by attaching values to what he/she sees, hears, smells and feels.

The child's world of the imagination is, however, just as, if not more, important, than the reality of the sensory world. In this way, the child can cross the boundaries of confining circumstanses, either physical or emotional. The child who grows up in a loving and secure world will easily venture into flights of imagination and transform his/her already meaningful world as if by magic into one in which the child creates meaning.

The world of the traumatised child is, by comparison, insecure, uncertain, alarming and inaccessible. In order to render meaningful aid to such children and enter their disordered world, adults ought to be able to know the child, that is to say, to understand the world of the child.

The writers of this professional work are such people. They can link up with the world of the child and even enter the world of imagination, and, with the aid of supplementary play therapy techniques, relieve and heal the pain and confusion of traumatised children.

Prof E.A.K. Hugo

Contents

Introduction

1 Knocking at the door: theoretical background

Summary 3

Chapter 1: Basic components of play therapy 6
           M van der Merwe

Chapter 2: The art of the relationship with children —
           A Gestalt approach.. 29
           J P Schoeman

Chapter 3: Sensory contact with the child........................ 41
           J P Schoeman

2 Entering the child's world: forms of play and techniques

Summary 61

Chapter 4: Projection techniques 64
           J P Schoeman

Chapter 5: Relaxation play 77
           M van der Merwe

Chapter 6: Fantasy, metaphor and imagination 85
           J P Schoeman

Chapter 7: Assessment play... 98
           M van der Merwe

Chapter 8: Biblio-play.. 108
           M van der Merwe

Chapter 9: Dramatic play... 128
           M van der Merwe

Chapter 10: Creative play 138
           M van der Merwe

3 Problem solving through play: intervention in specific problems

Summary 153

Chapter 11: Street children 157
P Matsemela and M van der Merwe

Chapter 12: Handling aggression in children 171
J P Schoeman

Chapter 13: The use of play techniques when counselling young children in a divorce situation 184
M van der Merwe

Index 201

Part **1**

Knocking at the door:

Theoretical background

Summary

Introduction (Definition)

There is an abundance of energy and strength hidden in children. The authors of this book are constantly amazed at children's ability to cope with threatening and frightening life events. Children are not as fragile as is often thought. Nonetheless, it is important to help hurt and traumatised children to use their limited energy constructively to work through their feelings, whereafter they should be helped to focus their energy on normal development.

The first part of this book presents basic theoretical knowledge regarding direct work with children. The authors believe that there is nothing as practical as good theory. They also agree with Compton and Galaway (1979:38) that professional social workers should be able to select from available theories an approach appropriate to the problem or need requiring professional attention. Applying knowledge differentially to specific situations and using theoretical knowledge as a strong foundation for practical outreach strategies is one of the strong points of the social work profession. The techniques and principles described in this book should be suitable for use in a variety of settings and with different systems and disciplines of various proportions and types.

Therapy is expensive and time-consuming. In the light of dwindling resources and overwhelming problems in Southern African society, child therapists should always evaluate the cost-effectiveness of their service. Working with the family or subsystems thereof, and with children in a group context is often more effective than working on a one-to-one basis. Working with bigger systems has the additional advantage of dynamic transactions that can lead to individual growth and development. Learning from people in the same situation can be very convincing. Within the group context, there is strong social energy, urging individuals toward better social functioning.

Components of therapy

Chapter 1 focuses on the essential components of therapy with children. The special characteristics of the child client is one of the main components determining the unique character of direct work with children. Adults in therapy seldom show the directness and innocence that is found with young children in therapy. A young girl of about six years old once expressed herself as follows, within the first ten minutes of the first interview: "I am going to visit you lots of times, hundred times, until you die." This little girl's mother died when the child was about four years old and the therapy was focused on helping her to work through her feelings and to cope with a new life situation involving remarriage of the father. So much could be read in her statement. Another boy was seen in a group with a few other children having to cope with divorce and remarriage. When the therapist reminded them of the termination of therapy following the next week, he lightly tapped her on the head, saying: "Bad dog, bad dog." Their comical ways with words can be very humourous. A little girl once told the therapist that her cat laid kittens in her cupboard. These unexpected moments make therapy with children interesting and very satisfying.

Child therapists should have specific knowledge, skills and the correct attitude. They should have mastered the basic knowledge of interviewing, communication, building of therapeutic relationships and problem solving so well that they can adapt it with ease to this specific target group. Other components discussed in this chapter are the use of limits in therapy and the nature of play material.

The therapeutic milieu is an important aspect. At times, it will be necessary to enrich or simplify the therapeutic milieu according to the child's needs. Children younger than four years often need a very basic setting for therapeutic inputs to have a chance to work against their wandering attention. They tend to focus on irrelevant material, such as the pictures on the wall, and especially the "wonderglue" keeping the pictures there.

The therapeutic relationship

The therapeutic relationship is described in more detail in chapter 2, from the point of view of a Gestalt approach. Therapists working from a Gestalt approach study the whole of the Gestalt, with the idea that the total is more than the sum of the parts (Van Niekerk, 1986:7).

As Perls (1969:16) has stated, "Gestalt is as ancient and old as the world itself." According to Gestalt theory, the free functioning of the body in nature forms natural and healthy behaviour. A Gestalt approach can therefore be seen as a self-regulating, natural approach.

The therapeutic relationship based on a Gestalt approach is an important tool in helping to unlock the child's deepest feelings, fears and frustrations. It is the instrument used to heal the child through meeting him in the therapeutic milieu. In such a relationship, the child is handled in a natural way, thinking, feeling and acting freely. It is important for the child's needs to be met, largely through the therapeutic relationship.

Sensory contact with the child

Chapter 3 highlights ways of getting into contact with the child. It is important that the therapist is also in contact with the child within, sorting out own past hurts and traumas. Counter-transference in therapy is a very real thing. When working with a child of alcoholic parents, the therapist who experienced the same situation will find that it reactivates own unresolved feelings. This may contaminate therapy. On the other hand, where the therapist has come to terms with her own experience, it may enhance inputs, especially regarding empathy and teaching coping skills. Burns (1988:3) views self-awareness as a vital part of the ability to form meaningful relationships.

Somewhere in every adult there are still residues of the child that he or she once was. Some people can remember the sensations and smells of childhood clearly, whereas to others childhood is simply a blur. It can be helpful to therapists to think back to their childhood, to try and recall their first memories and then to try and remember traumatic experiences with the feelings that they had in those situations.

Burns (1988:3-4) emphasises the value of having an awareness of the sensory modalities when trying to keep in step with children. People are inclined to prefer specific sensory modalities. As part of assessment, it would therefore aid therapy to know whether the child tends to be more visual (using visual words and focusing more on the visual aspects of what he observes); auditory (using words that primarily involve sound); or kinesthetic (learning best through the sense of touch and emotions). According to Burns (1988:4), kinesthetic children usually enjoy crafts, whereas auditory children's verbal skills are well developed. Visual imagery is a strong point in visual children. People tend to prefer specific personal distances and may feel uncomfortable if their preference is not taken into account. When assessing children, this aspect should also be taken into account.

Conclusion

Whatever the approach and techniques used in direct therapy with children, it is important to have a sound knowledge of the components of therapy with children, especially the therapeutic relationship and how to make contact with the child. Primary focus on the strengths of the client and his surrounding systems when striving for the realisation of goals should also be a basic premise.

Bibliography

Burns, M. 1988. Rapport and relationships: The basis of child care. *The Child Care Worker*, 6(2): 3-6.

Compton, B.R. & Galaway, B. 1979. *Social work processes*. Illinois: Dorsey Press.

Perls, F. 1969. *In and out the garbage pail*. Moab: Real People Press.

Van Niekerk, P.A. (Ed.). 1986. *Die opvoedkundige-sielkundige*. Stellenbosch: University publishers and booksellers.

1 Basic components of play therapy

M VAN DER MERWE

Introduction

The social work profession is aimed at alleviating people's problems and needs. This implies working with families, and therefore children are inevitably involved in the problem-solving process. Lieberman (1983:441) states that social workers are known to be the therapists who have been most involved with children through the years. Clinical work with children is an area of specialisation within social work. This work has a unique character which is, amongst others, determined by the special characteristics of the child client. Social workers dealing with children need specific knowledge and skills, as well as an appropriate attitude. This is in addition to the basic knowledge of interviewing, communication, the building of relationships and problem solving.

This chapter focuses on the unique character of counselling children, by looking at the components mentioned above. Other relevant aspects are the use of limits in therapy, play material, the therapeutic milieu, barriers that may be encountered and the involvement of significant people who are part of the child's world.

Characteristics of the child client

The unique characteristics of the child client give a special character to therapy. Greenspan (1981:1) states that children are complicated, but once the therapist understands their special language, they are found to be both uncomplicated and open. When contrasted with the adult client, the characteristics of the child client become especially clear. According to Porter (1983:114-120), there are three main factors that facilitate the differences between child clients and adult clients. These are the difference in age, the way the child handles the client role, and the child's unique experience of the therapeutic relationship.

Fraiberg (1952:77-60), Moore (1976:14), Smith (1979:175-176), Smith (1981:97-98) and the Group for the Advancement of Psychiatry (1982:49) all mention differences between child clients and adult clients.

Differences due to developmental level

- Children are in the process of development and their conduct will therefore be immature.
- There is an inability to conceptualise, especially concerning time and space. This may limit the structuring of the therapy.
- A child's span of attention is short. Moore (1976:14) refers to the "grasshopper mind" of the child client. When planning interviews, social workers should take this into account and allow enough variety in the program.
- As their intellectual abilities are still in the process of development, children usually take longer to gain insight than adults. This process may be helped by the use of visual aids.
- The use of fantasy is common, which makes it difficult to know when the child is giving a clear picture of reality. The child's ability to distinguish between fantasy and reality is still in the process of development. Inexperienced social workers may wrongly think that the child is telling lies.
- As his ego is still developing, the child's ability to handle internal impulses and external demands is limited. This is one reason why it is necessary to use limits in therapy.
- Children perceive their external world as being able to control them in a mysterious way. They may have unrealistic thoughts and fears concerning the social worker's power.
- Owing to a strong egocentric attitude, the child may act impulsively, seeking attention and self-satisfaction.
- The emotional influence of somatic and biological factors, such as thirst or hunger, is considerable and can be the cause of a low frustration tolerance level.
- As the child's self-identity is still unformed, his knowledge of himself and his aspirations is poor.
- Ambivalence is common, with the child showing no definite pattern in the handling of conflicts or problems.
- The cognitive ability to place himself mentally in someone else's shoes is lacking. As a result, the young child cannot feel empathy.

Differences in communication

- The child's style of communicating differs from the adult's. Non-verbal communication is especially prominent in the child and surfaces through play. Because the child's language skills are poorly developed, the use of simple language with appropriate voice tone and facial expression are necessary on the part of the therapist. Social workers may find it difficult to handle long periods of silence interrupted only by uncontrollable fits of giggling!

- Conversation is not always reliable, as verbal skills are still underdeveloped.
- The child does not usually respond well to questions.
- The verbalisation of feelings — even those on a conscious level — is difficult for the child as his knowledge of "feeling language" is usually limited.
- The use of language may shift between sophisticated language (possibly picked up from television), and childlike language. Moore (1976:14) describes this clearly: ". . . it is not always easy to attune oneself to the change between the tough, hardswearing four-year-old and the same child, crying and complaining that someone has taken his ball." This also demonstrates the lability of the child's emotions.
- Words like "helping", "helper" and "support" may have negative connotations when the child has heard that punishment is aimed at "helping" him.

Differences in the handling of the client role

- The child often finds the role of client strange. He does not see the social worker as a professional person with the aim of helping him. The structure of authority differs from the usual, in that the child may be in charge of the sessions. The acknowledgement of his right to self-determination and the prevailing permissiveness may be new to him.
- A formal atmosphere may be counterproductive, as children are so spontaneous. Usually, they have fewer defence mechanisms than adults do, and a relaxed atmosphere suits them.
- Children do not conform to the usual expectations of clients in a therapeutic situation. They will focus on irrelevant aspects such as the closing of the blinds or the number of tiles on the floor.
- Usually, a child is not involved in treatment by own choice, but because a grown-up has brought him.
- It is difficult for the therapist and child to formulate goals together, as the child does not have the necessary insight. Such formulation of goals is more effective when done visually.
- Children have problems in differentiating between long-term and short-term needs. Moore (1976:14) describes this: ". . . a child may wish to be placed with an aunt whose meals are a continuous round of baked beans and ice cream and could not be expected to be aware of his long-term nourishment needs."
- Children have difficulty in accepting the termination of therapy and are usually unable to determine when it is necessary.
- It is impossible to work with the child in isolation. Significant people, such as the parents, must be involved. Often, a child's problems can be directly associated with the parents' behaviour and circumstances.

Differences in the therapeutic relationship

- The individualisation and attention that the child experiences in therapy is in itself therapeutic even without any other inputs from the therapist.
- Children are more demonstrative and usually show their feelings clearly through words or actions.
- Children are honest and sincere in their communication regarding the relationship. When they do not find the sessions enjoyable, they will most probably say so. In this respect Moore (1976:13) warns: "Perhaps the greatest resistance to working directly with children is that they can spot a fake a mile off." When they do not trust the therapist, they are likely to show it in their attitude.
- Children are more spontaneous in the relationship than adults. During an interview with the author, a child made the following statement while drawing a picture of his mother: " Must I make-up my mother? Where is your make-up?" Once, while working on threatening areas, a child started to sing in order to stop the author.
- It is easy for a child to become dependent on the therapist.
- According to their needs, children will place the therapist in different roles.

Clearly, social workers working with children need to adjust to the unique child client to ensure that therapy will be successful. Apart from special knowledge and skills, special characteristics will help the social worker to reach the child and to handle the difficult task of meeting the child's needs successfully .

Characteristics required by the child therapist

It may well be asked if certain people enjoy hereditary characteristics which give them a natural touch with children. If this is so, it may then be asked if it is indeed possible for someone to learn to work with children. A good foundation for someone wanting to do this job is to have a basically positive feeling for children. In other words, the therapist should be able to work at the child's level of functioning. Ideally, the therapist's own childhood should not feel far away and unreal, but she should be able to recall her own feelings, fears and questions clearly. She must be in contact with the child within and should be able to assume the role of child again. This implies of course that she should not be upset by things like clay under her fingernails! Her appearance should not feature too significantly in the work situation, and she should dress in a way that creates a comfortable and informal atmosphere. She needs to master the art of professionalism combined with spontaneity and fun.

The therapist's training will already have proven that it is possible to learn certain skills by means of good supervision and practical work. This should, in any case, be true for motivated students who want to learn to work with children. Contact with young children affords the opportunity of refining techniques for reaching out and building relationships with children.

The characteristics of therapists in child care work are discussed below. (Holgate, 1972:xiii; Greenspan, 1981:1-2; Porter, 1983:141-154; Esman, 1983:18; Guerney, 1983:28; Jernberg, 1983:139):

- The therapist should be **emotionally mature** and balanced, with good social functioning. Her maturity should enable her to empathise with the child without over-identification.

- The child's behaviour is complex and the therapist should look out for hidden messages. She must understand what the child is trying to convey in therapy and must be able to devise a meaningful plan for counselling. Theoretical knowledge and practical experience should complement the **intelligence** of the social worker. Instinct and compassion are not enough.

- As the therapist sometimes has to continue the work under difficult circumstances, she must exhibit **perseverance**. It may take time to win the child's confidence and to open up the flow of communication.

- The therapist should be highly **responsible**. It is an enormous responsibility to help a child work through his feelings and to place him on the path to more healthy adjustment.

- **Friendliness** and **spontaneity** are necessary for the building of a relationship of trust. The therapist should be optimistic and cheerful.

- **Calmness** and **honesty** should be evident in the therapist's attitude, behaviour, thoughts and expression of feelings. Everything therapist does or says during therapy should be credible.

- It happens quite often that the child has lost confidence in the significant people in his life. It is the task of the therapist to help the child recover his trust in people. The therapeutic relationship should therefore also be characterised by trust and **reliability**. This implies, amongst others, that appointments should be strictly kept and promises be fulfilled.

- In order to make rapid decisions in the playroom, the therapist needs **self-confidence**. She must be able to trust her own judgement and devise relevant strategies and tactics as the situation requires.

- Complementing self-confidence should be **good judgement** and **the ability to make decisions**. The therapist dare not show signs of uncertainty in the therapeutic situation. Decisions sometimes rest on very little information. The kind of a person who needs overwhelming evidence before making a decision will most probably not be successful.

- **Love** and a positive feeling for children are necessary to enable the therapist to be honest, spontaneous, sincere and friendly. It is a good thing to be curious about the child's functioning and thoughts.

The therapist must be **sensitive** to the child's needs. She must be able to place herself in the child's shoes. A sensitivity to the atmosphere of the therapy will enable

her to know when to leave the child to work at his own pace and when to be more directive.
- The therapist's attitude should convey **warmth**. A positive outlook and a joy for living, as well as a good sense of humour, are all factors that influence the atmosphere of therapy.
- Good **interpersonal** and **communication skills** and the ability to build a relationship that will form the basis for special therapeutic events are necessary.
- **Self-knowledge** brings about control, understanding and acceptance. The therapist needs to acknowledge her own limited perspective.
- In order to maintain the child's attention, the therapist should be **creative**. Her initiative should develop in such a way that it surprises even herself. She must be able to move from one role to another in order to flow with the child's play. A good imagination is very functional.
- An exceptional **ability to listen** is essential. This encompasses the complete theory of correct listening. Listening is more than hearing. The emotional climate from which the child shares information should be "heard". The therapist needs to be able to place her own problems in the background and to open up all her senses when the child communicates.
- The therapist should move into the child's world with **empathy**. She must attempt to see situations through the child's eyes. Esman (1983:18), Mishne (1983:12) and Peoples (1983:80) see controlled regression, where the therapist reveals the flexibility of a child in cognitive thinking and behaviour, as a vital characteristic. The therapist should nevertheless succeed in maintaining her own identity, and she should keep in contact with reality.
- A good sense of **perception** and **observation** will aid the assessment of the child and the planning of treatment. Interpretations and conclusions should only be made after thorough observation.
- The therapist should not appear apathetic and tired, but must be able to keep up **energetically** with the child's pace.
- She must always aim at developing her skills and extending her knowledge. She should not become overconfident, but must in **humility** be prepared to learn from others, especially from the child client.

Naturally, the therapist cannot be expected to possess all the characteristics mentioned above. However, by taking note of the desired characteristics, the therapist can assess herself and work on areas of shortcoming.

Unique character of therapy with chidren

Various factors influence therapy with children. Possibly, the therapist will dress differently, and she will definitely communicate differently, than when working with adults. If the therapist uses the same office as for adult clients, it will possibly have to be arranged differently — the therapist's seating arrangements should be different, and she could have a variety of therapeutic aids and toys available. She may be lucky enough to have a separate playroom, otherwise she will have to make do with the available space and materials. It is quite possible to work with children while sitting on a river bank and playing with mud or clay. Expensive, sophisticated aids are not necessary.

Play material

The therapist's approach to therapy determines the nature of the play material to a great extent. Each child client with his specific problem should form the main criterion for the choice of play material.

Esman (1983:16-17), writing from a psychoanalytical perspective, proposes that it is not necessary to have a lot of play material, although there must be enough and it should be simple and durable. The therapist should feel comfortable with the material, and it should suit the space and other facilities in the room. This is in accordance with the psychoanalyst Klein's view that play material should be simple and non-mechanical (Mishne, 1983:280). Guerney (1983:27) adopts a client-centred approach. Her opinion is that the availability of play material is more important than the exact nature thereof.

Zwerdling (1974:7-8) warns that too much play material may lead to over-stimulation of the child and fragmentation of his thoughts. Only the material that the therapist can control ought to be allowed. Zwerdling compares this to a playwright who will not write a dog into a script if it would be impossible to control it on the stage.

Richards (1971:5), Rooney (1979:49-50), Kezur (1981:9), Mishne (1983:281) and Porter (1983:213) advocate relevant play material. This is categorised according to the different forms of play, namely, relaxation play, assessment play, dramatic play, creative play and biblio-play. However, the play material is not exclusively associated with a specific form of play. Certain items may therefore be mentioned more than once in the following discussion:

- **Relaxation play** aims at reducing the child's tension to open him up to therapy and the building of a therapeutic relationship. Common materials to use are musical instruments, tapes, puzzles, pets, games and finger paints.
- **Assessment play** is used to examine the child client's skills, phase of development, "feeling" language and other verbal skills, and his mastering of the environment. For this form of play, materials like games (ludo, chess and dominoes), incomplete sentences and pictures, wooden blocks and other building toys are used.
- **Dramatic play** has various functions, such as the remodelling of family life, expression of aggression or regression, playing out of feelings concerning gender, replay or working through traumatic situations, and preparation for anticipated difficulties. To help in achieving these aims, a variety of play material is needed, such as a play phone, farm and farm animals, cars, paper dolls, masks, glove puppets, finger puppets, inflated dolls, male, female and baby dolls, dolls' houses with enough dolls to portray at least two families, anatomically correct dolls, darts, games, soldiers, guns, clay, noisy instruments, hammer and nails set, trains, aeroplanes, kitchen utensils,

clothes for dressing up, doctor's instruments, and baby's bottle, bath and powder. Children can make their own dolls with clay or mealie leaves.
- **Creative play** is aimed at ventilation of feelings. For this, clay, sand, water, paint, paper, wooden blocks and mud may be used.
- **Biblio-play** leads to the development of insight and working through of feelings. Materials that may be used are books, comics, magazines, diaries, life books, camera, paper, calenders, maps and emotional barometers.

To hold the attention of the child and to make him feel at home in the therapeutic milieu, even general office equipment like paper clips, staplers, glue, scissors, tape, rope, a pencil sharpener and an eraser may be used as play material. Play material may be divided into **raw material** (clay and paint), **constructive material** (building blocks) and **completed material** (dolls and train sets) (Pringle, as cited by Crompton, 1980:56; Porter, 1983:216).

Controversial play material

Esman (1983:16-17) reasons that a therapist with a psychoanalytical approach should not use complicated games, play cards or construction toys as these may evoke resistance and limit communication. Gardner (1983:260) differs from Esman in that he argues that valuable observations can be made when playing board games. They are also relaxing and can be a valuable tool for relationship building. Esman (1983:18) does accept the value of simple games such as ludo or checkers.

According to Guerney (1983:35), the use of play guns is not acceptable to all therapists as they fear that this encourages violence. Guerney sees play guns as a helpful tool for the ventilation of aggression. When unavailable, children will often simulate by using their fingers as guns.

Not every therapist will find paint an acceptable medium as it can cause a mess. Guerney advises that paint only be used if the therapist doesn't mind the mess. It is better not to use paint at all than to show irritation and anxiety about it. Guerney is not in favour of the use of books in the client-centred playroom, as she believes that this discourages catharsis. Only when the child specifically requests it, will she allow books. The author uses a more structured, goal-directed approach and constantly finds that books and other biblio-therapeutic materials are the most effective in directing therapy to specific problems and needs.

Unusual aids such as pets and other animals are described by George (1988:400-416). Weiser (1988:339-376) describes the use of cameras, video-cameras and photos. In the chapter on children of divorce, a technique is described where photos are used to construct a lifeline, better known to child clients as a "washing line" of life events.

Criteria for choice of play material

Ginott (1961:240-245), Guerney (1983:33-34) and Thompson and Rudolph (1988:158) give clear criteria to employ when choosing play material:
- The material must have more than one function.

- ❏ It should encourage the expression of feelings.
- ❏ It should help to build the therapeutic relationship.
- ❏ It should be possible for more than one person to play simultaneously with the material so that the child can involve the therapist.
- ❏ It should aid the therapist in gaining insight into the child's thoughts.
- ❏ It should offer the child the opportunity for reality testing.
- ❏ It should help the child to express his needs symbolically.
- ❏ It should encourage catharsis and the development of insight.

Play material is an essential part of therapy with children. The material to be used with each child must be determined according to the child's personality, his problems and needs, the plans for intervention and the form of play. The approach of the therapist is also an important factor, especially the degree of direction given by the therapist. It must be stressed, though, that expensive material is not a necessity. Creativity and a willingness to make do with available material should adequately enable the therapist to reach the child client.

Counselling environment

It is difficult to give directions for the counselling environment. Instinctively, the child therapist wants to make the room colourful, cheerful and bright. Thompson and Rudolph (1988:33) warn that colourful items may divert children's attention. Even the fish in the fish bowl may prove disruptive. The therapist's appearance may divert the child's attention from therapy, especially when she wears conspicuous jewellery. Colourful ties or even the material of which a dress is made may prove to be a stumbling block. When the therapist is aware of this, she can use it to the advantage of the therapy — especially in the initial stages when the building of trust is essential. When she does wear a colourful dress, or a specific piece of jewellery that attracts the child's attention, it may be used as a general opener for the conversation.

The therapeutic milieu should help to make the child feel comfortable. It should offer the safe space that Kezur (1981:8) sees as a prerequisite for therapy with children.

Therapy rooms should be as soundproof as possible, preferably with washable walls and floors. To ensure the child's safety, electric plugs should be covered. Low cupboards with drawers are handy for storing material. As children feel more at ease when their feet can touch the floor, it is advisable to have low tables and chairs, as well as a big carpet. For storing material out of the reach of children, it is a good idea to have higher cupboards. Bulky cushions on the floor serve as places to sit, while at the same time contributing to a relaxed atmosphere (Kezur, 1981:8).

The author interviews children in a room adjoining her living-room. This particular room has no special features. There is no running water. Fortunately, it has an inexpensive carpet, as a few litres of cool drink have already been spilt there! The author does not serve cool drink during therapy, but children occasionally bring some along. (The author has not found it necessary so far to place limits on this practice.) Although a table and chairs are available in the room, the author and child client always sit on cushions next to a low table. Coming to a private home seems to help children to relax quickly in the beginning phase of therapy. When they come through the gate, they are welcomed by a lively fox terrier wanting to make friends. They then pass through a living-room instead of a waiting-room. Interviews are scheduled so that there is no waiting period.

Even though it is convenient when a welfare organisation has a playroom available, therapy and the use of different forms of play definitely do not depend on this. Moore (1976:14) and Porter (1983:215) support this view. Porter suggests that social workers always have a supply of play material available, to enable them to use it during home visits. Basic material does not take up much space. It should be possible to carry it around in a small bag.

According to Guerney (1983:36), play should not be restricted to the playroom. The outside playground may be used, as well as visits to places of interest, and hikes.

Use of limitations in therapy

A statement made by Moustakas (1953:15) concerning limitations in therapy has been echoed by numerous writers in the decades thereafter. He said: "Without limits there would be no therapy." The decades of the fifties and the sixties were, to a great extent, the golden age of play therapy, and they laid the foundation for current writing on the subject. The original sources are mentioned because much of what they say is still relevant today.

Limitations have various advantages, as indicated by Dorfman (1951:261), Axline (1969:130), Kezur (1981:9) and Guerney (1983:38):

- Limitations are a link with everyday life and therefore help the therapist and the child client to keep contact with reality.
- They give structure and set boundaries to the therapeutic relationship.
- They build the child's self-control, making him aware of his responsibility towards the therapist, the playroom and himself.
- Limitations offer security as they render predictability to the therapeutic situation.
- They ensure that the child is able to play safely and freely.
- They help the therapist to remain accepting of the child. It is difficult to accept a child bent on attacking the therapist or damaging the property. This is echoed by Dorfman (1951:258): "What therapist can feel accepting of a child who is in the process of flattening his cranium with a mallet?"
- Limitations ensure the child's emotional safety. Without limits, the child may move into unknown and threatening emotional areas, leading to anxiety and feelings of guilt. These feelings can block the therapeutic relationship.

Nature of limitations

The nature of limitations is discussed by various writers (Dorfman, 1951:257; Moustakas, 1953:15-16; Bredenkamp, 1953:40-41; Faure, 1966:33; Axline, 1969:131-132;

Joubert, 1970:49-53; Richards, 1971:6; Sloss, 1978:14; Rooney, 1979:49; Kezur, 1981:9-10; Rhoden, Kranz & Lund, 1981:191; Guerney, 1983:41; Peoples, 1983:82-83). The limitations that can be set in therapy with children are discussed under specific headings, described by Van der Merwe (1991:91-93):

Time limits

As the attention spans of young children are short and they tire easily, it is advisable to limit sessions to more or less 45 minutes. The child should be warned when there are only a few minutes left. If the child arrives late, the time should not be extended.

Limits on the use of material

Expensive and irreplaceable articles may not be damaged. Normally, the child should not be allowed to take material home. There are exceptions. The author usually asks child clients to bring an exercise book along. This is kept in the office for the duration of therapy. The therapist uses this to prepare therapeutic aids for the client, and important guidelines regarding problem solving and other skills are written or drawn in it. After the session, the child takes it home for further reference.

The application of this limit depends on the specific therapist and organisation. If they feel comfortable with children taking expensive material, such as crayons, paint, pens and other equipment, home, they should feel free to allow the children to do so. However, if restriction on this practice is placed early enough, it will avoid disappointment at a later stage.

Limits on aggressive behaviour

The therapist and her clothes may not be damaged. Any physical attack on the therapist should be stopped immediately. Dorfman (1951:258) offers a logical reason for this restriction, namely: "It saves wear and tear on fragile therapists."! There should be an absolute restriction on bullying.

Limits on movement

If the child leaves the room before the end of the session, except under certain circumstances, the session should be ended. Some children use endless visits to the toilet as an avoidance strategy.

Limits on people present

Usually only the therapist and the child are present, although parents, grandparents, friends and/or animals may be allowed, if necessary. Some therapists prefer to have parents in a passive role during interviews, while others involve the parents actively.

Health and safety restrictions

These limits are set for the protection of the child client and the therapist. It is, for instance, not allowed for children to climb through the windows!

Limits on affection

It is not acceptable for the child to keep contact with the therapist on a social basis between interviews. If this does happen, it can blur the role of the therapist. The therapist is allowed to show affection through touch and words when the situation requires it. Care must be taken that the child does not place the therapist in the role of a missing parent or other relative. When the child asks for gifts or if he has other special requests, it could be an attempt to bridge feelings of rejection experienced elsewhere. The therapist should not meet these needs in a superficial way, but should help the child, through play, to work through these feelings.

Moral limits

The child should not be allowed to remove his clothes; only shoes and jackets. Swearing is usually allowed in the playroom, but the child may not swear at passersby through the window.

There are alternatives concerning the time when restrictions should be discussed. Each alternative has certain implications. Limitations can be laid down in the first interview. If this is done at a later stage, after the child has behaved unacceptably, he may feel frustrated and cheated. On the other hand, if restrictions are discussed in the first interview, the child may see this as a challenge which could have a negative influence on his attitude. He may also inhibit the expression of negative feelings out of fear of the therapist's disapproval.

According to Axline (1969:132), the therapist should place restrictions as the need arises. She is of the opinion that children's experiences in everyday life do prepare them for limitations in therapy. It is helpful for therapy to limit the verbalisation of restrictions to only those situations where the necessity arises. This is underlined by Bredenkamp (1953:40), Guerney (1983:39) and Mishne (1983:285).

Van der Merwe (1991:93) concludes that certain limitations have to be mentioned in the beginning phase of therapy, for instance, time limits. This helps prevent disappointment and unrealistic expectations. Children need to know from the beginning that therapy is time limited, and they need to be given an idea of the duration of therapy.

Guidelines for stating and implementing limitations

Often, therapists have clarity on the restrictions that they want to place on the child in the therapeutic situation, yet they find it difficult to act when the child has broken a rule that has been laid down. The following are useful in this regard:

- According to Bredenkamp (1953:40), it is important that the therapist has clarity on the limitations she wants to place on the therapy. She must be able to put these limitations to the child in a concrete and simple way. Preferably, limitations should rest on an all-or-nothing basis. For instance, a total restriction on hitting the therapist should be made rather than telling the child that he may hit the therapist, but not too hard. A message like this may be confusing.
- When discussing and enforcing restrictions, the therapist should be as natural and

relaxed as possible. Peoples (1983:83) maintains that the therapist should avoid an attitude of aggression and of challenge to the child, as this can evoke defiance. According to Peoples, almost any form of punishment is acceptable, except corporal punishment.

- Concerning punishment, Moustakas (1953:16) advises that as a form of punishment, a toy or a part of the office be announced as a restricted area. The therapist can verbally reinstate the limitation. The child may be held firmly for a few minutes. If this is unsuccessful, he can be carried out of the room and the session will be over.
- According to Dorfman (1951:262), a therapist should be sincere when implementing limits. False reasons should not be given. When the child wants to play with the therapist's watch, for instance, it is better to say that the therapist is afraid that the child will break the watch than to say that the management is opposed to the child playing with it.
- The use of activity-channels to divert feelings of anger or to prevent damage to windows and other property is mentioned by Dorfman (1951:257). The child can scream as loud as he wants to, he may throw clay, hit something with a hammer or throw unbreakable toys. He has to learn in therapy that it is not necessary to deny feelings. However, there are acceptable ways of showing them.
- Guerney (1983:38,40) suggests that limits be sparse, clear and enforceable. To ensure the child's full attention, the therapist should use a firm tone of voice, eye contact, and address the child using his name.
- It is the responsibility of the therapist to maintain the limits. When a limit is not enforced by the therapist, it may threaten the child's sense of security within the therapeutic relationship, as breaking the rule may be his way of testing the therapist.
- The therapist must distinguish between a permissive attitude and the practical reality. The child cannot be allowed to hurt himself or to damage property. An attitude of exclusive permissiveness can lead to breaking windows and committing other damage. This can have a negative influence on the therapy, as the child may feel unsafe in the relationship. He may feel guilty. Another important factor to consider is that management and donors of welfare organisations will not accept intentional damage to property (Van der Merwe, 1991:94).
- Guerney (1983:39) describes a three-point plan for implementing limitations in therapy:
  - state the rule
  - remind the child of the rule and state the implications of breaking it
  - remind the child of the rule and the implications and implement punishment.
- In certain instances, mentioning a limitation may be seen as a challenge, for instance, limitations regarding physical attacks on the therapist. It is better not to mention the limitation if an attack on the therapist is not happening, and then to handle it firmly if it does occur. However, limitations on play material and other practical issues may be discussed, as this is part of the reality that confronts the child daily.

It seems, then, that those limitations that are part of the child's everyday life, like a limitation on breaking things, can be discussed freely. More unnatural behaviour, like undressing in therapy, or attacking the therapist, should not be discussed, as it very seldom occurs. it should be sufficient only to mention that the child is not allowed to damage property, and better not to be too specific. As soon as the therapist says, for instance, that the child is not allowed to break a window, the child may regard this as a challenge.

The therapeutic approach usually influences the therapist's use of limitations in therapy. Rhoden, Kranz and Lund (1981) have made a study of this. Therapists with a non-directive approach were found to be more open to allowing the children to leave the room, to put off lights, to make a mess with sand and paint and to physically attack the therapist. Limitations regarding symbolic expression were not used often by any therapists. In general, all the therapists were more open to the use of foul language and obscene drawings than usually prescribed by society. Children were generally prohibited from shouting obscene words to passers-by.

The use of limitations in therapy can be seen in relation to the principles of acceptance and adopting a non-judgemental attitude. Thompson and Rudolph (1992:48-49) stress that acceptance does not imply total permissiveness on the part of the therapist.

Being non-judgemental also does not imply total permissiveness. Although therapists should not be moralising, critical or accusing, they should encourage responsible behaviour that is in line with reality. The use of limitations, when used correctly, can be therapeutic when it develops ego strength and impulse control.

Communication with the child client

Communication with children differs from communication with grown-ups. This applies universally, but especially during therapy. Non-verbal communication is particularly prominent. This is expressed through gesture, facial expression, appropriate touching and playing.

According to Dennison and Glassman (1987:vii), a verbal approach is not effective with young children, especially when they are having problems. They recommend that therapists use play activities to help children work through sensitive and difficult problems.

Wardle (1975:429), Winnicott (1977:8) and Crompton (1980:13) refer to social workers' lack of direct communication with child clients. Social workers tend to do work *about* children instead of *with* them. Why then is an action that seems to be so obvious, so neglected? One of the main tools of social workers is communication. Even so, the "hasn't he grown" syndrome, as Wardle (1975:430) puts it, is still a common thing. Just as sighted people tend to talk in front of blind people as if they were deaf as well, adults tend to talk about children while they are present as if they could not hear. Wardle (1975:430) looks for an answer in the following:

> Combine busyness and interstaff tensions and avoidance of painful feelings and not-quite-knowing-how-to-talk-to-children and not-wanting-to-be-shown-up-in-front-of-other-adults-if-he-won't-talk-to-you and he-

won't-understand-anyway and the child whether two or twelve, has no chance of being communicated with, let alone of communicating.

Here Wardle points out a number of stumbling blocks in the path of successful communication with child clients. Social workers are expected to put a large amount of energy into the maintenance of the organisation. Fortunately, more and more social workers are working from private practices where they can run their practices without outside pressures.

Another problem is a lack of know-how in communicating with children. Possibly, social workers are simply expected to be able to communicate with children in need. The social worker who has suddenly been confronted by a young child in a wheelchair, who is terminally ill, will know the difficulty experienced in finding the right words. It is a myth that social workers are "good with children".

Fortunately, there are ways of improving communication with children. These are mentioned by Zwerdling (1974:3-7), Winnicott (1977:10), the Group for the Advancement of Psychiatry (1982:98-102) and Thompson and Rudolph (1992:44-45):

- Correct observation of the child client's non-verbal communication and active listening to his verbal communication are the essence of mutual communication between social worker and child.
- The therapist should be open to the message the child is trying to convey and should react accordingly. When a message is not clear, the therapist should clarify it. The young child's communication is often unclear with messages such as, "No, I want a biscuit." It is important to listen to the complete sentence and not only to react to the "no".
- Periods of silence must be allowed.
- The therapist should show respect and not adopt a paternalistic attitude in relation to the child.
- Giving advice is not always desirable. It is usually better to help the child make his own decisions.
- It is good to laugh *with* the child, but never *at* him.

  The therapist should take care not to overwhelm the child with his knowledge and power.
- The therapist should use language that the child understands, both verbally and non-verbally.
- Clichéd expressions should be avoided, as they can come across as insincere and artificial.
- Moore (1976:14) and Mitchell (1981:189-201) recommend the use of third-object techniques. Mitchell, for instance, uses letters to an imaginary kangaroo in order to reach young children.
- Active listening is crucial. Crompton (1980:34-35) writes that it is a pity that therapist are often so busy with the giving and receiving of information and facts that they do not really listen to the child. Even when a child talks about seemingly gen-

eral, meaningless happenings, there may be a deeper meaning behind the words. They can also be used as an opener for deeper communication.

- Therapists should work on conversation openers with children. In the literature, there are various examples, for instance: "Can you whistle?" (Holgate, 1972: xii), "Hallo, I am glad that you are visiting me with your red shoes on!" (Winnicott, 1977:9) and "What would you say if a fairy knocks on your door and grants you three wishes?" (Moore, 1976:14). An unexpected way of greeting can even be tried when the child meets the therapist for the first time. Look at the child and say something like "Good morning, Mrs Smith." Then point to the mother accompanying the child and say "I assume this is Mary who is coming to play with me." Every child therapist should converse in a way in which she feels comfortable. Finger puppets may be used for children who are very anxious during the first interview. For the first part of the interview, all the talking can be directed through these dolls. Lots of initiative and creativity are necessary.

- According to Holgate (1972:xii) and Winnicott (1977:10), a neutral zone must be created where the therapist and the child share mutual experiences. Such a joint experience is a form of non-threatening communication. When the communication and the relationship deepen, the therapist can refer back to this experience. This can strengthen the relationship and pave the way for therapy. Shared experiences should be planned, keeping in mind the child's unique personality, as well as aspects such as time and available facilities. These experiences need not be complicated or lavish. Even a drive in a car or a game can serve this purpose. A neutral zone is helpful in relieving the child's tension and it leaves him more open to therapeutic inputs.

- Various practical aspects are conducive to good communication with children. Guerney (1983:45) suggests that the therapist sit at the same height as the child. The power that is sometimes associated with height will then be replaced by a sense of equality through face-to-face and eye contact. The therapist should try to keep the tone of her voice even, irrespective of what the child tells her — the child can be inhibited if the therapist conveys shock through facial expression or tone of voice. The therapist's body language should show the child that she cares. Body language should be congruent with what is conveyed verbally.

- The physical distance between the therapist and child client should be determined by what they feel comfortable with. However, if a child therapist feels uncomfortable when a child wants to sit on her lap, she should reconsider her area of work. During assessment, a child's preferences regarding personal space should be determined.

- Spontaneous, timely and sincere physical contact is a very special form of communication. This conveys to the child that he is a worthwhile human being, while also carrying a strong message of comfort and consolation. When handling strong emotions and difficult problems during therapy, some children might seek close physical contact with the therapist in order to gain the strength to work through their problems.

To ensure meaningful, healing communication with children, therapists need to work through their own unresolved feelings concerning their childhood (Wardle, 1975:430; Moore, 1976:13; Thomas, 1977:1). Direct work with children in need is difficult. Their suffering cannot always be successfully alleviated through therapy. This may lead to counterproductive feelings of helplessness in the therapist. This will restrict communication. However, therapists have a theoretical basis regarding interviewing that can be used in direct work with children. Various play techniques can be used to enhance communication, as discussed at length in later chapters.

The therapeutic relationship

The therapeutic relationship is a crucial factor in the helping process. The quality of this relationship determines the child's susceptibility to therapeutic inputs. Gardner (1976:194) mentions various reasons for the necessity of a good therapeutic relationship:

- Within a good relationship, it is possible for the child to communicate with the therapist on a deeper level.
- Within such a relationship of trust, the child's identification with the therapist will be enhanced.
- The strength of the relationship should motivate the child to handle the frustration that often accompanies therapeutic change.
- The relationship should motivate the child to become involved in other healthy, corrective emotional experiences.
- The relationship should enable the child to strive for further therapeutic growth such as the development of his self-image.

Smith (1979:170-182) and Porter (1983:354-357) mention certain factors that are beneficial for the therapeutic relationship. The therapist should have a good knowledge of childhood development, including physical growth, emotional development and spiritual development. This will prevent her from having expectations that are too high and that will discourage the child. There should be consistent, empathic authority in the relationship. Furthermore, it should not only be a good relationship, but, indeed, a relationship of trust. This implies reliable, honest conduct by the therapist and acceptance of the child. Before the child can accept the therapist and her demands, he must first feel accepted.

Mutual communication is vital. This should include authentic self-disclosure. In the beginning phase of therapy, a simple visual questionnaire (see figure 7.1) can be used to find out what the child's preferences are regarding taste, colour, smell, sound and touch. The therapist can then disclose her preferences in this regard. Later in therapy, after the child has shown a readiness to work on a more personal level, the therapist can share more of her own experiences and feelings.

Moore (1976:13) stresses the need for objectivity in the relationship. The therapist must be able to handle intense feelings and fluid emotions without being thrown off balance. This also implies that she must be able to remain calm and clear headed.

According to Zwerdling (1974:5), the continuity of the relationship is important. The therapeutic situation should be more or less the same every time so that the child knows what to expect. The author has found a continuity object to be helpful. In one case, an old whistle was used. Each time the child came for an interview, he asked for the whistle. He played with it and kept it in his hand during the interviews, as if it gave him security. When a child brings his own exercise book to therapy, it is helpful for revising previous inputs and for continuity.

Children find it difficult to visualise the relief they should experience at the end of therapy. It is too abstract a concept, besides which children function on a direct pleasure-pain principle. Therefore, Zwerdling (1974:6) advises that the therapeutic relationship should be positive. One way of keeping it positive is by planning lots of pleasurable activities to ensure that therapy is fun.

Skills that therapists use in the building of relationships with adults can also be applied in direct work with children. However, the special characteristics of children should be kept in mind and the necessary adaptations be made. The therapeutic relationship is discussed in more detail in chapter 2.

Obstacles in therapy with children

Holgate (1972:xiv), Zwerdling (1974:10-12), Crompton (1980:13-24), Mishne (1983:12-13) and Van der Merwe (1991:100-103) name obstacles that may be encountered in therapy with children:

- When a therapist resigns during a critical stage of therapy or even takes leave, the child may feel rejected or abandoned.
- The therapist may feel embarrassed when the child asks awkward questions. When the child conveys with typical honesty that he does not like the therapist, the latter may feel rejected.
- Therapists may feel frustrated, bored or angry during interviews. This is a common human reaction. The child will most likely sense these feelings.
- The therapist may feel uncomfortable with her role and task. She may find it difficult to stay involved with the child's play or to communicate on an informal level. She usually feels safer within the boundaries of a more typically professional relationship. When she has to handle more or less the same problem with different child clients, her ability to observe may be negatively affected. The important principle of individualisation may be neglected, while she may tend to generalise too easily. Insufficient knowledge and experience may also prove to be a stumbling block.
- Working with children requires a great deal of energy. The therapist may experience physical problems, such as headaches or fatigue, thus reducing her involvement in therapy.
- According to Mishne (1983:4), therapy with children is multidimensional. Usually, the therapist needs to work with the child, as well as significant people in his envi-

ronment. Support systems, such as the school and church, are usually involved, and it is often necessary to change the child's environment. All these inputs are taxing and can elicit a variety of negative responses from the therapist, such as a lack of interest, pessimism and making inputs that are merely instinctive and aimless.

- As a result of personal, negative experiences, the therapist may encounter feelings of transference in relation to the child client. This will be especially prominent when she is helping the child to work through an experience such as a divorce, but still has unresolved feelings regarding a similar personal experience.
- The therapist's personal problems are a potential obstacle. Although it is difficult, the therapist needs to put aside her own problems during therapy with children.
- As working through children's problems is a slow process, therapist sometimes give false reassurances to their child clients in order to speed up the process.
- A therapist may not enjoy working with children for a variety of reasons. She may feel guilty playing during working hours. She may feel, too, that working with children is not really intensive enough and that she can spend her time more fruitfully.
- The child may become overly dependent on the therapist.
- Mishne (1983:4) sees children as so-called captive clients who do not come for help voluntarily, but are brought there by parents or teachers. This may lead to passive or more active forms of resistance.
- Within the current policy of welfare programming, individualisation may be lost.
- It is difficult to remain neutral towards child clients. Feelings that obstruct objectivity are anger, pride, rejection, anxiety, boredom, sexual stimulation and overprotection. When the child is antagonistic or suspicious, it may elicit subjective feelings from the therapist.
- In order to give immediate relief to parents, the therapist may tend to minimise the child's problems before a thorough assessment has been completed.
- When a child is difficult and emotionally draining, the therapist may feel trapped in the relationship.
- Parents are sometimes distrusting and prevent the therapist from working directly with the child. This may also happen when they feel guilty about their part in the child's problem.
- The child will experience problems with the relationship when he is uncertain about the therapist's role and function.
- When other professionals become part of the helping team, the therapist may lose confidence.

Direct work with children is definitely not easy. It is, however, important to make the relevant inputs at the right time to prevent problems in the long term. When therapists are aware of the obstacles that can obstruct direct work with children, they can work around them more easily by using supervision, taking leave on a regular basis and looking at ways of relieving work tension.

Involvement of parents and other significant people

It is not possible to work with children in isolation. Parents and other significant persons must be involved during assessment and also later on in therapy. Without this involvement, it is quite possible that treatment will be terminated before the helping process has been completed. Zwerdling (1974:14-20) and Mishne (1983:28) advise that the involvement of parents during assessment helps them to become more actively involved in the rest of the treatment. This also removes the mystery that may surround therapy. The parents can evaluate the therapist and decide if this is the best person to help their child. Zwerdling feels that parents must be seen before the first contact with the child.

The author always sees the parents first, and the basis of assessment is an interview schedule that focuses mainly on the family background (only briefly), the child's development (from before birth), his reactions to the stressful life event that brought them to therapy, the variables that influence the reactions and an overview of his play form preferences. Smith (1979:177) also views the involvement of parents in child therapy as a basic starting point in the approach to working with children.

Gardner (1976:50) allows parents to be present during interviews. This saves time, as he does not have to repeat what happened during the interview. When parents are present, they can learn from the therapist when she models certain managing techniques. When they have been present, parents often do the follow-up work with more conviction. They feel involved in therapy, and this may reduce feelings of guilt or helplessness. Parents should be involved as partners in the helping process. They are usually expected to put their own concerns aside and to try to remain neutral for the child's sake. The author leaves the choice to parents as to their presence during interviews. When using certain techniques, though, they are expected to be present, for instance when using the lifeline — the so-called washing line technique described in chapters 8 and 13. Quite often, parents prefer not to be present during interviews for two main reasons. They fear that their presence will inhibit the child. They also fear that they will not be able to control their own emotions.

Blitstein (1982:192) also involves parents in the therapy of their children. He demonstrates to them how to play with their children and how to have fun together. Often, parents can help with the interpretation of the child's play from their reference point. The therapist should be careful not to feel that she must save the child from his wicked parents and then offer the child a substitute parental relationship. She should rather help the parents to function more effectively in the parental role.

Gardner (1976:48-50) mentions certain contraindications to parental involvement:

- when parents have borderline psychotic behaviour
- when they are very dominating
- when the child is not ready to talk about or play out negative feelings regarding the parents in their presence.

Gardner acknowledges the fact that such parental involvement is taxing for the therapist. She may feel embarrassed and uncertain. Whilst in the waiting room, the parents may believe that the therapist works in a highly professional way. Even though this is usually the case, it is not so clearly recognisable when using low-level activities that look unnecessary or high-level activities that are too difficult to comprehend. The parents may think that all this playing is a waste of money and may terminate the therapy. Gardner takes this risk, as he firmly believes in the value of parental involvement. Furthermore, it is an incentive for the therapist to work effectively and efficiently.

The author finds it satisfying to see how parents gain insight into the child's behaviour while observing the interview. It is also encouraging to experience how enthusiastically they become involved in interviews after showing some apprehension at first.

The involvement of other significant people will differ for each child. Such people may include teachers, members of the extended family, friends, instructors or trainers. When children experience problems, the school and teachers are often the one stable factor. Before people outside the immediate family are involved, the parents and the child must first give their consent. There should be a reasonably free flow of information within the network involved in therapy.

Conclusion

It is clear that direct work with children is unique, but ordinary at the same time. It is familiar, but also unfamiliar and sometimes even unconventional. It is highly complicated, but uses elementary principles. It is therefore misleading in its simplicity.

For the non-professional, the fun and pleasure that are an inherent part of direct work with children may seem to be detrimental to the quality of the work. Child therapists, on the other hand, know that a formal, tense atmosphere is not conducive to the counselling of children. It is an art to use play correctly, so that something that is part of the child's everyday experience becomes the tool whereby his problems are addressed. The different components of therapy discussed in this chapter need to be adapted according to each child client's specific needs, problems and special features.

Bibliography

Axline, V.M. 1969. *Play therapy.* New York: Ballentine Books.
Blitstein, S. 1982. Playful therapy: The water pistol shootout. *Social Work*, 27 (2): 190-192.
Bredenkamp, M.A. 1953. Speelterapie. Unpublished MA thesis. Stellenbosch: University of Stellenbosch.
Crompton, M. 1980. *Respecting children: Social work with young people.* London: Edward Arnold.
Dorfman, M.A. 1951. In Rogers: 235-277.
Esman, A.H. 1983. Psycho-analytic play therapy. In Schaefer & O'Connor: 11-20.
Faure, J.S.M. 1966. *Die pedagogiese diagnostisering en behandeling van gedragsmoeilike kinders deur middel van spel, met verwysing na bepaalde pedagogiese kriteria*: Pretoria: HAUM.
Fraiberg, S. 1952. Some aspects of casework with children: Understanding the child client. In Holgate: 57-71.

Gardner, R.A. 1983. The Talking, feeling, doing game. In Schaefer & O'Connor: 259-274.
George, H. 1988. Child therapy and animals: A new way for an old relationship. In Schaefer: 400-418.
Ginott, H. 1961. *Group psychotherapy with children: The theory and practice of play therapy.* New York: McGraw-Hill.
Greenspan, S.I. 1981. *The clinical interview of the child.* New York: McGraw-Hill.
Group for the Advancement of Psychiatry. 1982. *The process of child therapy.* New York: Brunner Mazel.
Guerney, L.F. 1983. Client-centered (non-directive) play therapy. In Schaefer & O'Connor: 21-64.
Holgate, E. (Ed.). 1972. *Communicating with children.* London: Longman.
Jernberg, A.M. 1983. Therapeutic use of sensory-motor play. In Schaefer & O'Connor: 128-147.
Joubert, M.F. 1970. Die verhouding tussen die terapeut en die pasiënt in speelterapie met 'n tienjarige seun. Unpublished MA thesis. Stellenbosch: University of Stellenbosch.
Kezur, B. 1981. Play therapy as a mode of treatment for disturbed children. In Martel: 7-24.
Lieberman, F. 1983. Work with children. In Rosenblatt & Waldfogel: 441-465.
Martel, S. (Ed.). 1981. *Direct work with children.* London: Dorset Press.
Mishne, J.M. 1983. *Clinical work with children.* New York: Free Press.
Mitchell, J. 1981. Letters from a kangaroo: A third object technique for working with the young. *British Journal of Social Work,* ll: 189-201.
Moore, J. 1976. The child client. *Social Work Today,* 8(3): 13-15.
Moustakas, C.E. 1953. *Children in play therapy.* New York: McGraw-Hill.
Peoples, C. 1983. Fair play therapy. In Schaefer & O'Connor: 76-88.
Porter, C. 1983. Spelterapie met die sorgebehoewende kind. Unpublished D. Phil thesis. Pretoria: University of Pretoria.
Rhoden, B.L., Kranz, P.L. & Lund, N.L. 1981. Current trends in the use of limits in play therapy. *Journal of Psychology,* 107: 191-198.
Richards, E. 1971. Working with the inner worlds of children. *Social Work Today,* 2(15): 5-8.
Rogers, C.R. (Ed.). 1951. *Client-centred therapy.* Boston: Houghton Mifflin.
Rooney, M.J. 1979. Play therapy. *Adoption and Fostering,* 95 (1): 49-50.
Rosenblatt, A. & Waldfogel, D. (Eds.). 1983. *Handbook of clinical social work.* London: Jossey Bass.
Schaefer, C.E. (Ed.). 1988. *Innovative interventions in child and adolescent therapy.* New York: John Wiley.
Schaefer, C.E. & O'Connor, K.J. (Eds.). 1983. *Handbook of play therapy.* New York: John Wiley.
Sloss, J. 1978. Play therapy for maladjusted children. *Social Work Today,* 9(46): 14-15.
Smith, C.M. 1979. Die gebruik van inhoude uit die sielkunde deur maatskaplike werkers in gevallewerk met die kind. Unpublished D. Phil thesis. Stellenbosch: University of Stellenbosch.

Smith, C.M. 1981. *Leer die kind ken: Riglyne vir die maatskaplike werker*. Pretoria: Academia.
Thompson, C.L. & Rudolph, L.B. 1988. *Counseling children*. (2nd ed.). California: Brooks Cole.
Thompson, C.L. & Rudolph, L.B. 1992. *Counseling children*. (3rd ed.). California: Brooks Cole.
Van der Merwe, M. 1991. Maatskaplikewerk-beraad met jong kinders in egskeiding situasies met fokus op speeltegnieke. Unpublished MA thesis. Stellenbosch: University of Stellenbosch.
Wardle, M. 1975. Hippopotamus or cow? On not communicating with children. *Social Work Today*, 6(14): 428-432.
Weiser, J. 1988. Phototherapy: Using snapshots and photo-interactions in therapy with youth. In Schaefer: 339-376.
Winnicott, C. 1977. Face to face with children: Communicating with children. *Social Work Today*, 8(26): 7-11.
Zwerdling, E. 1974. *The ABC's of casework with children. A social work teacher's handbook*. America: Child Welfare Leaque.

2 The art of the relationship with children — a Gestalt approach

J P SCHOEMAN

Introduction

Research on factors contributing to therapeutic success consistently points to the importance of the therapeutic relationship. In this context, Buber developed a model in Gestalt therapy called "healing through meeting" (Yontef, 1993:31). Healing here refers to a restoring of wholeness, with the full engagement taking place in the here and the now. Therefore, the I-Thou relationship is very important.

In building a relationship, with a child client in particular, it is necessary to look at the level of the child's awareness. If the child is not aware of himself, his interaction and his sensory functions, the possibility of working on his recovery and of building a good relationship with him is very slight.

Furthermore, before the therapist and the child can start working on the objectives for building a relationship, the therapist has to identify the main aims of the relationship.

Main aims of the therapist in building a relationship

- It is necessary to know what caused the problem that led the parent to bring the child for play therapy.
- It is necessary to bring the child into contact with his sensory, emotional and cognitive needs.
- The child must be helped to fulfil his own needs through play therapy. He must also know if he is realistic in his expectations.
- The child must know that there will be situations that may be painful, but necessary for his recovery.
- The child will also have to know that he will have to make choices and take responsibility for his own life.

- ☐ The child must be willing to relate to his environment and other people and accommodate his influence in the world.
- ☐ The therapist will have to make a study of the child's process. In other words, how does the child deal with his situation in the world? The child's self-regulatory system will have to be studied.
- ☐ The therapist will have to empower the child so that he can assume responsibility for his own life.

Stabilising a relationship

To establish a relationship with a child, it is first necessary to become the child's friend, his playmate. This concept might be unfamiliar to some therapists. However, the most important issue concerning the concept is probably the professionalism (or lack thereof) in being a child's playmate. The author is of the opinion that no child will spontaneously be willing to play and share secrets with a total stranger. On the other hand, to a friend, a child can communicate his deepest feelings in a spontaneous manner, without fear of condemnation. This means that the therapist must also be a friend, in that she must also be willing to share of herself.

Objectives of a relationship

To become a child's playmate, the therapist must establish objectives or requirements for the relationship. These objectives must be accomplished by the child as well as by the therapist. If these objectives are accomplished successfully, they will serve to facilitate the development of and function as guidelines for the therapeutic relationship. Some objectives apply specifically to the therapist, others to the child client and, still others, to both. For the sake of convenience, these objectives have been arranged alphabetically. Note that this is not necessarily the order in which the objectives will be achieved.

Awareness

When a child comes for therapy, he has only a vague idea of what he is doing there. Therefore, it is often necessary to examine the structure of his experience and increase his awareness thereof. The therapist will have to find out what it is that the child experiences. She will have to find out why he behaves as he does and what his reasons are. The therapist will also have to look at why the child's functions and awareness are increased. Yontef (1993:203) explains awareness in this way:

> Awareness is a form of experiencing. It is the process of being in vigilant contact with the most important event in the individual environment field with sensorimotor, emotional, cognitive and energetic support.

Awareness is the means by which the individual can regulate him or herself by choice. It is thus necessary for the therapist to do experimental exercises with the child. These can help to build the relationship and can also serve to promote awareness. An example of an exercise follows. Ask the child to pay attention to his awareness now. His awareness must wander as he says aloud: "Now I am aware of . . ." This can also help the child to accommodate to his new environment. The therapist can go on with the exercise, continuing to prefix each statement with "Now I am aware of . . ." As the child goes on, listen to what he is saying, to sounds that he is hearing. Start to direct the child's awareness. Ask him to pay attention to a specific aspect of which he is aware. Every experience (looking, touching, smelling, listening, eating) has some emotional quality. Make the child aware of this.

Biding one's time

In building a relationship, there are various pitfalls to be avoided. One of these is haste. As the present is the central focus in the solving of problems, the therapist must take care not to hurry the child. An objective is therefore for the therapist to bide her time and let the child dictate the pace.

For a child, time is often a big frustration. The child needs more time than the adult to think things through and to make things workable in his mind. A child who is in the process of experimenting and trying out everything needs time to develop his imaginative background. He sometimes does not have the experience in his background to fall back on, therefore he has to create and imagine a picture that makes sense to him. The adult does not always bear this in mind, since an adult functions on a higher level of problem solving and therefore needs less time to complete these so-called pictures. However, if a child gets the message that he is unable to complete the tasks in the located time, he starts to feel incompetent. The outcome is often that the child refuses to play anymore and makes excuses that he is too tired or doesn't feel like it. The therapist should be aware of this and not hurry the child unduly.

Clichés and confluence

Another problematic area is that of confluence, often initiated through the therapist's use of clichés. Clichéd expressions often form part of the communication between children and adults. Sometimes, when a clichéd expression is put to a child, he may dismantle the boundary of his self and project his own existence into the person who has put the cliché to him. The privacy of his own isolated self is gone; instead, he allows another not only to share his experience, but also to make their experience part of his own self. At this stage, one may say that the child is in confluence with what has been put to him.

Confluence is the appreciation of sameness, and the openness of the child's boundaries allows him to appreciate the similarity between himself and the therapist. In other words, confluence makes the child and his therapist the same. This can be very dangerous, for it means that the child cannot form a self-image; he clings to his own lack of awareness; he cannot play a personal role and his own creativity is repressed. The child becomes helpless, in a trance, without will, without functioning of the ego mode at all. The resulting peril is that the child does not take responsibility for his own decisions.

A good example of confluence is where a child is taught to believe in Jesus Christ from childhood. When he becomes an adult, he still goes to church and believes in Jesus Christ, but is in confluence with the people who imposed this on him, not with himself. The right and healthy thing is for a person to be in confluence with his or her own beliefs, believing in Jesus Christ because of personal choice and involvement. When the child is being told how he ought to feel or act as a Christian, this is referred to as "laying a trap" on him. Traps are laid on those who will accept them. Latner (1988:89) is completely correct in saying that "we get traps laid on us in accordance with our willingness to give up our gestalt digestive process and gulp in another view of oneself."

It is thus clear that the therapist must be in confluence with the child and not the other way round.

Dialogue

One of the most important objectives of any relationship, particularly the therapeutic one, is achieving dialogue. The therapist must encourage the child to bargain about his circumstances. He must learn to think, talk, and to negotiate, and to experience all possible perspectives of a situation. In other words, the child must participate effectively in dialogue. Yontef (1993:132) emphasises four characteristics of dialogue:

Inclusion

This means putting oneself as fully as possible into the experience of the other without judging, analysing or interpreting, while simultaneously retaining a sense of one's separate, autonomous presence.

Presence

The play therapist must share experiences with the child, regularly and judiciously. The therapist always shares feelings, preferences and personal experiences.

Commitment to dialogue

Contact is more than something between the therapist and the child. It is important that the two have bargained (agreed) to allow contact to happen.

Dialogue is live

The participants can choose how they want to communicate. It can be by dancing, songs, words or any modelling that expresses and moves the energy between and among the participants. The child can thus choose to include any form of nonverbal expression. The creative therapist can initiate a wide variety of possibilities.

A fifth aspect may be added, namely, that of *resistance* in the communication process. A child has to have resistance: if there is no resistance, he imbibes all the new information and swallows it without "digestion". The digestion process is seen as resistance to the external and occurs with every new topic. The therapist must be aware of this, for it has nothing to do with the personal relationship, but is rather resistance to new information. In this way, resistance is needed for good integration, as discussed under confluence.

Equilibrium

To be in equilibrium is a very important factor for every child, especially for a child in middle childhood. The child in this age group is frequently concerned about what other people think of him. Therefore, he wants to be in equilibrium, albeit more with his external system than with his internal system. The child will sometimes even brutally ignore his own needs just to get this facet stabilised. At this stage, the child client sometimes makes promises that are not really part of his own needs just to get the goodwill and acceptance of other people. Often, because the child is also not ready or mature enough to admit his own needs, there is a continuous repression taking place between acceptance and own needs. This is a big obstacle to his own organismic functioning. The therapist will have to be sensitive to this kind of behaviour for through it, the child can easily give the wrong message.

Friendship

The therapist should become the child's playmate and friend, which is the main objective of the relationship. Although this concept often sounds wrong to a professional therapist, the relationship in Gestalt therapy is based on a horizontal level. The therapist treats the child as an equal as much as possible. For instance, when the child is unfair in his attitude, the therapist has full permission to draw his attention to the unfairness. A relationship of friendship is one of give and take, and once the child realises these dynamics, he feels at ease and experiences a sense of fairness and equality. A child will also prefer to tell his secrets to his friend and play them out, rather than tell a complete stranger about his private life.

Guardianship

The therapist must not only fulfil the role of friend to the child client, but also that of guardian. The therapist must be able to fulfil this role in such a way that the child does not get the impression that he is unable to look after himself or to make his own decisions. It is depressing for the child to gain such an impression, since, if he is constantly reminded that he is unable to look after himself, he will become uncertain and insecure. On the other hand, if the child knows that the therapist is there for him, to help him and to assist him, it gives him the security to escape and to go a little bit further than he would have, were he alone.

Humility

To become a child's playmate and guardian, the therapist needs to be humble. Children, just like adults, disapprove of an attitude of haughtiness. If a therapist is humble, the child generates the candour to try and take a risk and to enter a positive therapeutic relationship.

Information

An aspect of the role of guardian is the issue of supplying the child with information. If a child asks for information, it is usually because he needs to have it. A child will not ask about things that do not concern his functioning. If information is given to a child and the sensitivity required for certain information is explained to him, he will get the message that he is a trustworthy and reliable person. This can serve as a self-image builder. Furthermore, a child has the right to know about aspects concerning his life. If there is information that he is not conscious of, or if it will not serve to better his life, the therapist will have to make the decision whether or not to withhold the information. However, the therapist should bear in mind that half-knowledge of a situation is often more dangerous because the child builds his own story around the facts and may sometimes blame himself without reason.

Joy

An important aspect of any relationship is joy. It must be enjoyable for the child to play with the therapist. If the play sessions are not pleasant, the child will not be eager to come back for follow-up sessions. As Oaklander (1988) declares, play is fun.

Kindness and honesty

These are personal objectives of the therapist. In order to be a friend and guardian, the therapist must treat the child with both kindness and honesty. For example, if the child tells the therapist a secret, this information must remain confidential. The child relies upon the therapist's integrity. If it is, however, in the child's interest that the information be dealt with, and if other persons or officials are concerned, this must first be worked through with the child. The ideal situation is that the child has the chance and choice to deal with the information on his own, when he is ready to do so.

Laughter

Another aspect of a friendship is shared laughter. The therapist may under no circumstances ever laugh *at* a child. A child is not in a position to integrate shame into his self-concept. But to laugh *with* a child is a therapeutic tool. Humour can be used as a valuable instrument, serving as a mechanism for reducing tension and stress.

Making contact

According to Moustakas (1959), Landreth (1991) and Oaklander (1969), making contact with a child can (or being sensitive as a friend or guardian) only happen when therapy is approached with a passion, with the courage to pursue in depth, and with the determination to stay on the path with the child, no matter what.

(The concept of) Now

The present is the focal point of awareness, contact and the creation of new solutions. To understand the functioning of the child, it is thus essential to know what a child needs now, at this very moment. "Now" is a functional concept referring to what the organism is doing at the present time. What the organism did five minutes ago is not part of "now".

Remembering is not "now". This concept is also associated with the gestalt, since, in building the relationship with the child, it is important to remember that Gestalt therapy starts from the obvious, the things that the child can see for himself, the realistic. The obvious is so frequently overlooked by the adult. However, the opening gambit of the child — that smile, look or handshake — which is usually obvious behaviour is often laden with meaning.

To be in contact in the here and now also means that the therapist must be aware of her own emotions, feelings, preferences and dislikes and must share these willingly. To be with the child client in the here and now therefore means that the therapist should have the ability to be her natural self and communicate her own feelings. The child will know if the therapist is trying to be someone or something else. With therapy based on an awareness of and contact in the here and now, solutions can thus be created.

Organismic self-regulation

This objective is the personal objective of the child client in therapy. Although of great importance, there are many problems associated with it, especially for the therapist. Children have specific needs that must be met if they are to develop healthily. For example, children need sensory stimulation, movement, nutrition, affection, sleep, play, etc. Perls (1947:7) comments that "the organism is straining for the maintenance of an equilibrium which is continuously disturbed by its needs and regained through their gratification or elimination." It is therefore the task of the therapist to explore what the needs of the child are and to make it possible for the child to meet his needs. When the needs are not met, the child experiences a disturbance and the relationship can therefore not flourish.

However, Latner (1986:13) mentions that organismic self-regulation does not ensure health, but only that the organism does all it can with what is available. The therapist must thus keep in mind that the child client always comes first. His needs come first. The situation often arises that the parents want to be the most important persons in the situation, wanting to prescribe the intervention of how, when and under what conditions the therapist ought to take action. If this happens, it eliminates the child's ability to grow in his own organismic self-regulation, unless he and his needs are always of primary concern.

Polarities

A further objective of the therapeutic relationship is for the child, through effective dialogue, to gain an understanding of opposites and polarities. Children function in terms of opposites: light is known in relation to darkness; heat is known in relation to cold; left is the opposite of right. These are known as poles of distinction. Such dualism pervades our behaviour and understanding. Even our emotions are split into happy and sad, disappointed and satisfied; our morals into good and bad; our aesthetics into beautiful and ugly. Each of us divides our world into our likes and dislikes, friends and enemies.

Importantly, the relationship of opposites necessarily requires the existence of the other. The building of a relationship with a child works on this same basis, as the child's understanding of these concepts forms and develops as he grows. However, a child often feels confusion about that which he experiences and cannot understand how it is possible for him to feel respect and hatred for the same person.

The therapist, as friend and guardian, must guide the child client towards such an understanding.

Critique

A role of the therapist as guardian is that of critic, but of a wise and sensitive critic. Nobody likes criticism, but a child often experiences criticism more harshly than adults do. Children respond very negatively to criticism, especially when it comes from a stranger. It makes them angry and aggressive, which prevents introspection.

The therapist must therefore emphasise that it is the action of the child, and not the child himself, which is at fault. In a holistic understanding of the child, the functioning of his physical body, his emotions, his thoughts, his culture and his social expressions are unified into a single picture. All are aspects of the same event — the child. However, when a child is criticised, it is the deed that is criticised, even though the child as a person is part of the whole process. A child cannot understand how his brain (cognitive system) and nervous system (emotional system) operate as a whole, and thus reacts angrily to what is perceived as a personal threat.

Thus, when a child is criticised, the question to be asked is *how*, instead of *why*, since, if the child is asked how something happened, it stresses the activity itself and concentrates on the here and now.

Responsibility

To take responsibility in the relationship is to grow in self-image, and self-nurturing. As soon as the child can learn to take responsibility for himself, he will be able to overcome his own obstacles and problems. However, children often want to blame others for their failures. The wise therapist promotes the taking of responsibility by the child himself. This can largely be accomplished by refraining from being an answer source for the child. Furthermore, it is sometimes necessary to make the child aware that he talks without taking any responsibility for what he says. If the therapist can teach the child to speak for himself, he has already taken a step towards responsibility.

A further aspect of responsibility is for the child to take responsibility for his own selfhood. This, of course, is a primary aim of any therapeutic relationship. To give a child permission to be himself is to give him permission to feel, to be. According to Landreth (1991:195), "Children cannot discover and develop their inner resources and, in the process, experience the power of their potential unless opportunities to do so exist. Responsibility cannot be taught, responsibility can only be learned through experiencing." If a child has permission to be himself, he can be free to experience.

Sincerity

In developing the true and honest self, one comes to the experience and expression of unity within the self. It is only when all the parts of the gestalt become one that the child and the therapist can truly be themselves. When the whole self that concerns every activity, each moment, every situation or experience is reunited in the true and aware self, a child can be in contact with himself and with the person with whom he is in a relationship.

The child thus knows when the therapist is not being sincere. Therefore, it is necessary for the therapist rather to keep silent than to say something that she does not mean just to ease the situation. If a child gets the impression that an adult is false, he also starts to play roles and the therapeutic milieu comes to serve as a drama theatre and not as an honest and natural playground.

Introjection is obviously important here since a child learns through introjection. If the introjection stands to interfere with what he really likes or dislikes, it is unhealthy. Clark and Fraser (1987:42) see introjects in the following terms: "Uncritical acceptance of rules or patterns of behaviour which are imposed by parents, teachers, organisation etc". In building the relationship, try to free the child from introjects. Parents often force children to be as they wish. What is essential to know is that if an introject is not the desire of the child, it serves as a control mechanism over the child.

However, introjection can be healthy in a child's development. Imitation, copying and role-playing are healthy kinds of introjection. When the child acts situations out and they become real parts of him, the knowledge is assimilated. However, before the child can make it his own, there is a definite boundary to be crossed. The behaviour of the client will indicate a block in his awareness. This is because the child cannot distinguish between the fantasy of another person and the reality of the therapist. The here-and-now contact between the therapist and child is one of the basic means of increasing the child's awareness of this. Through this actual encounter, the child learns the difference between the insistent beckoning of the past and the freedom and clarity of the present. However, this relationship will not flourish unless based on sincerity and honesty.

Transference

A further stumbling block in the relationship of which the therapist must be aware is transference. Sometimes, a child finds many obstacles in his way, obstacles in the form of persons. Until these obstacles can be worked through, a relationship cannot be formed. Thus, when the therapist tries to build a relationship with the child client, she finds herself being treated though she were someone else. When this kind of transference happens, the therapist ought to realise that the child is not in the present, he is not in the "now". However, to warn a child or even forbid him to be with his feelings is to take control from him. This merely demonstrates the inability of the therapist to help the child to take control of his own life. Instead, the therapist needs to be aware of and deal with the issue of transference.

Unfinished business

Associated with the issue of transference is that of unfinished business. Unfinished business can be explained in terms of unexpressed feelings or concerns and unsatisfied needs. This factor litters relationships with other people and is one of the biggest problems that a child has to face. Unsatisfied needs may arise if a person is out of touch with his potential. When that happens, his gestalt cannot fully reflect his needs and the resolution is unfulfilling. Another characteristic of unfinished business is that it accumulates. When a child gets into the habit of organismic indigestion, he becomes clogged with incomplete gestalts which interfere with free functioning. The child begins carrying around his repressions. With his awareness blocked and his energies diminished, he cannot bring enough of himself to new situations. The child sometimes tries to participate, but, because of his gestalt weakness, his participation remains incomplete. Over time, the child collects a stream of incomplete situations, fantasies, dreams and unexpressed needs. Importantly, unfinished business never goes away: it sometimes appears as a hidden agenda or is manifested as a symptom. This can jeopardise the therapeutic relationship and thus the therapist ought to assist the child in dealing with his unfinished business.

Violence

Unfinished business may be manifested in violence or aggression. Behaviour which attempts to hurt others is actually an attempt to evade the child's own dysphonic feelings. Thus, acting out anger in violence is antithetical to increased experience. In Gestalt therapy, clients are therefore encouraged to work through negative feelings by directly expressing them in verbal response. For this purpose, it is sometimes necessary to give the child mechanisms for getting rid of his anger. If he can get rid of the negative energy, the level of aggression will be reduced.

Warmth

The actual process of making contact with the child begins the very first time the therapist comes into the child's presence. The therapist must experience the challenge of giving of herself. However, to come into the child's presence too quickly, or to get too close too quickly can damage the establishment of the relationship. The child will notice such things. Warmth therefore must come into the tone of voice, and gentleness into the face and posture. The therapist has to evaluate her own approach — is the warmth that the therapist feels being communicated, that is, are the words conveying the caring?

"X-ray vision"

The therapist must be highly sensitive to the child client. It is necessary for the therapist to "look beyond" just the verbal communication of the child. The building of a successful relationship depends on the therapist's sensitivity and ability to plumb the depths of the child's experience. However, the child's attitudes, feelings and thoughts must be taken into consideration. If the therapist is successful, she enters the child's world.

Yes, I can!

Both the therapist and child must be willing to believe in themselves and to take risks. The therapist may sometimes have to take the lead and demonstrate to the child that she is prepared to take risks. If the child has a role model, it is always easier to take chances. The child client can, at the same time, learn to take responsibility. For instance, in a negative situation, the child can learn that to take a chance sometimes means to lose. The therapist must give him permission to fail sometimes, since the most valuable lesson is that he can learn from his mistakes and that no one can blame him for his failure. If a child is too hard on himself and allows himself no mistakes, it is the responsibility of the therapist to guide him and help him to find a safe place where he can sometimes nurture himself.

Zest

The therapist in particular must have her own zest for life. This will manifest itself as a source of energy. The child must become aware of the zest in the adult's life so that it can be contagious. If a child sees that an adult has zest left for him, it gives him the confidence to claim some of the energy for his own situation. The child client who evaluates that the therapist is keen and willing to play with him takes the chance with more enthusiasm.

Conclusion

Building a relationship with a child is one of the most difficult therapeutic interventions. However, if the therapist is sincere and puts the child first, she will reap great rewards. Landreth (1991:5) in his child-centred approach offers the following principles for relationships with children, which all child therapists should take to heart:

I am not all knowing,
    Therefore, I shall not even attempt to be.

I need to be loved.
    Therefore, I will be open to loving children.

I want to be more accepting of the child in me.
    Therefore, I will with wonder and awe allow children
    to iluminate my world.

I know so little about the complex intricacies of childhood.
    Therefore, I will allow children to teach me.

I learn best from and am impacted most by my personal struggles.
    Therefore, I will join with children in their struggles.

I sometimes need a refuge.
    Therefore, I will provide a refuge for children.

I like it too when I am fully accepted as the person I am.
    Therefore, I will strive to experience and appreciate
    the person of the child.

I make mistakes. They are a declaration of the way I am—human and fallible.
    Therefore, I will be tolerant of the humanness of children.

I react with emotional internalization and expression to my world of reality.
>Therefore, I will relinquish the grasp I have on reality and will try to enter the world as experienced by the child.

It feels good to be an authority, to provide answers.
>Therefore, I shall need to work hard to protect children from me!

I am more fully me when I feel safe.
>Therefore, I will be consistent in my interactions with children.

I am the only person who can live my life
>Therefore, I will not attempt to rule a child's life.

I have learned most of what I know from experiencing.
>Therefore, I will allow children to experience.

The hope I experience and the will to live come from within me.
>Therefore, I will recognize and affirm the child's will and selfhood.

I cannot make children's hurts and fears and frustrations and disappointments go away.
>Therefore, I will soften the blow.

I experience fear when I am vulnerable.
>Therefore, I will with kindness, gentleness, and tenderness touch the inner world of the vulnerable child.

Bibliography

Clark, D. & Fraser, T. 1987. *The Gestalt approach. An introduction for managers and trainers.* (2nd ed.). Raffey Park: Management College.

Landreth, G.L. 1991. *Play therapy. The art of the relationship.* Muncrie, Indiana: Accelerated Development. Inc., Publishers.

Latner, J. 1986. *The Gestalt therapy book.* New York: The Gestalt Journal Press. Inc.

Moustakas, C.E. 1959. *Psychotherapy with children. The living relationship.* New York: Harper and Row.

Oaklander, V. 1969. (Second edition: 1988). *Windows to our children. A Gestalt therapy approach to children and adolescents.* New York: Gestalt Journal Press. Inc.

Perls, F. 1966. *Ego, Hunger and Aggression.* New York: Vintage Books.

Yontef, G.M. 1993. *Awareness, dialogue and process.* New York: The Gestalt Journal Press. Inc.

3 Sensory contact with the child

J P SCHOEMAN

Introduction

Human beings are sensitive, irritable creations of God. Actions can irritate, hurt or even caress us. Taking snuff makes us sneeze, lights shining in our eyes blind us and when an aeroplane breaks through the sound barrier, it feels as if our eardrums are bursting. However, when one is caressed softly, it is comforting, and a baby can even be rocked to sleep.

Levine and Shefner (1991) maintain that:

> Sensation refers to the process of detecting a stimulus (or some aspect of it) in the environment. It is the necessary collection of information about the world from which perceptions can be made.

People thus appear to be calm and tranquil until some or other impulse disturbs their peace. On account of their uniqueness, people react differently to these impulses. The impulse can be repressed or the person may act it out.

People make contact through their involvement in the world. Even with closed eyes, people know where to find their hands. They know the exact position of their body without looking. People also know when they are hungry or thirsty. It is possible to know all these things without seeing, smelling or hearing because everyone has an internal set of sensory mechanisms.

The human sensory mechanism was created so skillfully and incredibly that a multitude of physiological transactions take place before a person can really experience an impulse. The human brain can be compared to a very complicated computer program. Each cell is a world of its own, while also being in contact with the other cells.

Human beings are so unique that the slightest anomaly or irregularity of the sensory faculties is incorporated into a unique sensory interpretation. Loss of sight, for instance, can be compensated for by another sense organ, such as smell. Loss of hearing can be supplemented by more sensitive non-verbal observation.

However, people can also experience distortion of sensory impulse. The visual impulses that is experienced when looking at spiders behind glass may cause one to feel spiders walking on one's back. People may experience bizarre sensory impulses that are not real. They may hear voices, smell aromas, taste or even feel ants on their skins without it really happening.

It is clear that the human sensory system is a highly complex system which enables human beings to experience the world. It is therefore essential that the child's sensory skills be developed in order for him to make meaning of his surroundings.

The five senses

A newborn baby is totally dependent on its mother. Initially, a baby has a primitive sensory system, although it has lots of inherent developmental potential. The newborn baby can assume a feeding position, but cannot turn or move its arms or legs. It cannot lift its head, sit or walk. However, human beings, even very young ones, are dynamic and constantly react to internal and external stimuli. When it needs something, a baby cries. Its mother picks it up, cuddles it, smiles and hums. The baby reacts to this by laughing, kicking, crying or babbling with pleasure. The mother and child develop a communication system through which she welcomes him and introduces him to the world.

The mother can thus be regarded as the primary source of stimuli pertaining to the baby's sensory mechanisms. Compared to the child, the mother's sensory mechanisms are well developed. For example, when she observes the child, she sees colour, texture and forms — blue eyes, glowing complexion, pink mouth, chubby hands, whereas the baby sees the mother in shades of grey, white and black. The baby distinguishes indistinct shapes, rays of light and eyes watching it, without attaching meaning to any of these. A baby's eyes cannot focus or follow objects. He perceives objects as flat, not yet three dimensionally.

Even though a human is extremely helpless in its first few months, he can smell and taste. A baby's sense of smell can, for instance, direct him to the mother's milk. Research has also shown that babies can distinguish between sweet and salt tastes. Babies are also sensitive regarding cold, heat and touch. The baby can feel when he is touched with love or when someone handles him with apprehension.

As a child matures, sensory curiosity develops. Often to the embarrassment of parents, young children tend to stare boldly. Oaklander (1988:11) confirms this: " They see, observe, notice, examine, inspect everything, and often seem to stare."

As part of their socialisation, children learn that they must make choices that will also be acceptable to the community. It is thus important that they have the opportunity to make sensory contact with the external environment. A child who is unwilling or unable to observe what is going on around him finds it difficult to position himself in the world. Therefore it is important that the child explores, tests and realises what he finds agreeable or disagreeable.

Sight

All people have different perceptions. According to Gestalt theory, humans are pattern-forming beings, using forms, lines and shapes to make sense of observations. Certain parts of an image are grouped together to form a whole, the gestalt. However, certain inborn, forms are present that are always seen as a whole, for example, circles, triangles and straight lines. Even when such forms are incomplete, the human brain tends to complete them — in other words, the brain completes non-existent lines.

Other schools of thought, such as cognitive theory, state that people see only those aspects that have been integrated by learning. According to this approach, such patterns are not inborn, but compiled by raw material processed by the brain. Material may also be adapted to suit specific needs.

Either way, vision is the main coordinating sense, helping the child to understand the world around him. When the therapist is working on visual stimulation, she should remember that brightness and darkness, movement, shape and colour are important.

Tear (1993:70) lists ten exercises for advancing a child's visual sensory perceptions:

- peeping through fingers
- looking down a cardboard tube
- looking through coloured cellophane from a sweet wrapper, or perspex from set of paypax plastic building shapes
- looking through homemade "rose tinted spectacles" — frames made from pipe cleaners, lenses from coloured cellophane
- looking through a piece of paper with a hole in it
- using a magnifying glass or a microscope
- playing with a mirror: a plastic baby mirror, available from many toy shops, is double-sided and very robust for young children
- looking through a telescope or binoculars either way round
- looking through a kaleidoscope
- looking through an octoscope: this is held in front of one eye like a kaleidoscope, but, instead of seeing a palette of coloured shapes, the image in front of the octoscope is reflected eight times. This could be a person's face, the view from the window, or the child's own hand.

Visual skills may also be used to enhance the child's total sensory perception. A relevant exercise is to ask the child to look at an object and to project all the feelings and memories that it evokes, through a medium such as clay, sand or drawing.

Hearing

The child uses his sense of hearing before he is born. In the womb, the baby can hear the sounds of his mother's body and voice, as well as noises from the outside world.

As children develop, they learn to hear what they would like to hear. They withdraw from information that they find unpleasant, just as a deaf person would close his or her eyes to avoid comprehending what is said. Similarly, when parents scold their child all the time, the child tends not to hear it any more.

A child who represses his hearing faculty deprives himself of intensive sensory observation. Furthermore, a child who does not have contact with sound will have difficulty in making contact with connected feelings. Feelings and sound are often interrelated. When a child is asked to make joyful, sad and exuberant noises, his skill in portraying feelings can be observed. Sound can be used as an expressive symbol, for instance when a child is asked to write down what he associates with certain sounds. Several sounds can be combined to form a rhythm as an expression of emotions and feelings. Tear (1993:72) emphasises the importance of listening by stating: ". . . most necessary of all is the need to encourage all children to listen, so that they can have the maximum amount of pleasure from whatever degree of hearing they have".

Control is another important quality connected to the ability of producing sound. The child must be in contact with himself to generate sound.

There are specific exercises that can be done to enhance sensitivity to sound:

- Household articles can be banged together.
- The child can be made to sit quietly and try to identify everything that is heard.
- Tear (1993:89) describes an example of a game as follows:

   This can be a good game to play in odd moments or on car journeys, etc. It consists of imitating simple sounds like a clock ticking, a fire engine, a car horn or an animal noise. You make the noise and your child echoes the sound. The noises can be longer and more difficult to imitate as the child learns to listen and remember.

- There are also games to use in a group context when the aim is to stimulate children's senses, for example: **Giant's treasure** — The "giant" sits blindfolded in the middle of the room with a noisemaker. The rest of the group sit in a circle around her. One of the children tries to creep forward to steal the giant's "treasure". If the giant hears him coming, she must point in the direction of the sound. If she points correctly, the child must return to his place. If the child reaches the "treasure", he becomes the "giant".

Music

Even though music and rhythm are ancient and primitive means of communication, they are often underestimated as communication media.

Children like listening to and making music. Music offers the child the opportunity to come into contact with what he hears and experiences. When reacting to music, the child can come into contact with his own body, particularly with the muscles in his body. He learns to release emotions in healthy ways that are more beneficial than internalising those feelings.

Bonny and Savary (1990:13) are rightly of the opinion that:

   Human consciousness is like a many-storied skyscraper. Its ground floor represents normal consciousness — the state of mind we ordinarily use in thinking, problem solving, feeling, sensing, remembering, communicating and so on. In this skyscraper of the mind there are many higher and deeper levels of consciousness — realms of creativity, insight, self-realization, deep memory, the unconscious, dreams, transpersonal and religious experience. Few people, however, probe for deeper, hidden levels.

Music can thus create new dimensions of awareness for the child, in that it can bring out things in the child that nothing or no one has ever elicited. Music can bring out what the child is trying to verbalise.

Music can be used effectively in the therapeutic milieu. It can put the child in a specific mood, while also having a calming and reassuring effect. It can even soothe hyperactive children. In group therapy, games such as musical chairs, musical hats and musical mats can be played:

- **Musical chairs:** A chair is needed for all the players except one. While the music is playing, the players move around. When the music stops, they must find chairs. The one without a chair is out.
- **Musical hats or mats:** The person without a hat when the music stops is out. When playing musical mats, children run in a circle and jump over a mat as if it is a bridge. The last child to jump over when the music stops is out.

The author readily uses music in therapy when working with adolescents. The familiar sounds as background create an atmosphere of ease and security. This helps the client to feel at home and not so totally strange in the world of the adult. By discussing his choice of music and why he likes the specific piece, the ice can be broken. Adolescents tend to attach more meaning to the words than to the melody of the music. As parents are more inclined to listen to the melody than to the words, parents and children may lose each other at this point.

Songs can thus be used in the same way as stories in therapy. Younger children usually like to sing along and can identify with some of the words. There are songs to accommodate almost every situation and mood. According to Oaklander (1988:117), songs that touch children add vitality, beat and power to their emotions, imaginations and experiences. Children can even create their own songs, suited to various situations. The utilisation of music in relaxation play is discussed in chapter 5.

Smell

Humans have a well developed sense of smell. Denziloe (1994:49) is of the opinion that some people have an acute sense of smell and others hardly any. The sense of smell is used to gather information about the surroundings, what is happening and to discriminate between pleasant and unpleasant smells. The role of the sense of smell is often underestimated.

However, it is possible to connect smells with memories from the past. There are endless aromas reminding people of hospitals, churches, schools, shops and childhood places. These aromas are connected to certain emotions evoking pleasant memories, anxiety, or sadness. Helen Keller, as cited by Willentz (1968:129), summarised this meaningfully:

> Smell is a potent wizard that transports us across thousands of miles and all the years we have lived. The odors of fruits waft me to my southern home, to my childhood frolics in the peach orchard. Other odors, instantaneous and fleeting, cause my heart to dilate joyously or contract with remembered grief. Even as I think of smells, my nose is full of scents that start awake sweet memories of summers gone and ripening fields far away.

To stimulate a child's sense of smell, a few bottles can be filled with substances with various aromas. The child can guess what each is. He can also relate what the smell makes him think of. The child can even smell assorted flowers and choose the one with the most pleasant scent. He must give at least two reasons for his choice.

Aromatherapy

Aromatherapy is the use of essential oils for therapeutic principles. This is a form of alternative medicine. As the essential oils are placed on the skin, they are absorbed into the body and travel to various organs. Aromatherapy is based on a holistic approach as the oils affect the physical, mental and emotional state of the person.

Aromatherapy has been in use for centuries, even though the term itself was not used as such. For instance, brides used orange flowers in their hair; oils were added to a bath; oil-burners are widely available in craft shops; air spray is used in homes to freshen up a room.

Denziloe (1994:53) is of the opinion that aromatherapy massage has many benefits in that it

- encourages relaxation
- improves circulation, muscle tone and mobility of limbs
- increases bodily awareness
- allows opportunities for choice (different oils, which parts of the body are massaged, when and how)
- encourages interaction and communication
- increases tolerance of touch and provides age-appropriate opportunities for personal attention and contact which are not connected with functional touch (toileting, washing and dressing).

Massage is very personal. The therapist has no right to invade the child's private space and touch his body — even his feet and hands. This sensory contact suits the relationship between parent and child. It is recommended that if a child needs this type of attention, a parent should be informed as to how to carry out the performance.

Taste

The word *taste* originates from the Latin word *taxare*. It means being distinctly in touch, to assess or evaluate. Taste is a sensory observation that is linked to several other impulses. Having a cold can, for instance, influence taste. Taste is also influenced adversely when something smells bad. Taste is a combination of temperature, texture and smell.

The organ associated with taste is the tongue. The tongue is an important organ as it also helps with the processing of food and is necessary for talking. As such, it is an instrument for the verbalisation of emotions and feelings. In an endeavour to make contact with their environment, children often lick their arms or hands and other objects, such as ice creams.

It is part of every person's uniqueness to develop a taste for certain foodstuffs and liquids. Individual tastes should be encouraged and respected. Each child should be stimulated to make choices and to decide what he finds acceptable, as people who do not value food lose out on an important opportunity to be in contact with the environment. Willentz (1968:153) has the following to say about people who do not value food and tasting it:

> Those . . . from whom nature has withheld the legacy of taste, have long faces, and long eyes and noses, whatever their height there is something elongated in their proportions. Their hair is dark and unglossy, and they are never plump; it was they who invented trousers.

To stimulate the child's sense of taste, the following exercise may be performed. Assorted sweets, such as a peppermint, chocolate, almond and dried fruit can be mixed in a dish. The child then chooses a sweet, especially one that he used to like when he was younger. He can then describe an incident related to the taste.

Touch

Even though the skin is the biggest organ of the body, it very often remains unacknowledged. To show that people tend to take touch for granted, the following exercise can be done: place the child's index finger against your own and tell the child to stroke both fingers. This creates the same sensation as when a limb has pins and needles!

People do depend a lot on their sense of touch. When people touch something, either with hands or feet, they get the feeling of what it really is. The world is explored to a great extent by touching objects.

A baby's development depends a lot on his physical contact with other human beings. In a sense, physical contact being reciprocated is necessary for survival. The delicate interplay between the physical and emotional is thus necessary for development. Especially during the first years of existence, socialisation takes place through touch.

Certain body parts are more sensitive to touch than others. The fingers are more sensitive than the back, and the lips are more sensitive than the top of the head. The outer layers of the skin cannot convey impulses to the brain. This is possible only for the deeper layers. Thus, the thinner the skin, the more sensitive the observation.

It is possible to discern the precise locality of touch and to determine whether the touch is multiple or restricted to one spot. Touch by another person always carries sensory messages influencing observation. The internal and external environment also influences sensory encounters.

Temperature

The skin is a remarkable organ, regulating heat and cold to keep the body temperature constant. Temperature does play a role in the functioning of the child. When feeling hot, a child will possibly be apathetic and tired. When feeling cold, the child will possibly use accumulated energy in activities that will warm him. It is known that people generally feel cooler in the morning.

Pain

It is difficult to describe the sensory experience of pain. Usually, such descriptions are unspecific, subjective and influenced by cultural background. The most common view of the pain sensation is that it is caused by nerve endings that are sensitive to irritation or injury. Pain is controlled by nerve endings that are far from where the pain is localised. Pain can have a real basis or be somatic. It can surge or cramp. Sometimes, it is so intense that it can only be alleviated by drugging the nerves. The intensity of pain cannot be determined as people's pain tolerance differs.

The significance of pain as a sensory modality should not be underestimated. Pain is the body's alarm system. A person who experiences pain always wants relief. However, the experience of pain is variable. When a person falls, the first experience of contact is usually sharp pain, followed by a dull, burning sensation. There is, however, a whole chain of reactions in the body, such as sweating and a change in the colour of the complexion, as well as an increase in heartbeat. The person is unaware of most of these reactions.

It is possible to inhibit pain. After reaching a peak, pain usually subsides when the sensory nerves stop conveying the impulse to the brain. A person experiencing pain may also be so preoccupied with something that he or she does not realise the extent of the pain at a given moment. Rugby players, for example, often suppress the pain of an injury to prevent it from interfering with the game. When the game is over, the player will experience the pain.

Attention may be diverted from pain to more pleasurable sensations. A dentist, for instance, can use soft music to calm patients. Some cultures describe childbirth as an extremely painful experience, preceded by emotional preparation, with the result that the mother is often afraid of labour even before its onset. Other cultures perceive childbirth as a natural and pleasurable phenomenon and carry on with everyday activities as soon as possible after the delivery of the baby.

The exercise on page 49, known as **the pain ladder,** helps the child to acknowledge the modality: the child must write down on the steps of a ladder, all the words and phrases that have to do with ways he has had pain in his body or in his heart. The child must try to reach the top of the ladder.

Corporeality

Touch is more than just the tactile sense. It also implies corporeality. Jennings (1993:25) states in this regard:

> The body and its relationship with other bodies – through touch and the other senses – forms the basis for the development of identity in all human beings. However, it is important to remember that our identity depends on

Figure 3.1: **The pain ladder**

the relationship between bodies, not only on touch and senses; therefore there needs to be a balance between touch and seperation, between the we and the I.

The child cannot develop a body self before a body image has developed. The body self develops when the child comes into contact with the external world. This again points to the importance of the baby's first few weeks. The contact with the external world is enhanced by holding, cuddling, bathing, dressing and cherishing the baby.

It is important to determine in therapy where the child stands in terms of his own corporeality. The following exercise is useful in this regard:

The child must circle the words that describe how he looks at the moment:

skinny / fat	tall / short
straight hair / curly hair	unfriendly face / friendly face
nice nose / big, ugly nose	unattractive / attractive
good build / inferior build	bright eyes / lifeless eyes
ugly hands / pretty hands	caring / cold
unattractive posture / pleasant, proud posture	

Sensory tactile stimulation

Water, sand, bubbles, dough, clay and paint serve as substances to introduce children to natural media. They create a bridge between sensory experience and creative thinking. A child who has been deprived of such stimulation needs a lot of time to experiment with these media. He must have the opportunity to explore the wonders that other children have discovered over the ages. All children should have the opportunity to play with natural substances by splashing, scooping, shovelling and pouring. Jennings (1993:59) refers to this kind of play as "repair play". Children enjoy playing with wet or dry sand and often combine it with other natural materials, such as sticks, shells, leaves and grass. This offers the opportunity for elementary enjoyment.

Water

Water can be contained in a sink, bath, bowl or water tray. Sponges, plastic tubing and buckets will add to the fun.

Add food colouring, food essences or washing-up liquid for sensory stimulation. Denziloe (1994:78) mentions the use of coloured lights and shining torches, if you have a transparent water tray. She also mentions a foot spa, as it keeps the water warm and has possibilities for vibration.

Sand

Sand is very versatile. It has different properties when it is dry, damp or wet. Dry sand feels cool and silky. Wet sand can be moulded and sculpted. Sand should be clean and sterilised. A child can make a sand castle in the sand tray and the therapist can use it therapeutically.

Bubbles

Bubbles are fascinating to old and young. The attraction is provided by the making of the bubbles, their movement in the air and the splash when they burst.

A recipe for bubble mixture:

```
1 cup washing-up liquid
1 cup water
5 drops of glycerine (for some colour
   and stronger bubbles)
```

Dough and clay

Dough can be used instead of commercial play dough. It can be squeezed through the fingers, kneaded, pummelled, cut into pieces and put together again.

A recipe for dough:

```
2 cups plain flour
1 cup salt
2 teaspoons cooking oil
pinch of alum
water to bind
```

Potter's clay is also very versatile and easy to obtain. It can be recycled and used over and over by being soaked in water. Children like to take their models home and dry them in the sun.

Clay is a favourite material used by Oaklander (1988:67). She is of the opinion that the flexibility and mouldability of clay makes it suitable for many needs. She states further that clay is messy, mushy, soft and sensuous, appealing to every age group and that it offers both tactile and kinesthetic experience.

It is important to build a bridge between the medium and the child. When a child is not in touch with his feelings, he will find it hard to create something with the clay. It is especially helpful to use clay with the aggressive child as he can punch and pound the clay as much as he wishes. According to Oaklander (1988:67), using clay also contributes to a sense of control and mastery in children. The child can create as he feels, he can erase as he feels and he can even find mastery in his "mistakes" because of his own unique mastery or creation.

Paint

Finger paint serves the same goal as clay. It is messy and gives great pleasure to the child. He can create and express his feelings without making or drawing real things. The child can be requested to look at something for a few minutes and then to draw his feelings. He can use any colour(s) to make shapes and lines.

Recipe for finger paint:

> Mix equal amounts of plain flour and powder paint. Add cold water until the mixture is thick and smooth.

Intuitive perceptions

Some people view perception or intuition as a so-called sixth sense. This is, however, not supported by research. Nontheless, Oaklander (1988:120) indicates that the child can use this sense meaningfully to learn to trust the safe spaces. She describes an exercies as follows:

> I call it the yes-no exercise, or sometimes the true-false exercise. I will suggest a statement to the child such as: ' I like string beans.' I instruct the child to answer true or false from that part of the body that gives the answer, rather than from the head. For me, the source of the answer is sometimes in the chest and sometimes just above my navel. With practice, one can learn to tune into those places that seem to embody intuitive truth.

It is sometimes necessary for a child to tune into his inner self for answers to his problems. A feeling of what is good, acceptable and correct is part of every person's creativity. Everyone has an instinctive knowledge of threats and flaws in his or her life. These can be seen as the "monsters" in one's life. When these obstructions are named and given a certain character, they are in the process of being resolved. Some people have more than one monster. It is, however, the monster that figures most strongly at a certain stage that will come to the fore in the striving towards completion or gestalt. It is helpful to give the client a few examples of monsters to facilitate his identification of monsters in his life. When such fantasy is used in therapy, it is important to utilise the child's imagination and feelings. (For a full discussion of dealing with the child's monsters, see chapter 4.)

Feelings

The therapist may find barriers when trying to come into contact with the child's feelings. It seems that children have difficulty in verbally expressing the real intensity of their feelings.

However, it is important that the child should know the range of feelings that he can experience. It is helpful to show the child a card with no more than five faces reflecting feelings. He can then choose the face with which he can identify at that moment. (A choice between too many faces may confuse the child. See the example on p. 104.)

Oaklander (1988:122) also stresses the importance of offering the child the opportunity to choose how he wants to express or explain his emotions.

The child usually finds it interesting to hear how his body reacts to feelings. During therapy, the therapist can draw the child's attention to the reactions of his body to certain feelings. By being able to identify signs in his body, the child will be better prepared to identify and cope with feelings. Oaklander (1988:123) states in this regard: "It is only when we acknowledge our feelings and experiences that we can release them and use our total organism for other things." According to the Gestalt approach, unresolved feelings deplete the child's energy to such an extent that he does not have enough energy to cope with the rest of his feelings.

Magazines can be used to look at various ways in which people react to feelings and experiences. Children may see it as an enjoyable game to observe how breathing portrays feelings. Posture also illustrates feelings.

Oaklander (1988:123) describes the use of an "awareness continuum". This is aimed at making people more aware of their bodies and helps the child to release repressed negative emotions. When playing the game, the therapist and child take turns at reporting inside and outside awareness. The therapist may, for instance, state that she feels heavy inside. The child may report that he feels like a little, scared bird. After a while, the focus shifts to the external. The therapist will, for instance, state that she is embarrassed because a button is missing from her jacket. The child may say that he feels embarrassed because he forgot to bring a handkerchief to the session. They can also tell each other what they observe regarding one another, for instance, "I am conscious of your brown eyes and glowing cheeks. You are wearing a pretty dress and you have a nice smile. I see, however, that your shoulders droop and you avoid eye contact."

This technique implies that a lot of attention is given to the child's posture, facial expressions and interests. Sometime, the child's attention is focused on certain past actions.

The child may relate that he thought of his teacher when he pounded the clay. He can talk about his angry feelings. As the negative feelings are expressed, the child will often begin to talk about his troubles.

Sensory experience of the self

Most of people's actions are performed unconsciously. It is impossible for people to think about everything they do, as they react to impulses or signals. The way in which each person interprets and reacts to these signals is part of the individuality of every person.

Within a few weeks after a baby is born, he has used every part of his body. He swings his arms and kicks his legs. After a while, he tries to reach the toy hanging from his crib. Later, he is able to pick things up and control them. These actions are clumsy at first, but the child rapidly grows more competent.

The child may, at first, encounter obstacles, but usually keeps going until the actions are mastered. Sometimes, there are obstructions to this natural process when parents, for instance, do not allow the child to continue on his own until an action is mastered. They either do whatever must be done for the child or scold him when he engages in certain activities. A mother can, for example, show her annoyance when a baby touches his genitals. She may remove his hand and even talk to him in unfriendly tones. In this way, the child learns to suppress natural actions, and may even learn to suppress tears. Oaklander (1988:128) states rightly: "As children become disconnected from their bodies, they lose a sense of self and great deal of physical and emotional strength as well."

Sometimes, it is necessary to teach children in therapy to own their bodies. Those who are not in contact with themselves cannot feel comfortable with their own corporeality.

A child's maintenance of posture reflects a lot about his self-assertiveness. Poems can be interpreted with mime, for instance depicting the wind in the trees or a bird flying. The child may find it strange at first, but as the exercise progresses he usually enjoys it.

Another way of assessing where the child is on a sensory level is to do the following exercise. It will provide the therapist with an overall picture, even though not substantial.

The child must complete the following statements:

My favourite colour is . . .
My favourite smell is . . .
My favourite taste is . . .
My favourite thing to touch is . . .
My favourite sound is . . .

Relaxation

Children often think that to relax implies lying limply or doing nothing. However, to relax is to feel weightless. This means that the body's muscles are in equilibrium or balance.

To be comfortable is the first objective. Most children find that they relax best when lying supine on a floor or sofa. However, lying down is not enough. The child must "require" his mind to relax. The child can learn to relax his body progressively from the feet right up to the facial muscles and eyes.

An important part of relaxation is breath flow. The child can be helped to do breathing exercises. Deep breathing provides more oxygen and enables the child to control his body better. Regular, rhythmic inhalation and exhalation will help a great deal in securing complete relaxation, not only of the body, but of the mind as well.

Hyperactive children often feel that they cannot control their bodies. Therefore, they tend to engage in meaningless actions. These children need exercise and find it enjoyable; however, they also need to learn to relax.

Concentration

Once the body is relaxed, the mind is ready to concentrate. Guide the child to fix his concentration on a specific object. He must think of nothing else than that object, its colour, shape and smell. He must try not to analyse, describe or define the object — he must simply identify it and acknowledge its uniqueness. He must keep his mind on the object until he can recognise it and even with his eyes closed can "see" every detail of the object.

Children with no imitation fantasy will not be able to do this exercise. Some children may also fear a loss of self-control. It is therefore necessary to give the child the assurance that he need only block out those things that he feels comfortable blocking out. The child must also be told that a person in a state of concentration seldom loses consciousness of self. He or she knows what is happening around him or her all the time.

The process of making contact

The therapist must understand the process of making contact, as this process continually takes place. The play therapist should constantly aim at determining how the contact-making process affects the child's behaviour. Each child's experiences will be coloured by his own unique process. The quality of the experience of sensory stimulation will also be influenced by the way in which the child organises these stimuli. This will offer the therapist the opportunity of observing how the child copes with issues in his life.

The following are the stages in the process of making contact:

Awareness

The child becomes aware of a need to make contact. This becomes so intense that it influences his thoughts and behaviour. He integrates his total life experience in significant totality to form a unit. The need transcends his thoughts and forms a prominent motivation for him to take action.

Action

The child begins to mobilise his energy. He considers alternatives and makes choices. He moves towards fulfilment of needs.

Experimental contact making
The child develops a consciousness of the self. The boundaries that he keeps around him are expanded. He clarifies the content of meaningful material.

Making contact
There is interaction between the organism (child) and the environment. Exchange of sensory information becomes more prominent.

Assimilation
The child freely allows the new energy sensations . He experiences new stimuli spontaneously.

New meaning regarding consciousness
The child attributes new meaning to stimuli. There is the potential for the development of new perceptions.

Ferraro (1993), on the other hand, is of the opinion that the sensory awareness continuum can be divided into seven phases. Through these phases, the therapist can explore the experience process in the child. The sensory experience is mediated through how the child moves through the cycle: the child reflects his process in the way in which he organises and goes through the life process.

- **Phase one**: This is the sensation phase, where raw data is experienced. A child moves towards a figure.
- **Phase two**: Awareness starts to grow in the figure formation. The child starts to develop certain needs. He begins to organise his behaviour in action.
- **Phase three**: He begins mobilising his energy and begins to make choices to fulfil his needs.
- **Phase four**: The child makes contact with his own and inner self, as well as with the environment. He starts sorting out and clarifying his "theme".
- **Phase five**: The experience between the organism and the environment begins.
- **Phase six**: During the so-called assimilation stage, the energy exchange is experienced and the real contact is made.
- **Phase seven**: New learning awareness reorganises the "ground". New meanings are found and change has the potential to take place.

Woldt (1993) is of the opinion that if awareness and contact take place, the organism, and therefore the child, will be in homeostasis. He illustrates his homeostasis cycle with the diagram on page 56.

Conclusion
Many children lose contact with their sensory orientation. They tend to function instinc-

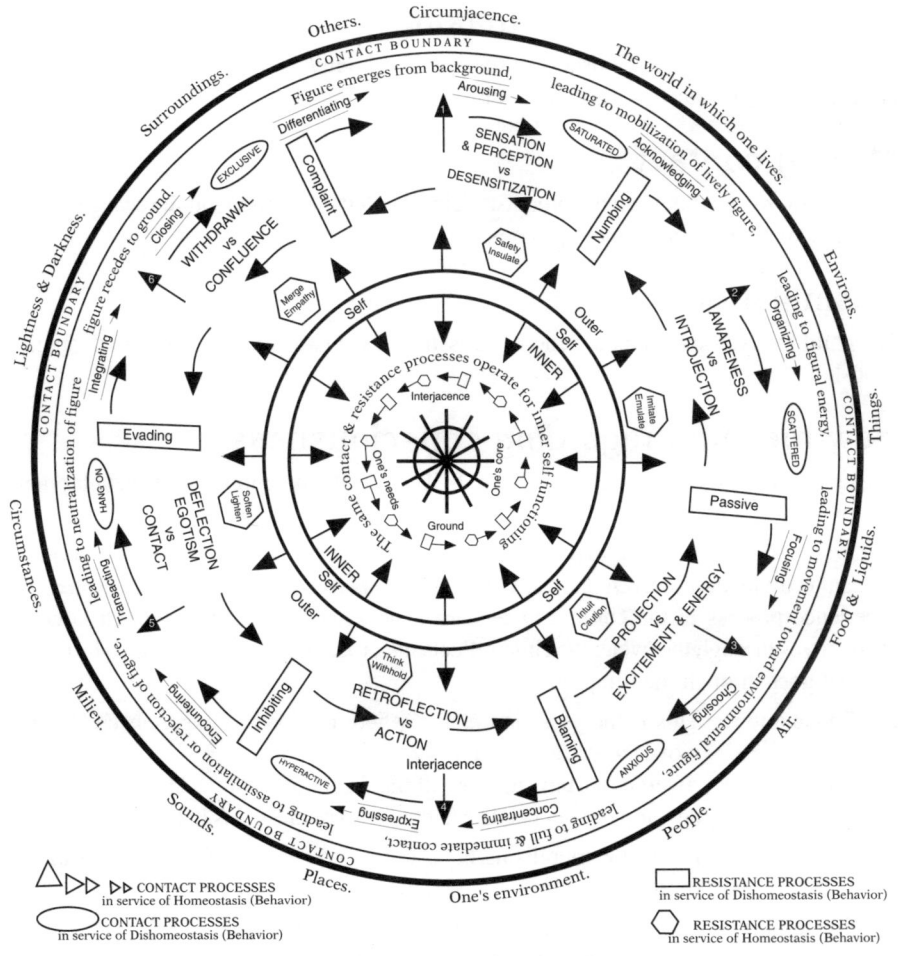

Figure 3.2: **The Gestalt homeostasis cycle**
(From Woldt, 1993)

tively and apart from their human wholeness. However, a human being should function as an absolute whole. When functioning as a gestalt, there is an abundance of power and strength.

Adults also need to be in contact with their sensory functions. If this is not the case, they will not be able to be in contact with their inner child. Play therapists who do not have contact with the child within are also often out of touch with their own corporeality, as Jennings (1993:25) explains fittingly:

Adults who feel uncomfortable with their own body identity may have problems in physical communication with children. Therefore it is essential for play therapists to have a good understanding and training of their own bodies.

The play therapist who does not appreciate her own body identity and sensory observation will not be able to reflect the child's experiences and perceptions. Making sensory contact is therefore of concern for both therapist and child client, in order to be able to give and take within the therapeutic relationship.

Making sensory contact is also an important process that should be assessed, so that the therapist can determine how the child copes with other issues in his life.

Bibliography

Bonny, H.L. & Savary, L.M. 1990. *Music and your mind. Listening with a new consciousness*. Station Hill Press.

Denziloe, J. 1994. *Fun and Games*. Oxford: Butterworth-Heineman Ltd.

Ferraro, J.M.S. 1993. *Gestalt technique continuum. Phasic approach to the cycle of experience*. New York: The Gestalt Journal Press. Inc.

Jennings, S. 1993. *Play therapy with children. A practitioner's guide*. Oxford: Blackwell scientific publications.

Levine, M.W. & Schefner, J.M. 1991. *Fundamentals of sensation and perception* (2nd ed.). California: Brooks/Cole.

Oaklander, V. 1988. *Windows to our children. A Gestalt therapy approach to children and adolescents*. (2nd ed.). New York: The Gestalt Journal Press. Inc.

Tear, R. 1993. *Play helps. Toys and activities for children with special needs*. Oxford: Butterworth-Heinemann Ltd.

Wilentz, J.S. 1968. *The senses of man*. New York: Crowell.

Woldt, 1993. Paper delivered at the 16th Annual Conference on the Theory and Practice of Gestalt Therapy. Toronto.

Part 2

Entering the child's world:

Forms of play and techniques

Summary

Projection techniques

The child is natural and spontaneous. When he experiences an emotion or need, he reacts according to his real feelings. In the process, he not only tells all about himself, his own functioning or way of handling things, he reveals a part of himself.

The development character of projection is part of this undifferentiated state of the child. Because the child's environment is part of him, confluent with him, he projects his own personal thinking in a unique way.

Projections will differ from child to child. However, projections usually reflect the state of the child's unfinished business. Because children are often helpless to change their situations, they make use of projections to cope.

Projection can be seen as functioning in two ways: on the one hand, the child can use projections to wipe out reality; on the other hand, he can fill the spaces with projections. These spaces may be within, inadequacies and voids. They may be external aspects of his environment which are scary or frustrating.

The role of fantasy is clear in that a fantasy can replace an unpleasant reality.

It is through play that the child projects his feelings and needs. In this section of the book, projection techniques will be discussed, as well as the forms of play in which the child can act out his needs.

Formulation of goals

The theoretical base of chapters 5 to 10 is founded on a goal-directed and structured approach. When planning an intervention program for a specific child, the child therapist will already be able, in the beginning phase of therapy, to tentatively plan for the incorporation of certain techniques. Other techniques will be used as the situation arises. The forms of play that are described can be used in individual therapy, but also when there are parents involved, as well as in group therapy. The five forms of play, namely, relaxation play, assessment play, biblio-play, dramatic play and creative play, should fit within a goal-directed framework. These forms of play are usually used in short-term treatment. As the formulation of concrete, specific goals is so important, this will be discussed in more detail.

The model that Dennison and Glassman (1987:3-15) propose for counselling children is easy to understand and to use. They distinguish between content goals and process goals. The main focus on the two different goals shifts according to the stage in the helping process.

In direct work with children, the attainment of process goals is especially important in the beginning and final phases of therapy. Process goals are directed at the helping process. When a child is not motivated for therapy, it is difficult to handle his presenting problems. Process goals therefore support the process. Process goals are maintenance goals focusing on the helping process. They pave the way for the content goals that focus on the specific needs or problems.

Process goals for the beginning phase of therapy may be
- motivating the child to become involved in therapy
- attaining the optimal level of tension that is necessary for effective helping
- building a relationship of trust
- encouraging the child towards self-disclosure.

For each of these process goals, various aims can be planned. In order to enhance the relationship, for instance, the therapist should be warm and honest, plan entertaining activities and emphasise confidentiality. As part of the plan to encourage self-disclosure, the therapist can employ appropriate self-disclosure, or use visual aids such as the examples on page 98.

In the final phase of therapy, the process goals could, for instance be
- helping the child to acknowledge growth and progress
- emphasising the attraction of other support systems after having investigated them together
- working through feelings concerning termination of therapy.

Content goals are more prominent in the middle phase of therapy. According to Dennison and Glassman (1987:7-10), assessment and tentative goal-formulation are content goals, as they are directly connected with the presenting problem. These two functions are an integral part of therapy, as they are a prerequisite for constructive work on problems. They separate problems into manageable parts and ensure purposeful work on each specific problem and need (Francisco-La Grange & Joubert, 1988:5; Compton & Galaway, 1989:430-433; Hepworth & Larsen, 1990:193-194).

For the child who has encountered loss, a content goal could be stated as follows:
- encourage communication between parents and child concerning the loss.

The "how" of the goal, or the aim could read as follows:
- Teach the child appropriate feeling language and encourage him to use at least three feeling words concerned with loss every day in his communication with his parent(s).

Individualisation is especially important when formulating content goals. Content goals will be determined mostly by the child needing help and his specific problems or needs. Process goals are more general and repetitive — they concern certain tasks that should be dealt with in the beginning and final phases of therapy.

Contracting can have components of both content and process goals (Rankin, 1985:25-27; Compton & Galaway, 1989:433). Where the contract focuses on the involvement of the child, regular attendance and self-disclosure, it is process-directed. Where it focuses on aspects concerning the child's specific problem, loss or need, it is content-directed. Even young children should be involved in the formulation of goals, when planning can be drafted in a simple contract, as this teaches decision making and responsibility. It is also necessary to involve parents. However, it must be stressed that the involvement of the parents will always be secondary to that of the child.

Forms of play

In the beginning and final phases of therapy, the focus is on techniques aimed at relaxation and assessment. Relaxation play and assessment play are therefore prominent forms of play in these phases. Certain techniques that are part of biblio-play, dramatic play and creative play have elements of relaxation and assessment too. In the change-oriented phase, assessment and relaxation are still relevant, even though the focus is more on the specific problem, with biblio-play, dramatic play and creative play as main forms of play.

In part 2, the five forms of play are discussed with pratical descriptions of relevant techniques. Most of these techniques can be adapted according to the specific child client's circumstances, problems, needs, cultural background and the time available for therapy.

Even though the different play techniques described here can be categorised into the various forms of play, some fit into more than one category. Certain techniques will suit a structured, directive approach, whereas others are more suitable for an unstructured, non-directive approach. Generally, the techniques of a biblio-therapeutic nature are more directive than those used in dramatic and creative play.

Conclusion

In the following chapters, the five forms of play will be discussed, highlighting metaphors, fantasy and projection techniques in separate chapters. Relaxation and assessment play are especially relevant in the beginning and final phases of therapy where there is a primary focus on process goals and a secondary focus on content goals. Biblio-play, dramatic play and creative play are applicable in the change-oriented phase where the primary focus is on content goals and the secondary emphasis is on process goals.

Biliography

Compton, B.R. & Galaway, B. 1989. *Social work processes.* (4th ed.). California: Wadsworth.

Dennison, S.T. & Glassman, C.K. 1987. *Activities for children in therapy: A guide for planning and facilitating therapy with troubled children.* Illinois: Charles C. Thomas.

Francisco-La Grange, F. & Joubert, M.F. 1988. Assessering in maatskaplike werk. *Maatskaplike werk/Social work,* 24 (1): 5-12.

Hepworth, D.M. & Larsen, J.A. 1990. *Direct social work practice: Theory and skills.* (3rd ed.). California: Wadsworth.

Rankin, P. 1985. Die aard en wese van die kontrak in maatskaplike werk. *Maatskaplike werk/Social work,* 21(1): 24-31.

4 Projection techniques

J P SCHOEMAN

Definition of projection

Yontef (1993:142) states that projection is a confusion of self and other that results from attributing to the outside something that is truly self. More simply stated by Clark and Fraser (1987:42), projection is imagining that our own (unwanted) feelings belong to someone else. Serok and Levi (1993:111) quote Polser and state that projection "... contributes to the development of artistic and creative qualities; it is at the same time a primitive defense mechanism, used when one cannot accept his feelings and actions because one should not feel or act that way."

Healthy projection is an art; pathological projection, on the other hand, results from one's not being aware of and not accepting responsibility for that which is projected. It is therefore very harsh on a child to confront him with a projection. He may feel robbed and unwilling to admit that a projection is part of him.

Projection serves the following objectives in the life of the child:

- Projection gives the child the space to sort out the expectations with which the world confronts him.
- It is an attempt by the child to dispel that which he cannot yet handle.
- Projection offers the child a means of maintaining his self-respect.
- It offers an escape when the child is unready to accept criticism and rejection.

The nature of projection

In a situation where a child makes use of projection, he is busy dismantling the boundary of himself. The child takes his own experience and puts it into another person or object. The other person or object serves as a "video screens onto which he "projects" the aspect of himself that he cannot handle.

Projection is thus closely linked with fantasy. Latner (1986:57) explains: "in a normal functioning, this is the fantasy process by which we visualize the environment in a different form than it presently has, in order to test out ideas for remaking the field." This is a way in which a person can change reality in accordance with desires. For example, when you ask a child to place his family in a sand tray, he sometimes rearranges the family members in other positions than they fill at home.

To abstract or recast a situation to meet needs is central to all creative thought. When a child can complete this type of exercise, it is far more valuable and problem solving than when a child refuses to create any situation. The child who can create something new through fantasy opens his options for better interaction with all his systems involved.

The process of projection is also important since, in projection, the child isolates those aspects of the environment that are important in the hope that he will meet his needs. However, because a child often feels the inability to own feelings, anger, or demands, he projects his needs into something else. Children are often discontented and believe that they cannot accept or feel that which someone else is experiencing. it is then necessary for the child to project his feelings, in order to determine whether this is really how he feels. This is one of the reasons why children so enjoy listening to stories. In this way, they get the opportunity to experience not only that which is universal, but also that which the characters are experiencing.

The basic principle underlying this technique is that the child must use natural media to communicate his responses, in cases where he would otherwise find it difficult to respond. The child organises the material in terms of his own perceptions, motivations and attitudes to adapt to his own uniqueness. He uses the familiar and reformulates situations to suit himself.

Some authors question the validity of the projective technique. However, these techniques offer the child the opportunity to provide additional information which would not usually have been given willingly, due to fear, feelings of inadequacy or a belief that it is unimportant.

Projection and normal development

The transition from embodiment (stage one of the child's developmental phases) to projection is a gradual one. This happens at the end of the first year and is heightened by the child's exploration phase and the capacity to symbolise. The child now, for the first time, explores sensation of media outside his body.

The exploration phase is a period of discovery and sensory stimulation. Therefore, a child in this stage is not in a position to create something. Later on, when he has control over all the media (sand, water, soap, sugar, faeces and so on), he will begin to create patterns, shapes and groupings. The child may need to achieve the ability to play with and through media before he can symbolise situations through projective play.

As the child develops, he starts to play symbolically: objects become toys; a box, for example, can become a car. The child starts to recreate and formulate new constellations of past, present and future experience. Importantly, not all projective play is symbolic play; it can also be exploratory, sensory and manipulative. However, if the child cannot develop an imagination through symbolic play, this cannot happen. The child will not be able to develop this means of handling a situation. The child will not be able to make sense of his world. Jennings (1993:54) is of the opinion that clients of all ages make use of their capacity to project as a way of looking at their lives and life decisions and at the possibility of new outcomes.

When the child creates, it is essential not to criticise and thus destroy the aesthetic urge. This will make the child feel insecure and may strip him of self-confidence. Adults often think that they are obliged to "teach" a child to draw properly. This cannot be justified as it hampers the child in feeling free to communicate through his creation. A child creates certain aspects disproportionately or out of context because he is experiencing that aspect in that way. The following picture, for example, illustrates a child's fear of her teacher's eyes. After this nine-year-old girl had undergone therapy, she was able to verbalise this fear. The size, colour and fearsome aspects of the eyes made the child so afraid that she could give no response in the class.

Figure 4.1: **Drawing by nine-year-old of fears (before verbalisation)**

The child saw her teacher as a monster and the eyes, particularly, aroused fear in her. Only after she identified the teacher's eyes as those of a cat could she verbalise the problem. She created the following picture as a result:

Figure 4.2: **Drawing by nine-year-old of fears (after verbalisation)**

The teacher had really become a cat to her. She could then further respond and explained why she didn't like cats, discussing the feelings they aroused in her.

The goals and objectives of projection

Projection in the here and now

To reach the child's actual problem area, he must be helped to direct all projections to the here and now: that which is making him unhappy *now*. Yontef (1993:185) comments that "the now changes each moment". Thus, it is important to support the child and deal with problems in the present.

Awareness is always here and now; therefore it is not magical, it exists. Everything that exists does so here and now. Even the past exists as now as a memory because it is of concern. That is the reason why the therapist has to bring the child into contact with the now in his life.

It is also easier for a child to exercise out the here and now. For a child, it is far more realistic if he can experience things now. Children live in the now rather than analysing the past. What is so refreshing is that children do often bring the unfinished aspect of things that happened in the past into the now. The therapist must facilitate this with techniques so that the child may explore it, taste it, act it, see it and hear it.

The here and now in the child's situation may be something only he is experiencing. That is, in the perception of the therapist, it does not exist. This is why the child must be supported to project a situation as he (the child) is experiencing it.

A projection is often an awareness, a new coming together which excludes an unchanging way of seeing the world. For this reason, a child may project a situation every day in a different way. The therapist must therefore allow the child to do his projection without interfering or pressing her goals onto the child. Interpretation of the projection can interfere with the child's focus.

Projection to stimulate self-growth

A play therapist who uses her own charisma to facilitate rapid change in the child that is not reflected in play or dialogue blocks out the child's potential for own growth and self-support. The therapist must keep in mind that although the client is only a child, he also has the potential to grow to self-regulation. If the therapist wants to dictate to him or do the interpretations of the projection, she is not treating the child as a person.

Oaklander (1992:9) stresses self-statements: "This is who I am and this is who I am not." This is a means of defining the self. An exercise to promote this kind of awareness is to let the child make a drawing of himself and then describe it. Little children also enjoy it when the therapist lets them lie down on a piece of paper and draws around their limbs to make a live silhouette. They can then be asked to name all the bad and good characteristics of "that" model. When a child gets the opportunity to project all his own characteristics into the model (knowing it is his own silhouette), he is busy growing and changing from the way he manifests himself to a fuller manifestation of his potential. Change can thus flow from acknowledgement of "is", rather than promotion of "ought".

If the therapist can succeed in giving this support to the child, it is the beginning of the child's dialogue with the world. If the therapist can give her unconditional support and acceptance, self-acceptance will come to the fore and determine the child's healthy growth.

Projection to solve unfinished business

A child makes use of projections to help him work through the traumas of his life. The child is often not allowed to express feelings in the open. Like adults, children also are forced in their families to "behave" themselves. They thus often carry unexpected resentment, incomplete awareness and anger.

Latner (1986:83) is of the opinion that "unfinished business" is organismic indigestion. We become clogged with foreign matter, the uncompleted gestalts that are the result of our interference with free functioning. Because of the unfinished business, the child is unable to establish organismic self-regulation.

At this stage, the child desperately tries to get balance; he has no confidence to participate; he is weak in himself; he leaves himself hanging. As the child strives towards closure, all the unfinished business remains, needing to be projected onto something else. The child, because of his lack of experience, projects all this unfinished business into his own body. He feels it physically as chronic aches, or any form of malfunctioning in his body. Thus, unfinished business creates both physical and other symptoms which represent expressions of unresolved conflicts. Unfinished business may become "monsters" in a child's life.

It is essential for the therapist to help the child name the monster in his life. The author often shows the children pictures of some of the monsters in our lives just to give them an idea of what a monster may look like. Children may then be asked to identify the monsters in their lives.

Figure 4.3: **An example of a tongue-tied monster**

Figure 4.4: **A monster who makes use of masks**

Figure 4.5: **The monster of the intellect**

When the therapist deals with the monster in the life of the child, the following steps can be followed:

❐ The child must create a monster that deals with his life situation.
❐ Start a discussion with the child, asking him the following:
  • For how long has the monster existed?
  • Are there other people who know about the monster?
  • Is there something about the monster that scares him?
  • Is he prepared to have the monster in his life and live with it?
  • Can he name his monster?
  • How old was he when he got the monster?
  • Is it possible to draw or make the feelings about the monster in clay?
  • Ask the child to talk to the monster. (Put the monster in the hot chair — chair work is described in chapter 12.)

VALUE

Reasons why children make use of projections

As said, projection is one of the child's mechanisms for dealing with problems. Children make use of projections for different reasons:

- A child sometimes wants to get rid of certain feelings or may actually want to own the feeling, but something is in his way. This is not necessarily unfinished business. The feeling or emotion is acceptable to the child and therefore he wants to make it his own.
- A child sometimes wants to try something out, but does not have the courage to try it immediately. He first wants to give something else the characteristic. If it is acceptable to himself and other people, he will then integrate it into his own gestalt.
- A child sometimes chooses projection as a method of escape. His own world is dull and not really exciting, therefore he creates a projection with fantasies in it to make his life more glamorous. This gives him a safe place to go to when reality is too overwhelming for him. There are adults that forbid a child to daydream like this. This is very hard on a child, for daydreaming makes his world a better place and thus gives him pleasure. It also generates his energy level to enable the child to handle the real world later on.

Adults, however, do the same thing. They often wish for something, for instance, that their holiday were not so far off or that they could win an overseas trip. Elderly people often wish to die because they want to go to heaven.

If a child wishes for a better place, it is not the therapist's responsibility to keep him in the state of unrealistic dreams. The dream world is an absolute clue for the therapist as to where the needs of the child are projected. The child creates alternatives in his imaginary world because of the lack of experience in the real world.

Dreams

Dreams (as opposed to daydreams) can be used to integrate the child's situation. A dream helps the child to put all the parts of his life in position. Dreams can also be very helpful in starting communication with the child.

A dream can thus be regarded as a projection. As Yontef (1993:83) states, each fragment of the dream person, prop, or mood is considered an alienated part of the individual. The person takes each part — and an encounter ensues between the divided parts of the self. Oaklander (1988:145) also feels very strongly about dreams:

> . . . the dream is an existential message. It is more than an unfinished wish, it is more than a prophecy. It is a message from yourself to yourself, to whatever part of you is listening. The dream is possibly the most spontaneous expression of the human being, a piece of art that we chisel out of our lives. And every part, every situation in the dream is a creation of the dreamer himself.

What makes it so useful is that the part of the child that he disowns is put into the dream. If a child dreams a bizarre or puzzling dream, he tries to forget it as soon as possible.

Sometimes, children get confused between a dream and a wish. It does not really matter because in both situations, the child is projecting unmet issues.

Oaklander (1988:145) deals with dreams in the following way:
- Ask the child to retell the dream in the present.
- Ask the child to play out all parts in the dream as if it were a play. The child must speak for each person or thing — like the father, the mother, the food, the wine, the dog, and so on.
- Ask the child to imagine an ending for the dream.
- Ask the child what he thinks the message of the dream is.

What is very useful is that the child exposes his fear and gets the opportunity to experience relief in the process of sharing his dream and all the emotions in the dream.

Practical ideas in projection: working towards assessment

Projective tests

Apart from the fact that all projection tests may not be carried out by all child therapists, the diagnostic accuracy of such tests is also questionable.

However, their value as an expressive medium emphasises other uses. If a so-called projection test is used instead as a creative and expressive medium, it is not only more useful to all child therapists, but also creates the opportunity for each child's uniqueness to be respected. The child has a chance to make definitive statements about himself as projection is used as a connection with dialogue. Oaklander (1988:135) states that the child's "learning to spit out statements that don't fit for him is a crucial part of his process".

Helping aids

The following helping aids can be used in projection:
- Take any magazine and ask the child to find a picture he would like to talk about.
- The child can be asked to draw a picture, more specifically, a house-tree-person picture. The child must then be asked to discuss his unique creation.
- The child can be asked to draw a picture and tell a story about it.
- The author makes use of sensory stimulation to trigger the child's memories. Smell can be triggered through allowing the child to smell something with specific memories. The child could also taste a sweet and then recall a connected memory. Flowers can also be used.

    This sensory contact creates a unique opportunity for projection, as the child has the chance to talk about something valuable, or even unpleasant. This brings him into contact with feelings he is still experiencing. Furthermore, the fact that the child

makes specific choices here also indicates unfinished business in his life. The child may thus also have the opportunity to talk about present problems.
- Fables also create an opportunity for the child's reactions. What is important is not always the reaction itself, but the child's opportunity to share of himself. Through this technique, children often provide so much information to the therapist that it is hard to deal with it all.

Specific analysis of projective creation

When a child is given a projection assignment, certain tendencies often come to the fore which cannot be blatantly ignored. Machover (1949) was the first person to analyse the creation of a human figure as a projection of the self. She believed if one is given the instruction to draw a human figure, all one's associated emotions will also be depicted. Machover even paid special attention to the placing of the drawing, its size, form and colour. Graphic art and how lines are used were also meaningful to her. The foreground, background, spontaneity or reservedness were all meaningful to her. She even placed emphasis on whether the child had erased part of the drawing and how many times he had erased the drawing before he was satisfied. She regarded the head as the central part of the self and also of intellectual power. Social control and the impulses of the body which are reflected were also important to her. For instance, she believed that a big head was an indication of brain dysfunction, headaches or intellectual achievement. This test is known as the DAP (Draw a person) test.

The following aspects are important in the evaluation of the human figure: items associated with the quality of the drawing; the quality of the line; integration; shadows; size of the figure; transparency; unknown figures; large or small heads; squint eyes; uneven teeth; short or long arms; large hands; hands clasped together; legs pressed together; genitalia; monsters; snow and rain. The play therapist who is in confluence with the child will use such findings as hypotheses and will ask the child to interpret all the aspects mentioned (Di Leo, 1983).

Other authors emphasise different aspects in projections concerning the human figure. Klepsch and Logie (1983:12) divide the depiction of figures into four categories, namely:

- personality which can be measured
- relationships with other significant people
- the measurement of group values
- the measurement of attitudes.

Although these authors are right in applying such categories to drawings, they can also be applied to work in any creative medium, such as clay or sand. A point can also be raised in connection with the measurement of group values. It is important to see that the child does not include any person in his depiction who does not play a meaningful role in his life.

Gender identification

As a rule, children depict themselves according to the sex to which they belong. This indicates the personal identification of the child. However, the very young child will often depict his mother instead of himself. This is done because he is very close to his mother. If a child depicts himself as belonging to the opposite sex, the therapist must take special note of the child's current developmental phase.

Genitalia

A child who draws genitalia generally feels uncomfortable and tense about them because they are very private parts of the body. The therapist cannot interpret this as, for example, evidence of molestation, unless the child indicates this. Ask the child what his picture means and what he is trying to say. Any parts which have been left out, such as hands or feet, must not be taken as an indication of something being dealt with. This sometimes indicates a child's awareness of puberty.

The overreactive child

The child who finds the sandpit or paper too small or who wants to shift his boundaries to gain more space usually feels this way because he is too restricted. Again, however, the child must explain and the therapist must not offer subjective guidance.

Organicism

Parts of the child's body which have been injured or affected will obviously receive attention. These issues form part of the child's unfinished business. The author once had the opportunity to work with a group of newly diagnosed diabetics. The children were instructed to draw themselves. A boy of eight years drew himself as follows:

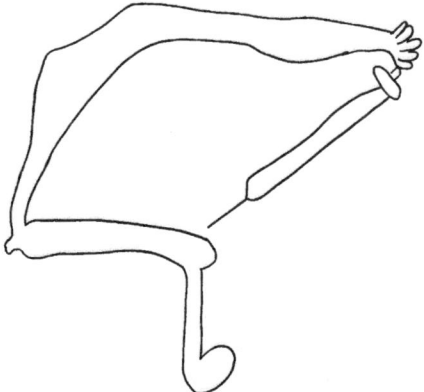

Figure 4.6: **Self-portrait by an eight-year-old**

The boy was clearly indicating that he didn't need a head or a body to survive. He only needed a hand to hold the needle — a hand larger than the needle. A leg was also needed to receive his insulin injections.

Anxiety

A fearful, anxious child will depict the sad, while an unfraid child will depict the pleasure in his life.

Self-image

The size and detail of decorations with which the child draws himself often reflects his self-image.

Learning problems

Children who find they have a problem with progressing sometimes unconsciously depict the cause of the problem in drawings or other creations.

Size

A very large or very small creation can also convey a message from the child. A large creation is often undertaken by an energetic child. Such a child is usually very creative and spontaneous. On the other hand, such an undertaking can also be made by a child who wishes he had more energy and depicts himself as large in an attempt to achieve this. Both hypotheses must be explored. Similarly, children who depict themselves as very small may do so because they have nothing to communicate or because they wish to make their problem invisible.

Absence or distortion of limbs

Those parts of the body causing the child discomfort are either overemphasised or underemphasised. The reason for the emphasis must be interpreted by the child.

The child as analyst

Only the child can say how he feels and thinks about something. The therapist must be sensitive in guiding the child towards an assertion. It is thus also important for the child continually to say how he feels and whether they are on the right track. Children, particularly in their middle childhood, are too frightened to say whether they feel different.

For this reason Oaklander's (1988:53) approach is useful as she leads the child through 14 steps to interpreting a projection. Oaklander terms this her working model:

- ❐ Have the child share the experience of drawing.
- ❐ Have the child share the drawing itself, describing the picture in his own way.
- ❐ On a deeper level, promote the child's further self-discovery.
- ❐ Ask the child to describe the picture as if it were himself, using the word "I".
- ❐ Pick specific things in the picture for the child to identify with.
- ❐ Ask the child questions, if necessary, to aid the process.
- ❐ Further focus the child's attention and sharpen his awareness by emphasis and exaggeration of a part or parts of a picture.

- Have the child create a dialogue between two parts of his picture or two contact points or opposing points (polarities).
- Encourage the child to pay attention to colours.
- Watch for cues in the child's tone of voice, body posture, facial and body expression, breathing, and silence.
- Work on identification, helping the child to own what has been said about the picture or parts of the picture.
- Leave the drawing and work on the child's life situations and unfinished business that come out of the drawing.
- Watch for the missing parts or empty spaces in the picture and attend to these.
- Stay with the child's foreground flow or attend to his own foreground.

Normal artistic development

However, it is essential for the therapist to be knowledgeable about the child's normal artistic development. Oaklander (1988:177) emphasises this: "Drawings, like dreams, tend to make accurate statements about what's going on in one's life at the moment."

The child's first attempt to create a human figure is often an incomplete attempt. Thus, the three-year-old will often depict a figure as a head only. The head is, naturally, the most important part of the human to a child. Sometimes, eyes, a nose and a mouth are also drawn. The four-year-old will draw a stick figure, while the five-year-old will distinguish a head and body. However, the arms and legs will often sprout from the head. As the child develops cognitively, more detail will be included, such as the neck, fingers, toes and even pupils in the eyes. The five-year-old still tends to draw the head disproportionately large. However, as the child gets older, he can handle pencils and other media with greater ability.

Conclusion

Projection is a mechanism that is used by children and serves a variety of functions. Projections may be expressions of anxiety or of unfinished business. They may be used to express feelings that children feel unable to express in real life. They may depict wishes, wants, needs, fantasies, questions, curiosities and attitudes.

The projection of a child may be a way of working through feelings and experiences that he is unable to deal with directly and openly. Therefore, the therapist has no right to interpret the projection. However, it is her duty as therapist to make the child aware of what the projection may be trying to say. Children are fully capable of learning to deal with themselves if only the therapist would give them the encouragement and the opportunity to do so.

Bibliography

Clark, D. & Fraser, T. 1987. *The gestalt approach. An introduction for managers and trainers*. (2nd. ed.). New York: The Gestalt Journal Press. Inc.

Di Leo, J.H. 1983. Interpreting children's drawings. New York : Brunner Mazel.

Jennings, S. 1993. *Play therapy with children. A practitioner's guide*. Oxford: Blackwell scientific publications.

Klepsch, M. & Logie, L. 1982. *Children draw and tell*. New York: Brunner Mazel.

Latner, J. 1986. *The Gestalt Therapy Book.* New York: The Gestalt Journal Press. Inc.

Machover, K. 1949. *Personality projection in the drawing of the human figure.* Springfied, Il: Charles C. Thomas.

Oaklander, V. 1988. (Third edition: 1992). *Windows to our children. A Gestalt therapy apporach to children and adolescents.* New York: The Gestalt Journal Press. Inc.

Serok, S. & Levi, N. 1993. Application of Gestalt therapy with long-term prison inmates in Israel. The Gestalt Journal, (XVI) 1:105-127.

5 Relaxation play

M VAN DER MERWE

Introduction

Relaxation play is mostly directed towards the attainment of process goals, namely, to prepare the child for the helping process by attaining the correct level of tension so as to ensure that he finds the helping process worthwhile. When a child's level of motivation is low and his tension too high, it will limit the attainment of content goals. The therapist's attitude should encourage trust, and the therapeutic climate should help the child to relax.

Relaxation techniques often have a distinct behaviour therapeutic quality, for instance, systematic desensitisation (Van Delft, 1980:119-121). It is important that the therapist should not see relaxation in the beginning phase as therapy in itself. Usually, it must be used together with other techniques. Its purpose is to open the child to the therapy of the change-oriented phase. When the child client is relaxed, it is easier to strengthen the therapeutic relationship. The other techniques can then be used more successfully (Van der Merwe, 1991:141).

In the final phase of therapy, relaxation play is used to reduce the therapeutic intensity. The child should be prepared to handle future problems on his own. The relaxation techniques he learns in therapy can be carried over to real life situations, especially difficult ones.

There are various relaxation techniques, including the use of music, puzzles, games, outings and animals, as well as progressive muscle relaxation and systematic desensitisation techniques. Various other techniques, as described under the other forms of play, also have relaxation value.

Music

Music therapy is a comprehensive field of study. According to Krout and Tischler (1986:145-146), music therapists usually have a thorough musical education, as well as a background in psychology and education. Even when child therapists are not experts in the music field, they should be able to use techniques based on music. Smith (1981:113) mentions two ways in which music can be used in therapy, namely, that it can be instrumental in creating the correct therapeutic climate and that it can serve as an opener for further discussion. In the latter case, the choice of words that form part of the music is important. According to Oaklander (1988:115), music and rhythmic beats are ancient forms of communication and expression. Therefore, they are appropriate in therapeutic work with children.

Crompton (1980:150) also stresses that music can be used for reduction of tension in child clients and for relaxation purposes in order to ensure effective communication. The use of music can bring an element of fun into therapy that will enhance the child's motivation.

It is unlikely that therapists will use music for direct counselling in the change-oriented phase of therapy unless they have had intensive education in music. Music will be used especially in the beginning and final phases of therapy and for the attainment of process goals. It may be used at the beginning and end of each session for relaxation purposes.

Research has shown that certain music affects brain rhythms. It may have a calming or a stimulating effect. It may also influence other bodily functions, such as blood pressure, heartbeat, muscle tone and abdominal functioning (Hanser, 1988:211). Individualisation is still important as a specific piece of music will not have the same effect on different people.

The child may listen to the music passively or may combine this with movement. Payne (1988:68-97) uses dance movements in therapy with youth. These can be adapted for younger children. Movement with the music can help the child to relax, while also using excess energy. This may enable him to sit quietly and to concentrate during the working part of the interview. Oaklander (1988:118) suggests that children enjoy using coloured chiffon scarves as they move to music. Similarly, Crompton (1980:149) believes that social workers do not utilise music enough when working with children, and also recommends the use of music and dance simultaneously. Furthermore, Dunne (1988:140) sees creative movement as a valuable relaxation activity, especially for people who struggle to verbalise their feelings.

Music can even be used in combination with drawing. The child may make big movements on paper when using finger paints or crayons. This may lead to the expression of feelings, to catharsis and may serve as an opener for communication when the drawings point out feelings or facts.

Musical lyrics may be used metaphorically. A well-known song describes various fairy tales, such as *Jack and the beanstalk*. In this song, Jack's victory over the giant is described. This can be used as a metaphor for the child's victory over his problems. Combined with creative play, a huge beanstalk can be drawn and the various steps necessary to combat the problem can be written on the drawing. On top, a drawing of a giant can be fastened in such a way that the child can punch it. This action may also give him a feeling of being in control.

Well-known songs may also be adapted to convey certain messages. For example, the song *Brother Peter* can be adapted as follows to various languages to address the self-image of the child:

English

I am smart, I am smart;
Very smart, very smart;
I am very smart, I am very smart;
Smart am I, smart am I!

Afrikaans

Ek is oulik, ek is oulik
Baie oulik, baie oulik;
Ek is baie oulik, ek is baie oulik;
Oulik is ek, oulik is ek!

Zulu

Ngiyathandeka, ngiyathandeka;
Ngithandeka kakhulu, ngithandeka kakhulu;
Ngiyathandeka, ngiyathandeka;
Ukuthandeka ngiyathandeka, ukuthandeka ngiyathandeka!

Tswana

Ke ya ratega, ke ya ratega;
Ke ya ratega gagolo, ke ya ratega gagolo;
Ke ya ratega, ke ya ratega;
Go ratega ke ya ratega, go ratega ke ya ratega!

According to Oaklander (1988:115-117), there are songs about every feeling and life situation, as well as nonsense songs and songs that tell stories. She has experimented with various musical instruments in therapy, and found the guitar to be the most effective, especially when combined with her ability to be expressive with the songs she chooses and her ability to involve the children. She believes that the guitar holds some special magic for children. When working on children's knowledge and skills regarding the use of feeling language, it could also be meaningful to follow Oaklander's (1988:118) suggestion that drums can be used to depict feelings, and to ask the child to portray different feelings with drumbeats.

In the final phase of therapy, music can have a definite function when the child learns to use it as a support system. It can be used in combination with muscle relaxation and imagination games. The use of music can help to reduce the therapeutic intensity that usually typifies the change-oriented phase, in order to prepare the child for the termination of therapy.

Muscle relaxation training and progressive muscle relaxation

Through these techniques which are described by Van Delft (1980:119-120) and Hepworth and Larsen (1990:512-520), the child learns to relax different muscles, with the aim of ultimately being able to relax his whole body. Therapists should have a sound knowledge of these techniques before attempting to use them.

Progressive muscle relaxation heightens the child's awareness of tension and relaxation, through the alternate contraction and relaxation of muscles. His attention must be focused on a specific group of muscles at a time. He is then asked to contract those muscles and to keep them tense until the therapist directs him to relax (usually after five to seven seconds). While the muscles are contracted, the child must be aware of the sensation. The comfortable feeling of the relaxed muscles must then be contrasted with the discomfort of the tense muscles. Hepworth and Larsen (1990:515) offer guidelines for therapists using muscle relaxation techniques: for instance, the tone of voice should be calm and soft, without being dramatic. Breathing exercises are also helpful when learning progressive muscle relaxation (Graver & Morse, 1986:105; Fish, 1988:163-167).

These techniques prepare the child to relax before, during and after difficult situations, for instance, when there is conflict between his parents. The techniques can be practised through role-playing in the final phase of therapy, to prepare the child to handle such situations on his own.

Systematic desensitisation

This technique requires the child to be helped to think through various aspects of frightening and alarming situations, while he is in a relaxed state. He learns to handle such situations by working through them from the least frightening to the most frightening parts. Usually, he must first have mastered progressive muscle relaxation. Then, a hierarchy of fears is compiled, with items on the hierarchy being paired off with relaxation techniques (Van Delft, 1980:120; Fish, 1988:167; Thompson & Rudolph, 1992:181).

While this is a specialised behaviour therapeutic technique, it can be adapted for use in the treatment of young children. In the case of divorce, for instance, a child can be helped to think through the whole process of visitation. A hierarchy of frightening aspects can then be compiled with the most terrifying at the top. The child must then visualise the least frightening situation while he is in a relaxed state. This could, for instance, be thinking of visiting the other parent. The most frightening could be getting into the parent's car. As soon as the child can visualise a specific situation without being afraid, it is time to move on to the next situation in the hierarchy, until all the fears have been mastered completely.

In the final phase of therapy, this technique can be revised, and the child can be helped to generalise it for use in other threatening situations. It thus becomes part of his problem-solving skills.

Puzzles

Porter (1983:316) regards the building of puzzles as a relaxing activity. It can help to develop a relationship of trust and to create a relaxed atmosphere for therapy.

However, puzzle building can be used metaphorically when connected with the way in which therapy builds the child's life skills. A puzzle may thus be built throughout therapy and serve as a parallel for the helping process. Working on it at the end of session will also help with the transition from therapy to real life. When the puzzle then completed in the final phase, it serves as a metaphor for the completion of the helping process. A connection can be made between the puzzle that is whole and the child that is whole after therapy. At the same time, by removing a piece of the puzzle, the child can be made to understand that he is not going to stay the same. A further connection can be made between his skill in the building of puzzles and his problem-solving skills. When he gets stuck whilst building a puzzle, he can ask for help. In the same way, he can ask for help when confronted by other problems. The therapist and child client can then look at possible support systems that he can use when he encounters trouble in the building of his "life puzzle" (Van der Merwe, 1991:147).

Games

Board games and other games are widely acknowledged for their therapeutic and relaxation value. they also bring the much needed element of fun to therapy (Porter, 1983:319; Frey, 1986:28; Gardner, 1986:41-73; Schaefer & Reid, 1986:4-11).

Games have relaxation value, but can also be used for assessment. For example, the child's reactions when winning or losing can render information regarding his general functioning and his personality. Communication is enhanced through the playing of games. Furthermore, it helps with the development of a rapport between the therapist and child client.

Especially during the first and last interviews, but also at the beginning and end of each individual interview, relaxation games can be used. The author often uses Ghiaci and Richardson's (1980:79) proposed activities, namely, that the therapist and child should pretend to be

- a rosebud opening its petals
- a sun rising
- a burning and melting candle
- a melting snowman.

Using an imaginary or even a real key to wind up children to be pretend mice or whatever they fancy works well. They can do the same to the therapist (Oaklander, 1988:19). Oaklander (1988) describes a lot of practical, fun-filled relaxation activities.

Trips and outings

Trips and outings may enhance the therapeutic relationship. Usually, the child enjoys such activities and this may influence his view of therapy as positive. When he relaxes during therapy, he often communicates more spontaneously and important information may come to the fore. Graver and Morse (1986:105) stress the fact that children need fun, even when they have difficult times.

The helping process can also be terminated with an outing. This helps to reduce therapeutic intensity. The trip should preferably be goal-directed, for instance, when the therapist and child cycle through the community to look for possible support systems.

It is often found, especially in the work of students, that they tend to view the last interview as one in which no work has to be done. They give the individual child snacks or the group has a party. However, therapy is expensive. This is especially visible when working from a private practice where parents pay for each interview. They can surely not be expected to pay for the therapist and child client to have a party! There are therapeutic ways of reducing therapeutic intensity and of reaching the other goals of termination. The last interview should be hard work with play included, but definitely not only play and fun.

Pets and animals

Smith (1981:111) refers to the value of pets in therapy with children. The relationship with an animal gives the child the opportunity for non-threatening interaction with another living being. According to George (1988:400-418), the use of animals in therapy can aid the child in developing his ego and inner strength. This will help him to handle stressful life events better. Furthermore, an animal gives a child love without criticism or reservation. While caring for an animal, the child also learns to be responsible.

George (1988:402) cites the research findings of Katcher (1985), namely, that when a child is in a strange room with a stranger, the presence of an animal can have a calming effect on the child, even causing his blood pressure to drop. The child feels safe in the presence of a calm animal and this may reduce his tension. Anxiety is also reduced when the child touches the animal. Especially in the beginning phase of therapy, the use of animals can be of great value in reducing the child's level of tension, strengthening the therapeutic relationship and getting the child involved in therapy. While doing relaxation or breathing exercises, for instance, the animal and the child can lie on the floor together.

The choice of the animal is very important, as it may be bad for a child's self-image if a dog ignores or bites him. Thus, George (1988:405) also discusses the work of Gonski, a social worker who uses German Shepherd dogs in her work with children. She finds that these dogs can involve even the most hostile or passive children in therapy. George (1988:407) also uses farm animals successfully, while Van der Merwe (1991:149) suggests that a child bring along his own pet if it will make him feel more comfortable. The author has used pets in therapy and found that they do have a calming effect on children. However, as soon as the animal becomes the centre of attention when other therapeutic work must be done, or the child uses the animal to avoid discussion of painful material, it would be best to remove the animal from the room.

Conclusion

It should always be kept in mind that therapy with children should contain elements of fun. This implies that it should take place in a relaxed atmosphere. Relaxation play is therefore an important facilitating form of play. It paves the way for the use of other forms of play. It also paves the way for the transition to life outside the therapeutic situation.

The techniques that are used should be adapted to each child's personality and preferences. If the therapist succeeds in teaching the child how to relax, this may be one of the most important advantages of therapy that can form part of the child's coping skills forever.

Bibliography

Crompton, M. 1980. *Respecting children: Social work with young people.* London: Edward Arnold.

Dunne, P.B. 1988. Drama therapy techniques in one-to-one treatment with disturbed children and adolescents. *The Arts in Psychotherapy*, 15:139-149.

Fish, M.C. 1988. Relaxation training for childhood disorders. In Schaefer: 160-192.

Frey, D.E. 1986. Communications boardgames with children. In Schaefer & Reid: 21-41.

Gardner, R.A. 1986. The Talking, feeling, doing game. In Schaefer & Reid: 41-72.

George, H. 1988. Child therapy and animals: A new way for an old relationship. In Schaefer: 400-418.

Ghiaci, G. & Richardson, J.T.E. 1980. The effects of dramatic play upon cognitive structure and development. *The Journal of Genetic Psychology*, 136: 77-83.

Graver, C.M. & Morse, L.A. 1986. *Helping children of divorce: A group leader's guide.* Illinois: Charles C. Thomas.

Grobbelaar, S.W.P. & Schoeman, J.M. (Eds.). *Benaderings in maatskaplike werk.* Pretoria: Publisher unknown.

Hanser, S.B. 1988. Controversy in music listening/stress reduction research. *The Arts in Psychotherapy*, 15: 211-217.

Hepworth, D.H & Larsen, J.A. 1990. *Direct social work practice: theory and skills.* (3rd ed.). California: Wadsworth.

Krout, R. & Tischler, B. 1986. Hands across the water: Impressions of music therapy in England. *The Arts in Psychotherapy*, 13: 143-146.

Oaklander, V. 1988. *Windows to our children: A gestalt therapy approach to children and adolescents.* (2nd ed.). New York: The Gestalt Journal Press. Inc.

Payne, H. 1988. The use of dance movement therapy with troubled youth. In Schaefer: 68-97.

Porter, C. 1983. Spelterapie met die sorgbehoewende kind. Unpublished MA thesis Pretoria: University of Pretoria.

Schaefer, C.E. (Ed.). 1988. *Innovative interventions in child and adolescent therapy.* New York: John Wiley.

Schaefer, C.E. & Reid, S.E. (Eds.). 1986. *Game play: Therapeutic use of childhood games.* New York: John Wiley.

Smith, C.M. 1981. *Leer die kind ken: Riglyne vir die maatskaplike werker.* Pretoria: Academica.

Thompson, C.L. & Rudolph, L.B. 1992. *Counseling children* (3rd ed.). California: Brooks Cole.

Van Delft, W.F. 1980. Gedragsverandering by wyse van gedragsterapeutiese beginsels en tegnieke. In Grobbelaar & Schoeman: 111-142.

Van der Merwe, M. 1991. Maatskaplikewerk-beraad met jong kinders in egskeidingsituasies met fokus op speeltegnieke. Unpublished MA thesis. Stellenbosch: University of Stellenbosch.

6 Fantasy, metaphor and imagination

J P SCHOEMAN

Introduction

> The infant is born with creative potential and the capacity to symbolize: indeed, it is this very capacity of human beings to pretend and make believe which enables them to survive. We cannot envisage a life within which we could not imagine how things are — how they were or how they might be. The creative imagination is the most important attitude that we can foster in a child; this is the basis of creative playfulness.
>
> (Jennings, 1993:20)

Fantasy forms a central part of the child's development. The word *fantasy* is derived from the Latin word *phantasticus*, which, in turn, stems from a Greek word meaning "to make something visible". It is therefore suitable that this concept is used to describe the making visible of a mental image to the child. The concept of fantasy thus incorporates various kinds of mental images, including fairy tales, fables, metaphors, symbolic and creative play, and products of the child's own imagination. What all kinds of fantasy have in common is that they create a secondary world.

Philosophers, such as Jean-Paul Sartre, have emphasised that this secondary world not only offers an escape from the primary world, but also a transformation of reality. For this reason, a child who cannot re-place himself into a fantasy world is infinitely poorer than a child who succeeds in doing so. Adults should thus offer children the opportunity of learning through fantasy and not make them adults too soon. Children need this opportunity for problem solving, creative thinking and concretisation, and the chance to deal with their fears in a harmless way. Fantasy thus offers the child a safe way of transforming his world.

Obviously, the child is dependent on his experiential or primary world, as his experiences serve as a point of reference. However, they form the basis for compiling imaginary pictures and for re-placing the child into fantasy situations. The fantasy world is thus a secondary world, as cited by Steenberg (1987:12). This subordinate world is therefore only a supplement to reality.

Some people see fantasy as illogical and try to take it away from their children. The experiences of the latter are then impoverished. Some parents are under the false impression that children are lying when they fantasise, and often reprimand children for such fantasising. The child who fantasises is actually busy organising and arranging reality as his imagination allows. This rearranging of his imaginary world is a creative action and an artistic expression. It is an interpretation of his abilities in imaginary form.

Another important facet of fantasy is that it allows the child to be displaced empathically. He thus becomes aware of the feelings, attitudes and opinions of others. This leads to empathic understanding and an understanding of alternatives.

The question often arises as to whether children do not hear too many fantasy tales and whether they are not overly involved therein. However, the child must learn so many life truths when still very young that there is almost no danger of overexposing him to fantasy. Fantasy helps him to handle life truths and knowledge of the world and to integrate these into an acceptable outlook on life.

It has been found that the world of a child who is exposed to fantasy insufficiently may be diminished and that the child may have difficulty in handling it. He becomes trapped in a colourless world where right and wrong dominate. Such a child often shows signs of disruption, as well as of deviant behaviour, for example, natural aggression or withdrawal from normal interpersonal relationship (Mills & Crowley, 1986:63). It is well known that children with little exposure to fantasy also have poorer problem-solving skills.

In this chapter, the value of fantasy will be discussed through different aspects: first, fantasy as metaphor; secondly, fantasy as imagination; and thirdly, dreams and fantasy.

The enchantment of "Once upon a time . . ." : fantasy as metaphor

Telling stories is as old as humanity. The most common are folktales or fables that are passed on from generation to generation. The question as to why fairy tales keep fascinating children has been asked for years. The answer lies in the fact that these stories function as metaphors. A metaphor may be defined as a way of communicating symbolically. Metaphors have been in use for centuries and their main function is to communicate a message as effectively as possible. Other examples of metaphors are the parables of Jesus Christ, or allegories which use imaginative imagery to convey meaning. Metaphors function by portraying objects and situations indirectly, often through paradoxical comparisons, in order to give them meaning.

The value of the metaphor for the child is not only that he can learn from it, but also that it forms his perception of the world in which he lives. The child's experiences should be facilitated in such a way that a milieu is formed wherein he can develop in a healthy way. The metaphor therefore offers him an imaginary experience from which he can learn.

The most important function of metaphors for the play therapist, as mentioned above, is that their use affords the child the opportunity of reasoning out alternative ways of behaving and of choosing the best possibility. He learns through metaphors that other people may follow different approaches to his own. This may lead him to conclude that his own choice is not necessarily the only alternative.

Metaphors are thus extremely useful as a therapeutic medium, as they enable the therapist to provide the child with the essential equipment he will need later in life, but without the child suffering any real consequences of his choices.

Furthermore, the metaphor is a valuable aid because it can be adapted to suit each child's unique needs. It can accommodate various temperaments and can serve as a filter. It offers a dynamic opportunity for adventure. In cases where the child's verbal skills are limited, the metaphor serves as a carrier of messages. Sometimes, children have visual pictures in their heads that they find difficult to verbalise. Yet one metaphor offers the opportunity to portray numerous non-verbalised images. The child can therefore use metaphors to give the therapist insight into what is happening in his world.

A useful summary of the nature and functions of metaphor is offered by Spies (1993: 14). She describes a metaphor as a carrier of information, which aims, on the one hand, to portray messages pertaining to acceptable behaviour, relationships, interactive processes and rules within a system and, on the other hand, looks at possible solutions. For the child who is in the process of learning and sorting out his world, forming and mastering the metaphor is a valuable aid as it can serve as a basis for comparison. The child then uses reality and his own imagination and integrates them into a whole in order to handle the situation with which he is confronted.

Functions of the metaphor

Empathic understanding

Mostly, children find it very difficult to discuss their unfulfilled needs. Verbalising their fears, for example, may evoke more anxiety. The request to verbalise emotions can also make a child anxious. The child experiencing negative emotions often protects the source as he finds it threatening to jeopardise a significant person in his life. Adults know the feeling and usually employ defence mechanism, as the verbalisation of unmet needs can be too painful.

However, even adults may find it comforting to read about people with circumstances similar to their own. In these stories, one often reads how other people cope with their problems and how they have bridged them. It is much easier to speculate about the fate of someone else, as the threatening content is then separate from the reader's personal level of experience, and it can therefore be regarded more objectively. The reader of the metaphor can relate to it, think it over and then distance himself again. The same applies to the child. When the child can look at an emotion without using extra energy for denial, he can enable himself to evaluate his feelings and can decide how to handle the situation. Sometimes, he can assess the source of his feelings and can gain more insight into his situation. Such stories may thus be regarded as metaphors for the child's life. When a therapist uses a metaphor and creates a situation similar to the child's own, it can demonstrate possible solutions.

The behaviour made possible by the metaphor gives the child the opportunity to consider and review emotions, feelings and problems concerning a situation without tension and fear. It offers the child a chance to learn without experiencing the real trauma and is a great relief.

The feelings that have accumulated are comparable with steam building up in a pressure cooker. Through the metaphor, the child is given the opportunity to vent his feelings within a safe environment. However, he still has the space to distance himself if he chooses.

Finally, the metaphor creates a platform for the child to experience his real needs more readily. The message that the child gets through the metaphor is that his situation is universal. Feelings of isolation are then controlled. The metaphor also has the advantage that it offers the child role models. When identifying with the character and experiencing empathic understanding, the child can learn from the metaphor.

Handling fears

Bettelheim (1976) suggests that fairy tales help children to handle various conflicts and fears in their lives. Many of the well-known stories, such as *Little Red Riding Hood*, reflect universal fears of children, for instance, that something will bother them when they are sent to do errands, or that a wild animal will catch them even if they are assured that the animal is as tame as a lamb.

Even in the therapeutic milieu, feelings (for example, of guilt) do not always surface. They are mostly repressed in the "respectable world". With the help of fairy tales, these feelings can be released. When the negative feelings are not allowed to come to the surface, more tension is built up, and the energy is experienced as negative. These feelings become too painful to discuss, and the child is not able to work them through. When excess negative energy takes this course, the child may develop psychosomatic conditions in an unconscious effort to handle his tension.

Adults would like to see children in a world where they are not constantly subjected to danger and disturbing situations. It is important that grown-ups try to remember that there were times when they were children and felt overwhelmed by a grown-up world that threatened to engulf them. There are certain fears that children commonly experience, for instance:

- fear of the world over which they have no control
- nightmares
- ghosts under the bed
- thieves at the window
- staying alone at home
- the fight for independence
- cruelty and ridicule by the peer group.

Even the happiest child has to experience these growing pains in order to develop normally.

It can be asked why the child needs to use fantasy to handle these fears. According to the psychonalytical approach, it is believed that the child grasps the part of the story that suits him. When his own feelings are too painful, he may still grasp the situation in the story as he can experience part of his pain through this channel. This action helps him to release his own feelings and pain.

Unfortunately, fantasy is not always fun and games. It may make the child anxious. On the other hand, the child may feel better when he returns from fantasy to reality to discover that his own circumstances are not really as bad as the circumstances in the secondary world in which he found himself. In this way, he may develop insight.

Adults may find it unacceptable to be in a fantasy world, as it brings them too near to the truth. This aspect borders on intellectual obstruction. The reader or observer does not want to allow himself to experience the unthinkable. Realism is important to such people and they may feel that it is childish to allow themselves to regress to previous developmental phases.

The consolation of the ego

The child must realise that he has control over his own life. He also has the right to make his own choices. He should be able to decide when something is threatening. By using the metaphor, the child learns to use imaginary characters to make the handling of his problem easier. By observing the ways in which characters cope with their problems, the child can adapt his actions accordingly.

The metaphor does not provide a magic wand that takes the problem away. However, it does give the child the opportunity of gaining self-knowledge in a way with which he feels comfortable. Offering a metaphor instead of the painful truth may soften the circumstances. The therapist does have the advantage that the child has some knowledge; he is not like a blank piece of paper. The therapist uses this basis to build on and tries to make existing information more gentle and manageable, because the child must be motivated to do something about his situation. Without hope of improvement, he will not be motivated to work towards meeting his needs. Thus, in the metaphor, triumph should overcome sadness in the end. Children frequently tend to want to hear a story over and over again. This is often to hear the process of triumph again. Sometimes, they will even change the content so that the metaphor does have a triumphant ending.

Even though children often realise afterwards that the metaphor is similar to their own history, it does not impede the effectiveness of the metaphor. It is still up to the child to decide if it is only a story distant from himself, or applicable to his own situation.

Concretising situations

Children sometimes seems to be small adults. They may also behave maturely. Adults may then wrongly believe that these children can think like grown-ups and forget that children do not have the experience to reason like them. For instance, adults sometimes think erroneously that a child is stubborn or intentional when he fails to understand something. Many adults have long forgotten how a child thinks and argues. The time when they were children and were functioning on a level where cause and effect had no meaning may feel far away.

For this reason, an adult may be surprised when a child clings to her when a big lorry drives past. She has possibly forgotten that a toddler does not yet have a realistic perception of the size of objects. Therefore, the child may find a big lorry overwhelming. It will take many hours of play to help the child to realise that the lorry will not harm him if handled correctly. Metaphors can build the bridge to make situations that are full of fear and emotion more concrete. A child finds it easier to discuss a concrete situation.

Examples stimulate new behaviour

The child needs to master many developmental tasks before moving over into adulthood safely. Besides learning, practising is necessary. Play is used for practising. The use of metaphors brings an element of fun and creativity to therapy.

Play helps the child to explore different feelings. He can live out his situation more comfortably in the form of a story. The metaphor may thus be used to stimulate creative thinking, as well as emotions and feelings. By playing, the child can experience how it feels to be a mother or a teacher, for example. These dimensions can illuminate new perspectives, and offer the child the opportunity to experience how the other person feels.

Through such play, the child may perceive himself as successful or in charge of himself and his environment. The metaphor helps him to encounter his strongest needs and develop creative behaviour and thus solutions to deal with them.

Teaching moral values

Fantasy stories are important to children because they aid in the establishment of moral values. This is especially true of stories in which good triumphs over evil. Other aspects that are prominent in fantasy stories are mastery and control, skill and hopelessness, and perseverance. This may be one of the reasons why the television character McGyver is so popular with both children and adults.

Children look for positive behaviour in characters, for instance, that Cinderella should complete her tasks faithfully. They also look for respect for nature, for instance, that the woodcutter does not chop down young trees. Respect for other people is another aspect that is often prominent in stories. Snow White loved the dwarfs and took care that they each got equal amounts of love and smiles from her.

These are important lessons to be learnt through metaphor, as the child will probably not believe an adult who only tells him this verbally. Messages, for example, of hope, strife and setbacks are absorbed by the child on an unconscious level.

Guidelines when choosing metaphors

Therapists need not fear that they will fail in their choice of metaphors, as the stories need not be perfect. Fox (1989:243) is of the opinion that there is no such thing as an inaccurate metaphor. Some metaphors are just more effective than others.

It is consequently possible to suggest that each story contains an element of truth and can offer someone something. The level of transformation is indeed not comprehended by everyone and all people would not be able to apply it to themselves. Herein, however, lies the effectiveness of the metaphorical fantasy.

Mills and Crowley (1986:65) have created what they call "phenomenological reality" that is to be shared between the therapist, child and metaphor. This can offer criteria when the therapist wants to create a metaphor that is suitable for the child with his unique problem situation:

- Establish an overall theme of metaphorical conflict in relation to the protagonist.
- Personify unconscious process in the form of heroes or helpers (representing the protagonist's abilities and resources) and villains or obstructions (representing the protagonist's fears and negative beliefs).
- Personify parallel learning situations in which the protagonist was successful.
- Present a metaphorical crisis within a context of inevitable resolution, by which the protagonist overcomes or resolves his problem.
- Develop a new sense of identification for the protagonist as a result of his victorious, heroic journey.
- Culminate with a celebration in which the protagonist's special worth is acknowledged.

Realism

The story or metaphor should be written in such a way that the child is able to experience it realistically. All the human elements and emotions should be portrayed. It must also be possible for the child to identify with the story, and there should be a possibility of spontaneous learning as required. The metaphor should take the child on a tour where he also experiences hope, understanding and support.

Simplicity

To meet the child in his world, the metaphor should be as uncomplicated as possible. An elementary story usually has more impact, reaching the child more effectively than a story with hidden agendas. The therapist should bear in mind that the metaphor acts as a mirror for the child to look at himself and it serves as something with which to compare himself. The situation, circumstances, friends and activities in the metaphor should correlate with those of the child so that he can relate to them.

The child as an individual

The following should be taken into account when choosing or writing a metaphor to suit a specific child and his circumstances:

- Each child needs to master certain developmental tasks. Each child also has a unique way of behaving. It is the responsibility of the therapist to understand the special way of functioning of each child client.
- Each child has a unique nature, disposition and personality. Family functioning often

influences the child's personality more than is commonly accepted. It aids the helping process if the therapist understands the child's preferences and behaviour.

- The active level and attention span of the child have a certain influence. If he is restless with a short attention span, it should be taken into account in the choice of a metaphor.
- The child's ability to adapt should be assessed, as children do not all adapt equally fast to changing circumstances. Some children are especially sensitive to change in their environment. They find it difficult, for instance, to make a new environment their own.
- The intensity of the child's reactions also plays a role. It may sometimes seem as if a child is apathetic, when this is actually not the case. Other children may act in an expressive way that creates the impression that they are more spontaneous. Some children seem to be more cheerful by nature, whereas others react more negatively when they do not find enough pleasure in something. For example, an expressive character should not be created for an introverted child as this may hinder identification.

Order and structure

The secondary world created by fantasy should have order and structure. The television character, Alf, for instance, can talk, as this forms part of his right to exist. He also eats cats, not out of deviance or a violent nature, but because he likes eating cats. Children should find this secondary world convincing and credible: they should be so convinced that they sometimes even believe that Alf really exists. According to Steenberg (1987:13), the consequences and the claim for constant rules that are put to fantasy emphasise the function of transforming the world and not necessarily of escaping from it. There is indeed another dimension involved.

Humour

The value of fantasy can be enhanced by building in humour. Humour offers the possibility of taking the sting out of the tale's tail! It lightens the spirit and allows for objectivity. The child who can abandon himself enthusiastically to humour finds life easier than if he looks at everything too solemnly. In a more cheerful atmosphere, the child may learn to laugh at himself. The self-centred child may find himself so stuck in a web of sombreness that he finds it difficult to free himself from a world that sometimes threatens to engulf him emotionally. Fantasy offers a role model in the sense that it enables the child to gain self-knowledge.

Portrayal of characters

The characters in fantasies are often not depicted strongly. The reason for this is that the child should get the opportunity to form his own imaginary images. Although fantasy characters should still be comparable to characters in the child's real world, they typically illustrate a more complex view of life that centres in the child's subconscious. The main character should receive prominence and should have contact with the primary world. For example, the main character may play a realistic role with fantasy happening around him or her or may undergo fantastical changes of form. The character can therefore have human authenticity when necessary. This is important since the character should have the power to convince. The child who must still learn a lot gains greater insight into his own latent and hidden feelings and desires when he can identify with the character. When the child observes the fantasy character struggling with something, he may often realise for the first time that he is battling with a similar situation.

Animals in fantasy

Children are usually enchanted by animals in fantasy. Furthermore, as they may see themselves as superior to animals, they may also feel protective towards them. One often finds, thus, that children become absorbed in fantasy stories that involve animals. In such stories, the animals usually communicate as if they could understand human language. Animals also take on human characteristics as tame animals may break in wild animals, or as dangerous animals display the characteristics of a protector rather than those of an attacker. Children often humanise animals in such stories. Through this process, they may work through their own ugly and unacceptable behaviour by attributing these undesirable characteristics to the animal in the story.

There are various ways of using animals in stories. They may be fully anthropomorphised, or they may retain their animal characteristics, but be able to hear, understand and talk. Animals may also be used symbolically, for instance, good and evil are often opposed in fantasies containing animals.

An important problem to guard against is when an animal is given excessive human attributes. In this case, some of the fantasy value is lost. The animal is then merely used as a mask through which a moral lesson is proposed. This offers only superficial entertainment and does not have much other value.

Fantasy and the supernatural

The imagination of a child often draws upon the supernatural to make a seemingly impossible situation more manageable. There is thus a switch from the primary to the secondary world. Magic and wizardry are often the focus of the fantasy story, which enables the positive forces to win. However, it is impossible to re-place wizardry to the primary world. Thus, when the goal has been attained through magic, the fantasy usually ends. Often, though, the wizardry found in the fantasy story remains within the rules of the world. These powers are usually confined to one person, or someone is granted only three wishes.

For the Christian, it is important to keep the supernatural only in fantasy. If not, it can reach an unacceptable dimension that is not in accordance with the Christian's norms and values. However, references to wizardry and magic in fairy tales are something completely different from evil powers or witchcraft. The power that the child does experience from the fantasy story should flow from the source from which he believes he gets his strength.

When a child is confronted with the question of where he gets his strength from to accomplish the so-called impossible, he will without exception answer from his own frame of reference. Children from Christian homes will usually and without hesitation connect their source of power to Jesus. Children without a religious background will rather tend to idolise television and movie characters. The question arises as to whether children may involve the Father Almighty in their fantasies. The author is of the opinion that the Father in his wisdom will know better than any adult the sincerity of the child's fantasy.

Children's reactions to metaphor

The child sometimes finds himself so drawn into the metaphor that he finds it difficult to distinguish between fantasy and reality. He may then bring negative experiences which he has not worked though to the fore. Unnecessary fear and anxiety may be generated, making his circumstances seem bigger and more intense than they actually are.

In spite of the fact that children can become so involved in the fantasy story, they can usually distinguish clearly between reality and make-believe.

The therapist must always be open to the child's reactions. Some children may be impatient and not interested in the details of the story, whereas other children want to know detail, for instance, how the dress of the princess in the story looked. In order to fulfil the needs of each child client, the therapist should be in contact with the child and should know the child client. While some children listen to stories quietly, others may comment on them constantly. The social worker should take note of the commentary and react to it as this ensures good rapport between therapist and child client.

Development and fantasy: the imagination

Symbolic play occurs from the second year of age. Intensive studies by Piaget (1951) have shown the symbolism in children's play clearly. Three aspects may be highlighted, namely, decentration, decontextualisation and integration.

Decentration

Centration and decentration focus on the child's need to divert the attention from himself onto something else. At this stage (from twelve months of age), the child tends to imitate everyday situations, for instance, pretending to eat or sleep. After a few months, the child incorporates other objects into his play and projects situations onto them by saying that the doll or dog must also sleep (Fenson, 1980). Similarly, when he has a dirty face, he may want to wash the doll's or dog's faces. By end of the second year, the child attributes life to the toys.

Decontextualisation

At this stage of symbolic play, objects are used as substitutes for others. For instance, a girl may use a dishcloth as a sheet for her doll and may be quite upset when opposed in this. In this situation, it is true that the one object does represent the other rather realistically, but this is not always the case. It is interesting that older children may sometimes be more unrealistic than younger children. A three-year-old may, for instance, follow the instruction to use a knife as a pen without objection whereas a two-year-old, when faced with the same symbolic problem, may point out that a knife is used for cutting and not for writing.

Integration

As children develop, their play becomes arranged in patterns to an ever-increasing degree. For example, a two-year-old may use all his cars on the same road, through the same tunnel and then down into the same abyss. Uncoordinated play therefore develops into an ordered scheme forming certain parallels.

Materials for fantasy play

The child's fantasy play is influenced by his developmental level, as well as by the availability of objects. If a child knows an object and understands how it operates, it is natural for him to incorporate it into his fantasy play. A child who has not made something within his world his own will find it difficult to fantasise regarding the specific item. Sometimes, children need such objects to enhance the fantasy: Hughes (1992:129) emphasises that realistic articles stimulate fantasy.

Gender and fantasy

There is a definite difference in the choice of subjects for fantasy for girls and boys. Thus, materials or objects that stimulate the imagination will differ according to gender. Girls will, for instance, rather play house and with dolls than boys will. Furthermore, according to Hughes (1992:130), the development of realism is more advanced in preschool girls than in preschool boys. Girls will rather choose a more realistic fantasy, for instance, that their children (dolls) are ill, while boys will be more interested in adventurous fantasies. Studies also show that girls depend more on verbal descriptions of their play, while boys support their play with sound (Hughes, 1992:130). Girls are also more passive in their play, while boys are physically active and tend to demonstrate details physically. The reason for these differences is gender identification and socialisation.

Fantasy and music

Schulberg (1986:211) is of the opinion that people have been aware for some time that listening to music is one of the pathways to the deepening and expanding of unusual levels of human consciousness. Music can thus make the child aware of sensory imagery, through the visual and auditory sensations it evokes. Music can also be helpful in going beyond certain defence mechanisms in a fusion of mental and physical awareness. Because of this, music has the ability to make the child face unfulfilled needs, but concomitantly creates a positive experience in problem solving.

Fantasy and dreams

A dream is a distinct example of the secondary world. The fact that people dream clearly demonstrates the need for a secondary world. No person can decide what he or she wants to dream beforehand. Even so, people often dream about aspects that can definitely only exist in fantasy. When dreaming, there are no borders. Dreams are typified by freedom. Troubles can become worse or better after dreaming about them. According to psychoanalysts, dreams are generated by the subconscious. Furthermore, problem-solving skills and wishes come to the fore from the conscious level and are re-placed to the subconscious. The dream is thus fantasy, but offers an opportunity for symbolic organisation.

Conclusion

Fantasy clearly has a central role to play in the development of all children. However, fantasy can also be utilised effectively by the play therapist in helping children to overcome fears, conflicts and problems. The therapist's role is essentially to create the correct atmosphere for fantasy to be effective. It is only through healthy cognitive, creative stimulation, enough emotional space and a milieu in which he can create spontaneously that the child can incorporate his secondary and primary worlds successfully.

One of the most effective fantasy media is the metaphor. The metaphor is an extension of the child's imagination. It serves as a supplement to those parts of the child's perceptual development that are not clearly identified. For this reason, the metaphor is not necessarily a simplified explanation or replacement of information or perception, but acts as a supplement to a given.

Other important aspects of the child's fantasy world relevant to the therapist are symbolic play and the role of the child's imagination, and dreams and the subconscious functioning of fantasy.

Bibliography

Bettelheim, B. 1976. *The uses of enchantment*. London: Thomas & Hudson.
Biffle, C. 1990. *The castle of the pearl*. New York: Harper & Row,
Fenson, L. 1980. Decentration and integration of the child's play in the second year. *Child Development*, 47: 232-235.
Fox, R. 1989. What is a metaphor? *Clinical Social Work Journal*, 17(3): 233-243.
Hughes, F.P. 1992. *Children, play and development*. London : Allyn & Dacon.
Jennings, S. 1993. *Play therapy with children. A practitioner's guide*. Oxford: Blackwell scientific publications.
Mills, J.C. & Crowley, R.J. 1986. *Therapeutic metaphors for children and the child within*. New York: Brunner Mazel.
Piaget, J. 1951. *Play, dreams and imitation in childhood*. New York: Norton.

Schulberg, C. 1986. *The music therapy sourcebook. A collection of activities categorized and analyzed.* New York: Human Sciences Press. Inc.

Spies, G.M. 1993. Die gebruik van metafore in die maatskaplike werk-praktyk. *Social Work Practice,* 1(93): 13-18

Steenberg, E. 1987. *Fantasie en die kinderboek. 'n Kernhandleiding.* Pretoria: HAUM-Literêr.

7 Assessment play

M VAN DER MERWE

Introduction

Before the change-oriented phase of therapy, it is essential to assess certain aspects. Hepworth and Larsen (1990:217-247) describe the assessment of intra-personal systems, including individuals. When assessing individuals, the relevant aspects are the bio-physical, cognitive, perceptual, emotional, cultural, behavioural and motivational factors. Cantrell (1986:163) stresses that the child's developmental phase must also be assessed as this determines the quality and quantity of his reactions to the stressful event. The developmental phase of the child should also be taken into account during assessment of needs and planning of treatment. Furthermore, his verbal and non-verbal communication should be examined to determine how conversation can complement play techniques. Various activities can be used to determine the play forms that are suitable for a specific child client.

The specific techniques that can be used for assessment play include various board games, bag games, line drawings, incomplete pictures, ecomaps and evaluation forms.

Board games

Board games are aids that are possibly not utilised enough by child therapists. Frey (1986:29) discusses the value of board games. While playing board games, it is possible to make observations concerning the child's thoughts, feelings and behaviour, verbal skills, attention span, perception, body language, purposiveness, ability to express feelings and level of development. Games can test fine motor skills, for instance, when playing pick up sticks. Games can also use bigger motor skills, for instance, when playing ball games.

Gardner (1976:68-70) has developed various board games, for example, the **Board of Objects game**. This is an uncomplicated game that is especially suitable for children in pre-primary or early primary school. Their reading skills are still poor and more advanced games are usually too difficult for them.

The Board of Objects game uses a board with 64 or 100 squares with a play figure in each square. These include figures of animals, family members, vehicles, baby's bottles, knives, guns, and clay. Although figures are chosen to evoke fantasy in a variety of areas, Gardner (1976:69) does not see the nature of the material as important. The usual variety that can be found in a toy shop should be sufficient.

Two dice are used, each with one red side. A player throws the dice and may choose an item from the board as soon as a red side is on top. He must then say something about the specific item, after which he receives a reward disk. When he can also tell a story about the item, he gets two reward disks. When both dice fall with the red on top, the player can choose two items. After use, a figure may be replaced on the board, or be removed. The specific item may also be used for dramatisation. The therapist also takes part. The person with the most reward disks can choose a prize at the end of the game.

When playing this game, the focus should be on the stories and not on the prizes. The therapist's stories should be connected to the child's stories or life situation. Gardner (1976:70) has found that few children will refuse to play this attractive game. Younger children are often satisfied with playing, fantasising and gathering rewards without giving the therapist a chance.

As social workers focus more on reality than on the unconscious, those articles that psychotherapists see as indicative of unconscious processes can be left out. A few articles of this kind, such as dragons, may be included merely to give the child the chance to project his feelings towards parents or other people through a fantasy article.

For use in social work the board can be reduced to about thirty squares. Specific, problem-directed articles can be placed on the board, for instance, small family dolls, pets, houses (e.g. the type of houses used in Monopoly), faces with different facial expressions, furniture and a few more symbolic items, such as ghosts and monsters. The time used should be determined according to each specific child and the progress made.

This game has various advantages:

❑ It connects with the child's life situation.
❑ It helps him to relax.
❑ New information may come to the fore.
❑ It is a fun-filled, entertaining activity that may increase motivation for therapy.
❑ It focuses the conversation on relevant aspects.
❑ Playing informally together can develop the therapeutic relationship.

A communication board game that is related to the Board of Objects game is the **Ungame**. This game encourages the exploration of attitudes, feelings, motives and values, as players draw cards with light-hearted, as well as more serious questions. Typical questions are: "What would you do with a magic wand?" or "Name something that bothers you" (Frey, 1986:23). These questions have assessment value, while they may also lead to discussion of different issues and help to rectify wrong perceptions.

The board game **Don't talk to strangers** has assessment value as it gives the therapist an indication of the child's knowledge of issues such as sexual molestation, alcohol and drug abuse and peer group pressure, as he answers questions. It can also be used in the change-oriented phase of therapy as it opens up communication. It has definite educational value and teaches children how to prevent unhappy and tragic situations. The skilled therapist can adapt the questions to focus on a specific child client's situation.

Bag games

Bag games were also designed by Gardner (1976:70-78). They have certain overlapping features with the Board of Objects game and the mutual storytelling technique. There are three bag games, namely, the **Bag of Toys game**, the **Bag of Things game** and the **Bag of Words game**.

In all three games, the same method is followed, namely, that a child must close his eyes and pull an article out of a bag. He receives a reward disk when he can make a remark about the article. When he can tell a story, he receives two reward disks. The therapist takes part. The winner is the one with the most reward disks.

The author has adapted this game. Within a structured helping process, it works quite well when articles suitable for the Bag of Toys game and the Bag of Things game are placed together in a bag. The author uses no rewards, except a few sweets sometimes, as she has found that the children she works with are usually so eager to play the game that they see it as a reward in itself. It is effective with children from about four years of age up to about twelve. For an older age group, it is necessary to build in more sophisticated elements. Articles are chosen according to the child's problems or needs.

Once, when the author was working with a child of divorced parents, a toy telephone was placed in the bag. The specific child used it as part of the game to phone her father regarding his unsatisfactory contact with her. Other objects that have been used successfully are a miniature skateboard, finger puppets, little houses, trees and links from a chain. The last two objects particularly facilitated good therapeutic material.

The story revolving around the tree was that the tree lost its branches through a traumatic event, a fire. After some rain (time and therapy), small sprouts started to grow from the scars and a few summers later, new branches with fresh, green leaves covered the scars. Even though the tree was still aware of the scars and still felt them from time to time, especially during the winter cold (new problems or the old ones rekindled), it was much better and it knew that growth was possible out of the pain. The therapist told this story and found that the specific child followed her lead by relating similar "life-stories".

Another child of divorced parents told a touching story about the links in a chain. She said that it was a chain of life. Whenever there were problems, the chain got tangled and broke in places. Some of the links went missing for good, or formed their own new chains. She expressed the hope that it would be possible to mend the chain, even if outside help had to be sought.

A further child used a miniature skateboard as a metaphorical vehicle on the road of life. He demonstrated dramatically how the vehicle sometimes left the road and went into patches of trouble. He gave a lengthy account of how it was eventually better to stay on the straight road, as it was very difficult to get back once it has been abandoned.

Another client's feelings of hopelessness about his situation became clear when he told a story about a key. He said that he had lost his key and could not get into his home. He went to the neighbours for help as they had an extra key. He got that key, but still could not get into the house. In the end, he just wandered around forever and ever. This child was so caught up in a negative life situation that he had clearly lost all hope. He could not believe that help from others, such as the therapist, could change his situation.

This game has elements of assessment play and also of dramatic play. Often, children use articles that were drawn out of the bag in earlier games in their stories. They dramatise freely during storytelling.

For the Bag of Words game, Gardner (1976:74-78) uses about 400 words on cards. Colour can also be used to make this game more attractive. Words that should evoke a good response are mother, father, anger, love, hate and crying. This game is obviously more suitable for older children with good reading abilities. In order to be both problem-oriented and goal-directed, the words must be chosen carefully to reflect the child's situation (Van der Merwe, 1991:154).

Checkers

Gardner (1986:215) and Mills and Crowley (1986:198) regard the game of checkers as a valuable technique with low-level therapeutic input. It is used mainly as part of assessment play, with relaxation value. The way in which the child plays and handles losing, as well as his comments while playing, may contain valuable information. The game also enhances the therapeutic relationship. Gardner (1986:215-230) gives a comprehensive description of the use of checkers in therapy with young children.

There are specific guidelines for the use of checkers in therapy with children:

- The therapist should not let the child win time after time in order to boost his self-image. Therapy must be realistic and must give the child the opportunity to lose in a safe environment.
- On the other hand, it may be anti-therapeutic if the therapist wins all the time. Even though sincerity forms the basis of the therapeutic relationship, Gardner (1986:219) views this as the one time when the therapist can manage the situation subtly to let the child win.
- The therapist should state clearly that her opinion of the child does not depend on whether the child wins or loses.
- Vague praise should be avoided. Praise should only be given for specific achievements in the child's performance.
- Cheating should not be allowed. The therapist should address the issue and use the situation as a learning experience.
- If the therapist finds the game of checkers boring, it should not be included in therapy, as the child may then experience therapy negatively.
- This game should not be used to give the therapist an easy session. A whole session should not be used for checkers.

Gardner (1986:215-230) discusses the reactions of children with different problems to checkers, specifically referring to children with self-image problems, passive and dependent children, egocentric children, reserved children, paranoic and suspicious children, those with anti-social behaviour and obsessive, compulsive children. A child with a poor self-image may, for instance, try to change the rules in the middle of the game to promote himself. He may also be a bad loser after being reluctant to play in the first place out of fear of losing.

In the beginning phase of therapy, playing checkers may give an indication of the child's comprehensive faculty. The occurrence of certain reactions when the child is playing the game does not necessarily reflect such behaviour, as discussed by Gardner. Observation of the child's reactions may merely serve to strengthen the assessment when compared with his reactions in other situations. Checkers may also be used in the beginning and final phases of therapy to help the child to relax and to reduce the therapeutic intensity.

According to Gardner (1986:23), the game of checkers can teach the child valuable lessons, especially when the therapist confirms this verbally. The child can learn that a person is responsible for him or herself and that everyone has to bear the consequences of his or her own actions. When one plans carefully, the result is usually better than when one leaves it all to chance. He will also learn that no one can be the total master of his or her own situation, as other people play a part, too. These lessons can be learnt in a relatively painless way in the microcosmos of the game of checkers.

Line drawings and picture completion

Line drawings and picture completion are useful in the beginning phase of therapy. They help the therapist to determine the child's phase of development and play form preference. They are also functional in leading the child towards self-disclosure. Dennison and Glassman (1987) give numerous examples of line drawings for use in the various stages of therapy with children.

A useful one with which to start therapy is a drawing that will interest the child and which may be combined with questions about his favourite colour, sound, taste, smell and touch, such as the drawing of the mouse on page 103.

This aid is usually amongst the first to be used in therapy, as it is useful as an icebreaker. It prepares the child for problem-directed self-disclosure and also gives the therapist the opportunity to disclose some information about herself.

Completion of uncomplicated pictures has certain advantages, especially in the early stages of the helping process. By asking the child to follow simple instructions, it is possible to get an idea of his ability to comprehend directions and explanations. This technique is also helpful in determining the child's coordination, his attitude towards failure, his observation abilities, attention span and energy levels. It further aids the therapist in assessing the child's skills regarding practical problem solving. By asking the child to count the pictures, it is possible to assess his conception of figures and numbers. This is important to know as the child must be prepared for the number of therapeutic sessions

Figure 7.1: **Line drawing for use in play therapy**

so that unrealistic expectations can be avoided (Van der Merwe, 1991:262). The following example (based on Van der Merwe, 1991) could be used for picture completion:

Figure 7.2: **Example for picture completion**

Dennison and Glassman (1987:84-90) use drawings of a space creature to depict the feelings of sadness, pride, anger and fear. They combine the feelings with colour, for instance:

- This space creature is **sad**. His feelers are limp, **blue** and wilted.
- This space creature is **angry**. His feelers are **red-hot**.
- This space creature is **afraid**. His feelers are trembling. They are cold and **grey**.
- This space creature is **proud**. His feelers are raised, shiny and **gold**.

The idea of the space creature can be adapted to suit each child client's specific interests and experience. It is useful to combine feelings with colour, as a child may then use colour to identify his feelings. He can, for instance, say that he is feeling red, when angry. When he is feeling dark red, it implies a more intense feeling.

Jewett (1982:53-58) describes some other techniques that test the child's mastery of feeling language and teach him new language. The first step is to point out the five main feelings, namely, **sad**, **angry**, **happy**, **afraid** and **lonely**. The relevance of certain feelings in specific situations is then discussed. The child can indicate with gestures how much of a certain feeling he experiences in a particular situation. Secondly, the feelings are expressed in drawings of feeling faces. The child is asked, for instance, to draw his face as it looks when he gets a present. By sketching different situations, a conglomeration of feeling faces can be assembled. These drawings can be used in all sorts of games. They can, for instance, be turned face down. The child must then choose one at random and describe a situation in which he felt accordingly. In the final phase of the helping process, the drawings can be used again to discuss feelings regarding termination of therapy.

The author has found that the use of feeling faces in therapy is very effective. It often helps to bring the discussion or play back to a feeling level. The author concentrates especially on the eyebrows, shape of the eyes and the mouth when drawing the various facial expressions. The facial expressions with colour codes in the next example are useful when teaching children feeling language connected to colour. This feeling chart may be expanded to include more feelings, according to a specific child client's situation (adapted from Social Work Practice: 1.93 by Van der Merwe, 1993: 31-32).

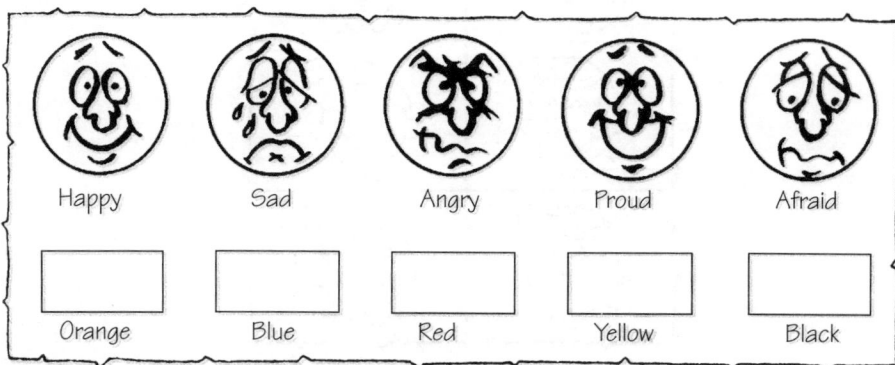

Figure 7.3: **Feeling faces**

Ecomaps

Hartman (1978:468-472) describes the use of the ecomap. It is helpful to complete an ecomap with the parents before treatment of the child starts. This gives an overview of the helping network that is available to the child and shows clearly where he needs more support. It is good to have the names of significant people in his life available.

A more visual ecomap can be used for children. Any form can be used. It can be depicted as a galaxy, as in the following figure based on Graver and Morse (1986:46):

Figure 7.4: **My universe**

The child fills in the names of significant people or places on the different planets.

Other variations of the ecomap are line drawings of a bunch of grapes or different fruit. Drawings of the petals of a flower or a variety of flowers can also be used. Child therapists need not be artists. Colouring books offer lots of interesting ideas which can be traced.

Assessment forms

A variety of assessment forms is available. For example, when used with young children, the forms should be visually attractive and simple. They should be designed for each client according to his problems and needs, as well as the aims and objectives that were stated for therapy. Van der Merwe (1993:31) discusses the use of individualised questionnaires to determine the child's feelings on various issues. The following is an example where feelings are marked by using different colours as on figure 7.3:

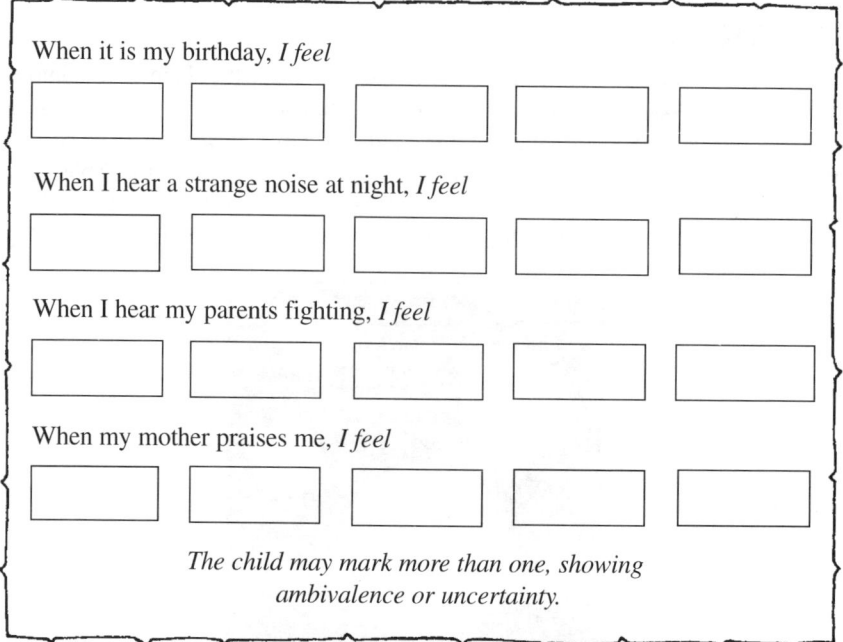

Figure 7.5: **Assessment questionnaire** (to be used in combination with figure 7.3)

Van der Merwe (1993:31) further mentions that this technique may serve as an ice-breaker regarding the handling of the child's feelings in therapy. It is a simple and easy way of establishing his comprehension of feelings, while it also offers the opportunity to work on his skills relating to feeling language. It directs the interview towards his feelings, while establishing the basis for the kind of language to be used in therapy.

Conclusion

The correct match between play form, technique, child and problem or need is essential for effective services to children. This match must already be accomplished in the beginning phase of therapy. As stated by Perlman (1974:4-5), the problem-solving process should fit the person and his problem. The process should also fit the professional person. It is no use for a therapist with no musical skills to try to play the violin in therapy! In the same vein, it is counterproductive to play checkers in therapy when it bores the therapist. The child will most certainly notice this, which may add to his feelings of worthlessness. It is essential to maintain an element of fun in therapy.

This is also true of the change-oriented phase of therapy that will be described in later chapters. When the intensity of therapy increases with the implementation of biblio-play, dramatic play and creative play, it is even more important to incorporate fun and pleasure into therapy. After all, the target group is children. They learn and respond best in a relaxed atmosphere that caters to their specific needs. Even though they are clients, they are children first.

Bibliography

Cantrell, R.G. 1986. Adjustment to divorce: Three components to assist children. *Elementary School Guidance and Counseling*, 20 (3): 163-173.
Dennison, S.T. & Glassman, C.K. 1987. *Activities for children in therapy: A guide for planning and facilitating therapy with troubled children.* Illinois: Charles C. Thomas.
Frey, D.E. 1986. Communication boardgames with children. In Schaefer & Reid: 21-41.
Gardner, R.A. 1976. *Psychotherapy with children of divorce.* New York: Jason Aronson.
Gardner, R.A. 1986. The game of checkers in child therapy. In Schaefer & Reid: 215-232
Gardner, R.A. 1986. The Talking, feeling, doing game. In Schaefer & Reid: 41-72.
Graver, C.M. & Morse, L.A. 1986. *Helping children of divorce: A group leader's guide.* Illinois: Charles C. Thomas.
Hartman, A. 1978. Diagrammatic assessment of family relationships. *Social Casework*, October: 465-476.
Hepworth, D.H. & Larsen, J.A. 1990. *Direct social work practice. Theory and skills.* (3rd. ed.). California: Wadsworth.
Jewett, C.L. 1982. *Helping children cope with separation and loss.* Massachusetts: Harvard Common Press.
Mills, J.C. & Crowley, R.J. 1986. *Therapeutic metaphors for children and the child within.* New York: Brunner Mazel.
Perlman, H.H. 1974. *Social casework: A problem-solving process.* Chicago: University of Chicago Press.
Schaefer, C.E. & Reid, S.E. (Eds.). 1986. *Game play: Therapeutic use of childhood games.* New York: John Wiley.
Van der Merwe, M. 1991. Maatskaplikewerk-beraad met jong kinders in egskeidingsituasies met fokus op speeltegnieke. Unpublished MA thesis. Stellenbosch: University of Stellenbosch.
Van der Merwe, M. 1993. Biblioterapie. *Maatskaplikewerk Praktyk/Social Work Practice*, 3 (93):31-32.

8 Biblio-play

M VAN DER MERWE

Introduction

Biblio-play is a form of play using books, reading, the written word and audio-visual media. Bibliotherapy is the specific approach of which biblio-play is part. Even though people may think that biblio-play entails only the use of directed reading, Howie (1983:303-305), Crompton (1980:118-141) and Van der Merwe (1991:166; 1993:32) are of the opinion that a bibliotherapeutic approach includes the use of life books, letter writing as a third object technique, compositions, maps, calenders, magazines, pictures, comics, diaries, self-descriptions and emotional barometers. However, therapists often work with illiterate persons, as well as with children who are unable to read. These people can still use books, by looking at the drawings or graphic material. Through biblio-play, the client is assisted in bringing forward feelings in order to work them through productively. This process leads to growth and insight.

Terminology

The term biblio-play is perhaps too restrictive to serve as a reference for everything that is classified under it. Possibly, a term such as media play would be more correct. Rubin (1978:76) in particular discusses the terminological problems with regard to bibliotherapy as a whole and refers to Axelrod's preference for the term *audio-visual therapy* instead of bibliotherapy, since multimedia are used. Howie (1983:289) agrees with Rubin and is of the opinion that various audio and visual materials may be used in the present multimedia phase.

It can be anticipated that the computer will be increasingly utilised for therapeutic purposes in the near future. A recent article by Schoeman and Botha (1993:307-318) has already examined the ethical dilemmas in social work with reference to the utilisation of computer technology. Computer games are particularly attractive to children: apart from putting them at ease, they also have assessment value. Computers and audio-visual media will soon have to be included in the terminology if practitioners continue to view their use as part of biblio-play. In fact, their use may develop to such an extent as to justify the development of a new form of play, computer play.

At this stage, though, broader activities are used to classify forms of play, for instance, relaxation, assessment, creativity and dramatisation. It is only with biblio-play that there is a more direct reference to the specific material that is used. In view of the general acceptance of the term bibliotherapy, the umbrella term biblio-play will still be used in this chapter.

Bibliotherapy is a comprehensive field of study. A number of sources on this subject were studied as background to the present discussion (Moody & Limper, 1971; Burt, 1972; Monroe, 1978). Although the origins of bibliotherapy can be traced to the ancient times, the term *bibliotherapy* was first used in 1916 by Crothers. Since then, various definitions have developed and persons from various disciplines employ this therapeutic method (Moody & Limper, 1971:7; Rubin, 1978:1,13; Howie, 1983:228). The application of bibliotherapy as described by Crompton (1980:118-141) and others will be examined below.

Stutterheim and Kroon (1991:180) and Stutterheim and Pretorius (1993:9) use the term bibliotherapeutic social work to describe the use of printed or non-printed material, fictitious or didactic, in therapy. This material is used as a therapeutic aid, where the interaction between reader and reading material, in individual or group therapy, leads to growth and problem solving. This is activated by a social worker and librarian in a team context, to enhance effective social functioning of individuals or groups.

Advantages of biblio-play

Bibliotherapy, including the use of children's stories and life-stories in the form of biblio-play, has various advantages, as referred to by Burt (1972:4), Crompton (1980:125-132), Smith (1982:231-232), Howie (1983:287), Porter (1983:271-316), Pardeck and Pardeck (1987:271), Thompson and Rudolph (1992:199) and Pardeck and Pardeck (1989:31):

- It leads to the development of insight.
- Verbalisation of problems is encouraged.
- It serves as an indirect communication medium between therapist and client.
- It offers enjoyable activities that can enhance the relationship of trust and increase the child's motivation for therapy.
- Feelings of isolation are reduced when the client realises that others have overcome similar problems.
- It results in clearer perspective with regard to problems.
- It presents a laboratory within which the client can control feelings, circumstances, wishes and thoughts in a symbolic world.
- It provides alternative problem-solving mechanisms.
- It offers possibilities for new behaviour patterns by providing models for positive behaviour modification.

- It has prevention value.
- It provides the opportunity for emotional release and catharsis when the child projects unresolved feelings onto the characters.
- It teaches the child the language through which feelings can be verbalised.
- It affords the child the opportunity to distance himself emotionally from his problems. The words "Once upon a time . . .", for instance, create such a distance.

In research with young children of divorced parents, Van der Merwe (1991:265) found that nine out of fifteen respondents reacted positively to biblio-play, by talking directly about the parental divorce after a divorce related story was read to them. The following are translated verbal responses:

> "Father is divorced. My mother is going to marry an old man."
>
> "This is just like my mother and father. I also cried a lot when my father left — nearly every day — but not any more."
>
> "We are also divorced, but we didn't know, because we were still too small."
>
> "When my mother got divorced, she got divorced in the lounge and we were with her. We were also there. We slept one night and then my father just went away. Even the stuff he bought for my mother, he took away."
>
> "We are the same as that little girl." (in the story)

The above should illustrate the value of biblio-play in opening the discussion on the child's feelings regarding the specific problem. Five of the fifteen respondents reacted to biblio-play with dramatic play. Possibly, biblio-play encouraged the children to act out their feelings. One respondent took dolls from the doll's house to act out the story. Later, he vented his feelings of anger towards his father by bombarding the father doll with clay. In other words, the story encouraged the ventilation of feelings through toys.

Van der Merwe (1991:267) raises further advantages based on this research:

- It has become clear that biblio-play is a good opener of conversations regarding divorce related issues. This should also be applicable to other problem situations.
- Biblio-play is therapeutic in the sense that it corrects misinterpretations, generalises and educates.
- It is a structured form of play. As such, it is cost-effective as it directs the conversation towards the problem.
- The use of biblio-play speeds up the therapeutic pace.

Limitations of biblio-play

There are also certain limitations attached to the approach of bibliotherapy. Howie (1983:301) refers to the following:

- Certain people may rationalise or intellectualise their problems when they read about them.

- Reading imaginative literature may activate certain people's defence mechanisms.
- Some people may believe that reading applicable literature is all you need to solve problems.
- The insight resulting from reading may be confused with the process of working through problems and the acquisition of coping skills that are necessary for actual problem solving.
- Certain people become anxious and nervous when they read about others' problems. This may result in new symptoms developing in themselves.

Notwithstanding the above restrictions, bibliotherapy offers many therapeutic possibilities to young children. However, it is important to check that they receive the correct message. During research with young children of divorced parents, Van der Merwe (1991:266) asked one respondent why the little girl in the story shook the mother and father doll. Instead of realising that she did this to vent her anger, the respondent answered that the girl had shaken the dolls as they were full of water.

Young children clearly need guidance when reading stories, and the therapist must take care to choose a suitable story. Van der Merwe (1991:267) based the following conclusions on practical research regarding biblio-play with young children of divorced parents:

- The choice of the story is very important.
- It is not always possible to use the same story for children with similar problems. Therapists should constantly be on the look-out for stories and should keep these in a resource bank. This will increase the possibility of finding suitable stories for a specific child client. Therapists with an ability and talent for compiling relevant stories should circulate them amongst their colleagues for the benefit of the clients.

Techniques and materials

The techniques and materials used for biblio-play include the use of life books, diaries, magazines, pictures, comics, poems and children's stories.

The use of children's stories

According to Smith (1981:114; 1982:231-232), the children's story offers the child an indirect channel for opening up obstructed and threatening aspects of his world. In a story that has been well-chosen, the characters will act in such a way that they do not hurt, frighten or disappoint the child. Furthermore, a children's story affords the client the opportunity of maintaining a distance, but of being involved at the same time. Reading opens him to therapeutic inputs, as his defences are lowered by his involvement in the story.

Criteria for the choice of material

The requirements for a children's story that is to be used for biblio-play are discussed by Smith (1981:114-115; 1982:229-230), Howie (1983:304-305), Porter (1983:276) and

Pardeck and Pardeck (1987:272). Rubin (1978:77-78, 90) also gives directions for the general choice of material for bibliotherapy, which are included here:

- The material should be known to the therapist.
- Long, complicated stories should be avoided, as they take up too much time. It is also more difficult for the child to remember the content. In the light of the limited attention span of young children, short stories which take no more than 30 minutes to read are suitable.
- Rubin (1978:69,89), Crompton (1980:121) and Howie (1983:304) agree that high quality books with literary value are not necessarily the most suitable. Therapists should look for books addressing the specific needs of every child client, whether through the illustrations or the story. It is clear that a thorough assessment should be done before choosing material for biblio-play. This should ensure that the correct choice is made for each child according to life situation, personality, chronological and emotional age.
- The story should be in line with the child's circumstances and developmental stage. A preschool child will quite possibly prefer a book with good illustrations and a simple format, while a primary school child prefers more character development in stories, as well as more detail. The therapist should know whether the child can read and, if so, how well.
- The story should relate to the child's feelings.
- Even though story situations need not be identical to those of the child client, they should be more or less comparable.
- Illustrations are important, as they hold the child's attention. Young children usually like a lot of big, colourful illustrations. The characters should preferably be illustrated in active rather than in passive positions. However, the therapist should take care that the illustrations do not distract the child's attention unduly from the content of the story. It is thus important to summarise and conclude the story to ensure that the correct message is transferred.
- The story should contain a character with which the child will identify, preferably also a child. The protagonist should be portrayed realistically and should therefore get angry, afraid, uncertain and be naughty at times, but still be accepted. One or more of the characters should also be unacceptable. This should enable the child to project negative feelings onto this character.
- The characters should offer positive ways of coping and working through their problems. Smith (1982:232-233) cites the following criteria for creating characters:
  - They should express feelings and work through situations even though these maybe negative or unacceptable.
  - They should examine the reasons for their behaviour and be willing to enhance their self-knowledge and self-acceptance.
  - They should gain intellectual insight into situations so that they can evaluate themin objective, realistic and cognitive ways.

- They should develop emotional insight, in other words, be able to acknowledge and experience emotions consciously. They should also relate to the stimulus of their emotions.
- They should use coping skills to encounter difficult situations in a positive way.
- They should determine positive life objectives and direct their functioning accordingly.

❏ The characters in the children's tale should display healthy functioning on physical, social, religious and self-conceptual levels.

❏ Stories about animals, fantasy and fairies allow for daydreaming and are good media for communication, especially with younger children.

❏ Stories should have comforting endings, but should not be falsely comforting.

The question may be asked whether children identify readily with books depicting characters of other cultural groups. Fortunately, more and more books portraying children of different cultural groups, such as black and Indian children, are available. One example is the book *Too small Themba* (Boucher, 1991). This book is about a small black boy, Themba, who does not like being so small. His experiences are described as he goes through a day and finds that no one really pays him any attention. In the end, the family gets locked out of their home and Themba is the only one who is small enough to get through the window to open the door. He becomes the hero in the family and realises that there are some advantages to being small. This book has a valuable message for young children in that it tells them that they need not feel powerless because they are small. They should look to their good points and utilise these to their own advantage.

Young children in the age group three to about six years usually find the books about Spot, a little dog, exciting, as these books have pictures hidden underneath doors that can open, etc. These books are also available in Afrikaans, with the little dog being called Otto. One of these books is also available in a dual language form, namely, in both English and Northern Sotho, with the title, *Where's Spot?/Tilo o kae?* (Hill, 1988). There is also an elementary dictionary, *Spot's books of words/Incwadi kaSpoti enkulukazi Gamagama* (Hill, 1991) available in Zulu and English. These books are especially suitable for relaxation play, and should help to get the child involved in therapy and to emphasise its fun element.

Books to help adopted children to accept their situation are also rather common. Good examples are *A book of life for an adopted child* (Anderson & Anderson, 1979) and *Horace* (Keller, 1993). The book by Aliki (1984), *Feelings*, is a valuable aid when teaching children about the different feelings.

However, it is clear that for children to identify with stories, the tales should function as metaphors. Mills and Crowley (1986:65-66) identify core elements that stories required to be used as therapeutic metaphors:

❏ There must be some form of **metaphorical conflict** (for instance, the ugly duckling that looks different from the other ducks and is rejected by everyone).

❏ **Unconscious processes** should come to the fore in the form of helpers, skills or obstacles (for instance, the ugly duckling is the best swimmer).

- Some form of **metaphorical crisis** that is manageable should develop (for instance, the ugly duckling flees to a swamp where hunters and dogs encircle him. When a dog discovers the duckling, the dog runs away because the duckling is so ugly).
- The story should offer **parallel learning** situations in which the character experiences success (for instance, the ugly duckling finds a home on a farm and learns to cope with all sorts of situations).
- A new feeling of **identification** should develop as the character learns to cope with his or her problems (for instance, the ugly duckling sees swans for the first time and then sees his own reflection in the water).
- The story must end with a **celebration** that emphasises the character's value (for instance, the other swans bow down to the once-ugly duckling, as he is now the most beautiful of them all).

When telling such a story to the child client, it is the task of the therapist to work metaphorically and to make the necessary connections. Often, the story is straightforward and the child should be able to make his own deductions so that he is able to identify with the situations and characters in the story. The metaphor is effective when the child's situation is reflected in such a way that he does not feel alone, but should not be so accurate that he finds it embarrassing.

Phases when using children's stories

Smith (1982:230-231) and Porter (1983:280-283) distinguish various phases in the therapeutic process regarding the use of children's stories:

Generalisation

Once the child realises that other people are experiencing similar situations to his own, he may feel less alone and overwhelmed by his circumstances.

Identification

This is the basis of projection and modelling which comes into operation once the child identifies with the character. For this reason, the child should be able to recognise himself in the story. Crompton (1980:125) prefers the term *recognise* to *identify*, as she believes that identification implies that the child should find a replica of himself in the character of the story, while recognition suggests that although the reader sees similarities between his life and that of the character, he is also able to see important differences. When recognising the similarities, his feeling of isolation will be diminished.

Projection

The child unconsciously transfers certain feelings, often unacceptable ones, onto the characters through projection. Hence, projection is applied as a defence mechanism and the child may feel emancipated from his unassimilated experiences as a result. Smith (1982:230) refers to four requirements necessary for the transformation from identification to projection:

which are clear from the child's story above, namely, his hope for reconciliation and his unrealistic hope that the father's problems are easy to solve. The therapist's story could be as follows:

> The father and mother dogs fought a lot on account of the father dog's temper. There were other problems too that the baby dog could not understand. The father dog left the family and he and the mother dog got a divorce. The baby dog wished that his parents would remarry. He fantasised about a good doctor who could solve everything with medication. One day, he realised that pills could not solve the problem. It was possible for the father dog to learn from a wise dog how to control his temper, but it would take a long, long time. Even if he succeeded, the mother dog would not take him back, because there were lots of other problems. Furthermore, the father and mother dogs had thought long and hard about a divorce. They knew that it was the right thing to do, even though it hurt everyone a lot.
>
> The baby dog realised then that the parents were not going to get together again. He thought about this for a long time and understood that he was still their child and that they loved him. He was glad to know that and decided not to hope that they would remarry any longer, as it was not going to happen anyway. In any case, whenever he started dreaming about that, he did not feel like learning to catch the ball, while his friend was getting better at it all the time. He would have to pull up his socks; he had some catching up to do. The moral of the story is that sometimes there are changes in a dog's life that he has to accept.

Naturally, the therapist should adapt her story according to each child's circumstances. It is clear, then, that this technique is really suitable for the change-oriented phase of therapy when the social worker knows the child client well.

The use of life books

A life book is a visual or written record containing important information on the child's situation, which is presented to the child. As described by Crompton (1980:135-140), Howie (1983:305), Porter (1983:289-308) and Harrison (1988:377-399), life books are usually used for children who have been taken away from their parents and who are in children's homes, foster care or have been adopted.

It is also possible to adapt this technique for use with children affected by violence and displacement. In these cases, the life book could be helpful in orientating children towards their new circumstances. It would help them to keep track of the changes in their lives and help them to plan their lives.

The life book can be closed off with a memory book. This can be compiled by the therapist and the child in the final phase of therapy. Elbow (1987:180) suggests that the helping process is mentioned or illustrated in this book, together with pertinent aspects of the therapeutic situation. This book does not replace the other termination tasks, but serves as an activator for the working through of these tasks.

The life book has certain functions, as mentioned by Crompton (1980:136-140), Porter (1983:291-292) and Harrison (1988:378):

- ❏ It enhances the child's self-concept.
- ❏ As the use of this technique breaks down emotional barriers and defence mechanisms, the child's view of himself, his environment and situation often becomes more realistic and accepting.
- ❏ The life book helps the child to develop a better understanding of the past and a sharper focus on the future.
- ❏ The life book provides the opportunity for reconstructing the past and developing an own identity.
- ❏ The child can work through and integrate unhappy, as well as happy experiences. He can develop a realistic image of the present and can build new relationships. Eventually, he can plan for a positive future.
- ❏ Greater tolerance of parting and change usually results.
- ❏ The life book can be beneficial to the therapeutic relationship and can stimulate communication between therapist and client.
- ❏ Between interviews, the child can keep the life book in order to maintain the tie between himself and the therapist.
- ❏ The parents can become involved by supplying information for the life book. With a family in a divorce situation, mutual future planning can even be done in such a book and the child may acquire a voice with regard to aspects such as visitation.

Content and modus operandi

Porter (1983:294-300) and Harrison (1988:385-393) offer particular suggestions with regard to content and modus operandi when constructing a life book:

- ❏ The preparatory phase should be spontaneous. The life book can develop out of the play situation or during conversation.
- ❏ The life book should cover the significant events of the child's life.
- ❏ The child determines where in the past or present the book should begin. Although a chronological order of events is preferred, the child sometimes works backwards from the present to the past. By observing where the child starts, certain inferences can be made.
- ❏ The child can request the therapist to compile a report on his life and can then illustrate it himself with photographs, pictures or drawings.
- ❏ He can provide his own chronological description of his life. This is usually a time-consuming process that demands special input by the therapist, since she has to attempt to fill in missing details.
- ❏ Simple drawings of faces with different emotional expressions can be of use to the

child in clearly identifying feelings with regard to certain incidents.
- The content of the life book can be restricted to important people in the child's life. Each person may be discussed individually and the influence that he or she has had on the child may be indicated.
- The content can be restricted to certain events in the child's life.
- The life book can portray the different homes and communities in which he has lived.
- It can focus on self-description. The child can be asked to describe his positive and negative aspects.
- An older child can even be requested to write an autobiography.
- A genogram can be used to compile a family tree. This may be visually attractive and may be, for example, in the form of a tree.
- Where possible, relevant photographs can be included. The therapist and the child can take the pictures together.
- Pictures from magazines or drawings by the child client can also be used to illustrate the book.
- Other aids that are used in therapy, such as drawings, poems, time schedules, letters and maps, may be stored in the life book.
- The life book is the child's book. He may use it as he likes.
- Even though the therapist controls the therapeutic pace, the child determines the tempo at which the book is constructed. When the child loses interest, the therapist should stop the work on the life book. Work sessions should, however, be regular enough to maintain his attention.
- It is up to the child to decide who may see the book and the degree of confidentiality with which it should be handled.
- The child determines how neatly the book should be constructed and how carefully the book should be handled.
- He determines whether he is going to keep the book or destroy it, and, if so, when he is going to destroy it.
- The therapist should share information sensitively and empathically. She should be as positive as possible.
- The use of a life book can form part of a slow, intense process that makes emotional demands on both the child client and the therapist (Crompton, 1980:136; Porter, 1983:293-294). A firm relationship of trust should offer the child security when working on the life book.
- Van der Merwe (1991:180) warns that therapists should be careful not to use the life book to avoid deeper conversation, as it is easy to look busy when using this technique.

Therapeutic aids and information

When compiling a life book, specific information and therapeutic aids are needed. Information is a **primary aid**. It can be obtained from various sources, for instance, casework files, documents, therapists who have worked with the family in the past, parents and other family, letters, postcards and photographs.

Secondary aids are, for instance, a camera, paper, crayons, books, pencils, glue and scissors (Jones, 1970:22-23; Porter, 1983:300-302; Pardeck & Pardeck, 1987:227; Harrison, 1988:394).

Weiser (1988:339-376) particularly discusses the use of phototherapy when exploring feelings and memories. Photographs can be used actively when they are taken during therapy sessions, but can also be used more passively, for example, when looking through old photos. The discussion of photos of happy family times can aid the child in grieving for the disruption of his family. Photos take him back to those times in a concrete way and his feelings should come to the fore.

Van der Merwe (1991:180) suggests the use of family photos in making realistic paper dolls that children can use to help them work through their feelings. The use of photographs can also be combined with playing with a doll's house.

The use of time graphics

When using time graphics, a child can get an overview of his life. Various developmental stages can be portrayed visually, as well as important people and events in the child's life. This can form a part of the life book (Smith, 1981:118; Porter, 1983:318).

When treating a young child of divorced parents, for instance, time graphics can depict a pregnant woman, followed by a baby in a crib and then a young child. The divorce event can form the centre of the representation, shown by a heart broken in two. The child can also draw his own version of the divorce. In this way, biblio-play and creative play are combined (Van der Merwe, 1991:184).

Jewett (1982:100-102) varies the use of time graphics, using a piece of string stretched between two chairs for the same purpose. Photos or drawings of significant persons in the child's life are pegged on the string in chronological order using clothes pegs. When divorce or death are discussed, the relevant person's picture is removed and placed on another line. Drawings of faces with different expressions can also be used to identify the child's feelings in certain situations. The use of this technique for children of divorced parents is discussed in chapter 13.

Harrison (1988:389) cites a similar technique that is a combination of a life book and a time line. Pieces of paper are stuck together to form a long piece of paper. When folded, this can form a life book.

The therapeutic process itself can also be outlined on time graphics. The helping process can, for instance, be portrayed as a treasure hunt between islands with the aim of recovering a treasure (the working through of a problem). In every interview, certain leads can be followed to unravel the mystery, for instance, in the case of parental divorce, clues can be how to handle visits to the absent parent, how to cope with new roles and how to tell friends about the divorce. This technique is especially effective in group therapy.

In an application of this method, Spies (1993:17) uses a chart depicting the various themes for group sessions. Specific times can be written on this chart:

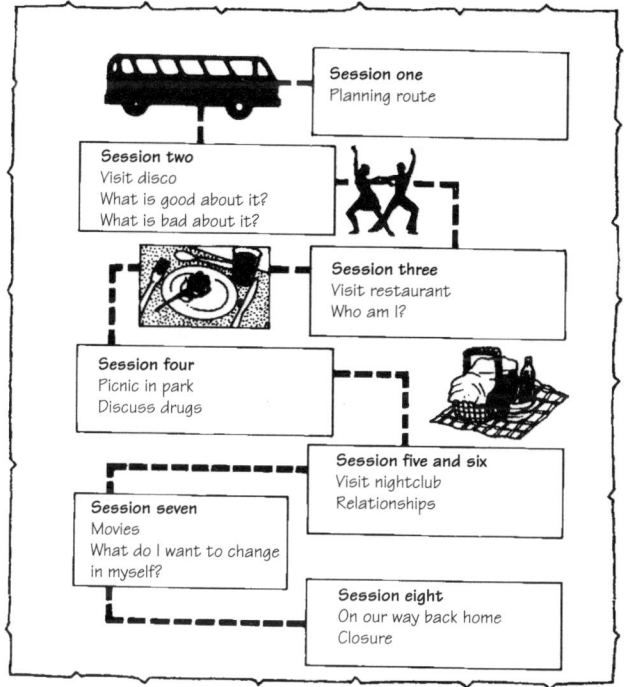

Figure 8.1: **Voyage of discovery**
(Adapted from *Social Work Practice* 1.93 March 1993)

Smith (1981:113) mentions calenders as a therapeutic aid, since these are useful in structuring the therapeutic program.

The use of diaries

Diaries can be used apart from or together with the life book (Smith, 1981:116; Porter, 1983:313-315). Younger children will not be able to give a complicated description of every day's proceedings, but they should be able to relate these by one or more drawings per day. The child can also place coloured stickers, portraying various feelings, in the diary. Stickers representing certain events can also be used. This record can be discussed during interviews (Van der Merwe, 1991:182).

The use of self-descriptions

This entails the child describing himself by writing about his positive and negative characteristics. The therapist can give him specific criteria. Self-descriptions can be useful as an opening for further discussion (Smith, 1981:117; Porter, 1983:317) and can be supplemented by self-portraits. Self-descriptions can also be used in conjunction with a life book.

The use of road maps

Smith (1981:112) mentions the use of road maps as an aid when working with children in children's homes. However, this technique can be adapted for use with other target groups. For children of divorced parents, for instance, it can be used to show the child where the absent parent lives. Miniature houses, like those used in board games like Monopoly, can be used to orientate the child to his new environment by placing the church, school, library, shops, etc., on the map.

The use of poetry

Burt (1972:6) stresses the escapist value of poetry, as the rhythms and symbolism that the poet works into his or her poem can evoke feelings in the reader. Crompton (1980:135) considers poetry a means of communication between the child client and therapist, while Rubin (1978:74-75) clearly distinguishes between therapy by means of poetry and bibliotherapy. On the whole, however, it would seem that there is a definite school of thought that argues that poetry alone, without other inputs, can be therapeutic.

Van der Merwe (1991:180) is of the opinion that poetry should be used as one of many techniques in working with children, particularly emphasising the use of rhymes. Poetry can be used in the beginning phase of therapy to put the child at ease and can be combined with rhythmic movement. As described in the discussion of the use of music, poems and rhymes can be used metaphorically to give the child more insight into his situation.

The use of magazines and pictures

According to Porter (1983:308-309), magazines and pictures can be used to

- reconstruct the child's family
- make him aware of the emotions of others, to explore his own emotions in different situations and to teach the child how to handle these emotions
- compile a model for behaviour modification
- illustrate the life book
- make comic strips
- make a scrapbook on a specific topic, for instance, rugby, to enhance the child's self-image.

Pictures (from magazines) can also serve as role models for children. A child in a children's home once chose a picture of a famous singer from a magazine. He said that he admired this man because he always dressed nicely, looked kind and was rich. It was obvious that the singer served as a role model to the child. This theme could be worked on in therapy as it was easy to encourage the child to follow the positive aspects of his role model's behaviour. This gave him something concrete for which to strive. The therapist's task in this case was to keep the child realistic in his expectations.

When trying to identify the various feelings in therapy, it is helpful to page through a magazine and to distinguish feelings depicted in the pictures. These can then be drawn in the child's exercise book by sketching the facial expressions using only the eyebrows, eyes and mouth. Therapists can even keep files of pictures of facial expressions showing different emotions. Hepworth and Larsen (1982:95-97) list numerous affective words and phrases that can be helpful when discussing feeling language with children.

Paging through a magazine with a child can also be relaxing. This can enhance the relationship of trust and also offers the child the opportunity of showing his feelings and wishes.

The use of comic strips and cartoon characters

According to Smith (1981:112), the creation of comic strips offers children an opportunity for fantasy and identification. Pictures must be chosen intentionally and placed in the form of a comic strip to make a story. Above each character, an empty circle is drawn. The child can write his thoughts there as if these belonged to the specific character. This is a form of projection. Porter (1983:312) has found that this technique is especially suitable for children in the age group eleven to thirteen years.

Mills and Crowley (1986:209-230) describe cartoon therapy, in which cartoon characters are seen as powerful symbols. They use them as living metaphors to aid the working through of feelings. First, the child is asked to identify and draw his favourite cartoon character. The therapist can then build a story around the character. In other instances, cartoon characters serve as imaginary friends that can function as support systems in difficult times – children often have imaginary friends in any case. (One is reminded of the child with the "broom-friend" named Heather Harvey.) It should therefore not be too difficult to involve children in cartoon-play.

In a practical application, the author once treated a child who loved the television program *Remi*. This cartoon character suffered numerous problems and losses in the course of the story. The specific child client identified with Remi. Thus, the author and child identified all Remi's losses and looked at the ways in which he coped. These were compared with the child's losses and the ways in which she coped. Although crying a lot, the little girl realised that her problems were not that overwhelming in the end, which gave her a feeling of controlling her difficult situation. It is thus important not to discard the child's problems as being of no significance when using this technique. However, the main advantage is that the child can learn coping skills by observing how the cartoon character handles its problems, much in the same way as characters in children's stories do.

Therapists can also improvise stories around cartoon characters, such as Popeye. Popeye's use of spinach for problem solving can introduce a discussion on ways in which the child handles his problems. South African characters, such as Liewe Heksie and Bollie, can also be used as positive identification figures. Importantly, for each child, a personal story should be developed, taking into account his unique situation. This implies that child therapists should know the children's programs on television, as well as cartoons in magazines. In general contact with children, the therapist can discuss their preferences and feelings regarding the cartoons on television as a means of keeping in contact with the children's perspectives on cartoons (Van der Merwe, 1991:182).

The use of incomplete sentences

The use of incomplete sentences in therapy is discussed by Porter (1983:317) and Graver and Morse (1986:50). Thompson and Rudolph (1992:115) describe incomplete sentences as one of the Gestalt techniques. These sentences can address aspects such as preferences and dislikes, family, friends, aims, wishes, and things that make the child happy or unhappy. Completing sentences of this nature can also be a point of reference for further discussions and can bring valuable information to the fore. This is a projection technique that should help the child to relax and should also facilitate rapport between therapist and client.

The use of letters

Children who find it difficult to verbalise can express their feelings in letters. Some letters will be written as a means of working through feelings, while others will be handed to relevant people (Harrison, 1986:392).

Mitchell (1981:189-201) has used letters as part of third object techniques in therapy with young children. Letters to and from a friendly animal character serve as an effective medium of communication for young children: they hold their interest while offering a safe, neutral way of entering the child's world. This technique is helpful in the building of a relationship between the therapist and client. For instance, in her work with preschool children, Mitchell (1981:192-193) used letters to and from an imaginary kangaroo. This kangaroo did everyday things with which the children could easily identify. Writing, drawing or dictating letters to an imaginary friend often evokes questions or discussion of problems and fears.

Porter (1983:263-271) cites the value of letters in therapy:

- The use of letters is especially effective for children in the age group three to nine years.
- Letter writing gives the child the opportunity of working through traumatic experiences.
- The child usually enjoys writing letters and when he finds therapy fun, the relationship with the therapist may be strengthened.
- The child does not always readily offer information to the therapist. Once he has built up trust in an imaginary pen friend, it is quite possible that he will also trust the person who introduced him to this pen friend.
- It is an easy method of communication for the child. The therapist should use the information that the child offers for further therapeutic work. However, the therapist should be careful not to jump to conclusions too early and not to ask inappropriate questions.
- This technique has a high success rate. As such, it is helpful in giving inexperienced child therapists more confidence in direct work with children.

After the termination of therapy, the therapist and child client can correspond a few times in order to monitor progress and to maintain positive changes.

The use of an emotional barometer

The emotional barometer is a graphic aid to counselling, described by Thompson and Elliott (1987:312-317). It is a visual scale with a happy face on top and a sad face underneath. The child is expected to mark his feelings on the ten-point scale. He may use initiative and mark his feelings by drawing a tie or facial expressions.

The main aims of using the emotional barometer are to assist children in identifying feelings and thoughts regarding problem areas in their lives and to help children to communicate thoughts and feelings in ways that lead to plans for problem solving. The barometer can be used in both individual and group therapy. It is particularly useful in the beginning of an interview or group session to assess children's moods and to direct the discussion to a feeling level.

The barometer may also be used to find out how the child feels regarding specific areas of his life. This aid is thus valuable in opening up avenues for further exploration. When a child places his feelings at six, for instance, exploration can be done regarding the stumbling blocks that prevent him from placing his feelings at ten. When evaluating marks on various barometers over a period of time, an idea can be formed of the child's progress.

Children may draw their own barometers, but it is a good idea to have some examples available, such as the following:

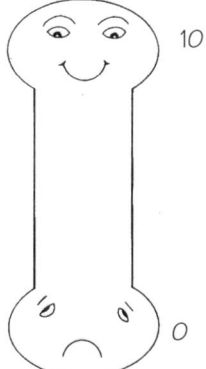

Figure 8.2: **Emotional barometer**
(Adapted from Van der Merwe, 1991: Appendix 11)

The use of computer games

Computer games, such as *Gorillas* and *Nibbles*, can be used for relaxation and assessment in particular. The first game concerns two gorillas who are throwing bananas at each other. This game is better suited to older children as they have to negotiate aspects such as speed and gravity.

Nibbles requires the child to navigate snakes around a game board on the computer screen, trying to eat up numbers and avoid running into walls or other snakes. The more numbers that are eaten, the more points the player obtains and the longer the snake becomes. This game can be played by two people simultaneously. It is especially suitable for checking children's fine coordination skills and can also aid in determining their tolerance of frustration. Children as young as four should be able to play this game.

A negative aspect of the use of computer games may be that the child client may grow like computer games so much that his motivation for the other aspects of therapy is restricted.

Conclusion

Biblio-play is a valuable form of play that has been proven to be effective in opening up communication regarding painful life events. It offers the opportunity of educating children on relevant aspects regarding their problems. Through biblio-play, children can generalise their circumstances when they see other people in similar situations. This will also help to reduce their feelings of isolation.

The real value of this form of play is that it usually directs the therapy clearly onto the child's problem or need in a non-threatening way, as it is structured and goal-directed. It is therefore an integral part of the change-oriented phase of the helping process, together with dramatic and creative play which will be described in the following chapters.

Bibliography

Ailiki. 1984. *Feelings*. London: The Bodley Head.

Anderson, A. & Anderson, M. 1979. *A book of life for an adopted child*. Cape Town: Harvard Timmens.

Boucher, S. 1992. *Too small Themba*. Pietermaritzburg: Shuter & Shooter.

Burt, L.N. 1972. *Bibliotherapy: The effect of group reading and discussion on attitudes of child inmates in two correctional institutions*. Published Ph.D thesis. Michigan: University of Wisconsin.

Crompton, M. 1980. *Respecting children: Social work with young people*. London: Edward Arnold.

Gardner, R.A. 1976. *Psychotherapy with children of divorce*. New York: Jason Aronson.

Graver, C.M. & Morse, L.A. 1986. *Helping children of divorce: A group leader's guide*. Illinois: Charles C. Thomas.

Harrison, J. 1988. Making life books with foster and adoptive children. In Schaefer: 377-399.

Hepworth, D.H. & Larsen, J.A. 1982. *Direct social work practice: Theory and skills*. Illinois: Charles C. Thomas.

Hill, E. 1988. *Where's Spot? /Tilo o kae?* Hatfield: Van Schaik.

Hill, E. 1991. *Spot's book of words/Incwadi kaSpoti enkulukazi Gamagama*. Hatfield: Van Schaik.

Howie, M. 1983. Bibliotherapy in social work. *The British Journal of Social Work*, 13 (3): 287-319.

Jones, W. 1970. Keeping the memories of childhood. *Social Work Today*, 1(5): 22-23.

Keller, H. 1991. *Horace*. London: J. MacRae.
Mills, J.C. & Crowley, R.J. 1986. *Therapeutic metaphors for children and the child within*. New York: Brunner Mazel.
Mitchell, J. 1981. Letters from a kangaroo: A third object technique for working with the young. *British Journal of Social Work*, 11:189-201.
Monroe, M.E. (Ed.). 1978. *Seminar on bibliotherapy*. Madison: Library School, University of Wisconsin.
Moody, M.T. & Limper, H.K. 1971. *Bibliotherapy: methods and materials*. Chicago: American Library Association.
Pardeck, J.T. & Pardeck, J.A. 1987. Bibliotherapy for children in foster care and adoption. *Child Welfare*, 66(3): 269-278.
Pardeck, J.T. & Pardeck, J.A. 1989. Helping children adjust to adoption through the bibliotherapeutic approach. *Early Child Development and Care*, 44(1): 31-37.
Porter, C. 1983. Spelterapie met die sorgbehoewende kind. Unpublished MA thesis. Pretoria: University of Pretoria.
Rubin, R.J. 1978. *Using bibliotherapy: A guide to theory and practice*. London: Oryx Press.
Schaefer, C.E. (Ed.). 1988. *Innovative interventions in child and adolescent therapy*. New York: John Wiley.
Schoeman, H.P. & Botha, D. 1993. Etiese dilemmas in maatskaplike werk met verwysing na die benutting van rekenaar tegnologie. *Maatskaplike Werk/Social Work*, 29(4): 307-318.
Smith, C.M. 1981. *Leer die kind ken: Riglyne vir die maatskaplike werker*. Pretoria: Academia.
Smith, C.M. 1982. Die gebruik van die kinderverhaal as biblioterapeutiese tegniek. *Maatskaplike Werk/Social Work*, 18(4): 229-236.
Spies, G.M. 1993. Die gebruik van metafore in die maatskaplikewerk-praktyk. *Social Work Practice,* 1. 93:13-18.
Stutterheim, H. & Kroon, S. 1991. Die gebruik van biblioterapie in maatskaplikewerk. *Social Work*, 27(2): 180-190.
Stutterheim, H. & Pretorius, C. 1993. The use of bibliotherapy in the treatment of abused children. *Social Work Practice*, 1. 93: 7-12.
Thompson, C.L. & Elliott, S. 1987. The emotional barometer: A graphic aid to counseling. *Elementary School Guidance and Counseling*, 21(4): 312-317.
Thompson, C.L. & Rudolph, L.B. 1988. *Counseling children*. (2nd. ed.). California: Brooks Cole.
Thompson, C.L. & Rudolph, L.B. 1992. *Counseling children*. (3rd ed.). California: Brooks Cole.
Van der Merwe, M. 1991. Maatskaplikewerk-beraad met jong kinders in egskeidingsituasies met fokus op speeltegnieke. Unpublished MA thesis. Stellenbosch. University of Stellenbosch.
Weiser, J. 1988. Phototherapy: Using snapshots and photo-interactions in therapy with youth. In Schaefer: 339-376.

9 Dramatic play

M VAN DER MERWE

Introduction

Porter (1983:216-233) and Dunne (1988:139, 149) regard dramatic play as a form of play that offers the child client the opportunity to grow by acting out situations and dramatising in a safe, non-threatening environment. Krüger (1988:15) uses pretention play and symbolic play as terms interchangeable with dramatic play. To use this form of play effectively, the therapist should have a clear picture of the child client's situation. A great deal of inventiveness is also required of the therapist. Dramatic play is especially suitable for use in the change-oriented phase of helping as it focuses on problem solving.

Advantages of dramatic play

Ghiaci and Richardson (1980:82), Porter (1983:219-225) and Dunne (1988:139) describe the advantages of dramatic play:

- It gives the child the opportunity to release his emotions while feeling less threatened and exposed owing to the distance that dramatic play creates from his problems.
- By acting out experience, he comes into contact with reality. It is constructive for the child to remember situations through play and to have the opportunity to repeat them and work through them. This may lead to emotional growth, development and mastering, for instance, when the child acts out the first visit to a parent after divorce.
- New or specific roles can be learned when exercising these through dramatic play. While the child is playing, the therapist has the opportunity of evaluating current role behaviour. This is followed by helping the child to practice new possibilities. The therapist may even model new roles.
- Dramatic play creates a special means of communication between therapist and child client. Important information can come to the fore, for instance, while playing with a doll's house.

- During dramatic play, the child can manage his world as he likes.
- By playing through situations over and over again, insight into certain aspects of his situation may develop. Often, the child's questions are answered during dramatic play.
- A tape recorder can be used in conjunction with dramatic play. While listening to his own play, the child may develop insight.

Porter (1983:229-230) claims that aids and apparatus are not so important for this type of play. They can be used, though, to make interviews interesting and full of fun. Therapeutic aids must be chosen according to each child's stage of development, age, motivation for therapy and intellectual ability.

For example, Van der Merwe (1991:268) has found that dramatic play was the ideal form of play for some of the respondents in research that she conducted on children of divorced parents. One child dramatised almost all the time. She was creative and had a good imagination. Her mother planned to remarry and the respondent would then go to boarding school. She acted this situation out with dolls. She also made a book containing all the pictures that she had drawn of the stories that she made up. Other respondents did not respond as well to this play form. They never progressed further than tidying up the doll's house. This again stresses the importance of individualisation when determining the forms of play to use in an intervention plan.

Van der Merwe (1991:269) also established that children generally personalise the dolls quickly by talking to and about them as, for instance, mom and dad. It was also a common occurrence for children to talk softly while they played with the dolls, therefore making it easy for the researcher to keep track of their playing. Some children talk to the dolls in a kind of a teacher/instructor manner.

Sequence of dramatic play

Porter (1983:229) distinguishes a specific sequence in dramatic play:
- The therapist should have a plan of action and should decide which form dramatic play is going to take.
- The method of interviewing should be explained to the child.
- The child must be motivated and joint planning should be done.
- A situation is then acted out by the child and the therapist.
- The play situation is discussed and facts that come to the fore are explored.
- The play situation is then assessed jointly and further planning is done.
- If necessary, behaviour is repeated and practised.

Dunne (1988:140-141) divides dramatic play into three phases, namely, warming up, dramatising and conclusion, also describing techniques which correspond to these phases, for example, focused fantasy and creative movement in the warming up phase, then change-oriented techniques as described below. These are followed by techniques for termination that reduce therapeutic intensity and imbue the child client with a feeling of progress. Techniques for dramatic play therefore display a particular sequence. If the techniques for relaxation play have been employed properly, the child client should be ready for more intensive dramatic play in the change-oriented phase of treatment.

Techniques of dramatic play

Role-playing

Role-playing can be used during therapeutic discussions. It can also consist of non-verbal interaction. The child may play himself or a reversal of roles may take place in that he plays the role of one of his parents or other significant people. This technique is of particular value for practising role behaviour.

Dunne (1988:141) describes the way in which hypothetical problem situations can be worked through by role-playing. The therapist describes various hypothetical situations that can serve as ways of handling a problem. The child client then chooses the situation with which he can best identify and acts it out. He can also play various roles of different characters in the situation to broaden his perspective. This will also help him to develop new and creative ways of solving problems.

A group of girls in a reformatory once acted out a court scene during a group session. They had to play roles of the social worker, magistrate and parents. One girl took the part of an extremely difficult adolescent and acted with great enthusiasm. The girls playing the social worker and magistrate could experience the feelings of frustration evoked by the difficult adolescent's attitude. They also gained insight into the "other side" of the situation. The girl portraying the social worker had to convince the court that the situation of the youth was so unsatisfactory that it necessitated her going to the reformatory. While being very negative towards social workers, the girl acted convincingly. In the process of role-playing, a small change of attitude was noticeable. The girls who played the roles of parents also reported more understanding for their parents' point of view. Clearly, one group session is not enough to change attitudes radically and convincingly. However, role-playing can be of value in starting this change and continuing it in follow-up sessions.

The Talking, feeling, doing game

Gardner (1976:79-85; 1983:259-273; 1986:41-72) developed this board game. According to Frey (1986:26), the game requires children to react to cards which focus on cognitive, affective and behavioural aspects. Tools that are needed for playing are dice, play pieces, 104 cards with different instructions, a wheel with various directives, reward disks and prizes. A child of about nine should be able to read the cards on his own. Children who cannot read can play along while the therapist does the reading. This game is suitable for use with children up to the phase of puberty whereafter their inhibitions often become an obstacle. Only persons skilled in therapeutic work with children should use this board game as specific therapeutic responses form the core of the game. It is therefore not possible for parents to use it with their children (Frey 1986:26).

The game starts when the therapist and child put their game pieces on **GO**. They throw the dice in turn and move along a curved path of coloured squares. Depending on the colour of the square on which they land, a card is drawn. Talking cards are white, feeling cards are yellow and doing cards are red. The questions or instructions on the cards lie on a continuum from low anxiety to medium anxiety. When the child reacts to the cards, he is rewarded with a disk. However, children are never forced to react. Then the card is placed back in the pack. If the same card is drawn later on, it does not matter, as it may bring new information to the fore through the dynamic therapeutic process.

Gardner (1976:83-85) gives examples of the kind of information that is requested by the various cards:

- **Low anxiety talking card:** Address, height, choice of present for next birthday, occupation of father.
- **Medium anxiety talking card**: Bad remark about mother, thoughts when unable to sleep.
- **Low anxiety feeling card**: Food dislikes, feelings when tickled, discussion of episode that made the child proud.
- **Medium anxiety feeling card**: Speculate why everyone in class laughs at someone.
- **Low anxiety doing card**: Pretend to blow out candles on a cake, make funny noises, pretend to eat ice cream.
- **Medium anxiety doing card**: Pretend to talk to someone on the phone and tell the therapist who it is, talk about the most stupid and selfish thing ever done and pretend to do it right now.

There are all sorts of rules and actions that aim at making the game fun, for instance, the spinning of a wheel that gives extra orders to the players.

The therapist should create a relaxed atmosphere and minimise the competition aspect. If the child does not want to react to a card, he must feel free to refrain from doing so. The therapist can also skip certain cards, while others can offer her the opportunity for self disclosure. According to Gardner (1976:89), clients often see therapists as being successful in many areas of life. This view can sometimes be an obstacle in therapy as it can have a negative influence on the client's self-image. Therefore Gardner sometimes seeks opportunities to state his own imperfections to clients. Cards asking about shortcomings often offer such an opportunity.

The child's responses usually bring out meaningful information. The therapist's responses and knowledge of the child's situation should accommodate this. Those aspects that come to the fore during reaction to the cards can be followed up by discussion.

Krüger (1988) translated the Talking, feeling, doing game into Afrikaans after obtaining permission to produce one copy through the Bureau for Continued Education of the University of Stellenbosch. Krüger (1988:42) used this game in the treatment of traumatised children in a children's home. As this game is not freely available in this country, therapists will have to improvise. This game has elements of dramatic play, especially in the doing cards. It can also be used as part of assessment play, and for relaxation.

Dramatising therapeutic communication

Children tend to dramatise their life-stories. Gardner (1976:67) started to imitate this with success. He found that it helped to get messages across to children, while keeping their attention. When dramatising therapeutic communication, the therapist should be able to let go of her inhibitions. According to Gardner (1976:67), the therapist should be choreographer, writer, actor and director at the same time. She should be able to think on her feet, and back and knees! This technique encapsulates the basic social work principle that social workers should adapt to the worlds of their clients.

Dolls, puppets and paper dolls

Dolls and puppets can be used for assessment and helping (Harrison, 1986:393; Mills & Crowley, 1986:199; Kruger, 1987:35). Usually, dolls or puppets are provided in therapy. The child then tells stories while playing with them. They may also be used in other ways.

Kruger (1987:43; 1990:8) distinguishes between ordinary dolls and puppets. Usually, dolls are not as mobile as puppets. The child often talks *to* the doll, but *through* the puppet. Both therefore have important and different functions in therapy.

There is a wide variety of tiny play dolls available. Van der Merwe (1991:194) has found that small Duplo dolls are most functional. There is a big set of these dolls available, including a fireman, a policeman, and family dolls (both black and white). These dolls can be used together with a doll's house and play furniture. Children tend to personalise the dolls by addressing them as mom and dad or using the names of other family members.

Van der Merwe (1991:269) has established that children, while playing with the dolls, "give a report" of what they are doing. One child acted out his feelings regarding the extra role responsibilities he had after parental divorce. He put the mother doll and the father doll on a play couch. He then took the little boy doll and let him kick the father doll out of his place on the couch. He put the boy doll in the father's place, stating that Pietie sometimes had to become the father. He switched the dolls a few times in this way. Then he took a mallet and hit pegs into the holes of a wooden toy with so much aggression that the wooden block cracked.

Kruger (1990:8) delineates specific characteristics of puppets, namely, that they are

❑ lifeless objects which are brought to life by a puppeteer using movement and speech
❑ an expression of fantasy

- not miniature persons or animals
- simplifications and expressions of the imagination
- symbols, and not realistic imitations of reality.

Puppets can be used in a number of ways. Cantrell (1986:167) describes the use of puppets in group therapy with children of divorced parents. Puppets are used to act out a variety of divorce related situations, for instance, longing for the non-custodial parent and anger towards the parents. Puppets can also be used in the same way in individual therapy.

According to James and Myer (1987:292-293), puppets offer children a safe way of sharing deep and private feelings with the therapist, even though the feelings are often vented in an indirect way. They highlight two skills that are needed when using puppets, namely that the therapist should be able to use her voice to portray the different characters and be able to move the puppets in such a way that they hold the attention of the child. The therapist should develop the puppet's personality to suit its physical appearance. When using puppets, it is essential that the therapist's skills in active listening and reflective responding should be well developed. Empathic responding is preferable to interpretation or giving of advice as puppets should convey warmth, empathy and caring. The therapist should practise her skills in handling the puppet as an integral part of overall proficient interviewing.

James and Myer (1987:295-298) cite various functions of puppets in therapy. A certain process can also be distinguished in these functions:

- Puppets can help to initiate a discussion. At first, the therapist will use mostly reflection techniques. When the child starts to acknowledge his feelings, more direct questions can be asked by the puppet.
- When using puppets, the therapist can enter the child's world in a natural, non-threatening way.
- Multiple dialogue is possible between the various puppets, the therapist and the child client. To confirm perceptions and hunches, the therapist can ask the puppets for feedback on what is happening during the interview.
- If the child finds it difficult to discuss ways of solving problems, the puppets can be used to consider alternative ways of coping. A puppet can also discuss his feelings in a similar situation to that of the child.
- Puppets can be used to combine fantasy and reality, so long as the therapist understands the symbolic meaning of the child's puppet play. The therapist should listen well to identify the emotions that the child is projecting. She should be skilful in determining whether she should talk to the puppet or to the child.
- When the child is ready, the dialogue should be focused away from fantasy and the puppets and the child should be addressed directly. Problem solving will then focus on the real problem.
- At the end of the interview, the child should be guided back to reality. He should be able to distinguish himself clearly from the puppet character that he played. He

should then be able to determine what is to be done in connection with his problems.

It is clear that therapists cannot use puppets without thorough preparation and practice. Moving between fantasy and reality is a fine art.

Kruger (1987:53-60) describes other kinds of puppets. **Glove puppets** consist of a head with hands and a "body" which consists of a glove. Van der Merwe (1991:195) regards dolls made out of socks or paper bags as glove puppets as well. The child can make his own glove puppets depicting significant people in his life. Then he can act out problematic situations with these puppets.

Finger puppets fit on the finger. They can be made to fit tightly or may be fastened with a rubber band. Children can make them quite easily. These are possibly quicker to make than glove puppets and are therefore more cost-effective. Small photos of family members can be used as faces for finger puppets. This should make the play very realistic, although the symbolic element of doll play will then possibly be lost. More realistic finger puppets should be especially suitable in the change-oriented phase of therapy, when moving past fantasy to reality is appropriate and when problems are addressed directly. Cheap finger puppets in animal forms are also effective when used in therapy.

Marionettes are figures with loose limbs attached to the body by wooden pegs, leather, metal hinges or wire. The limbs are also attached to vertical control sticks. If the therapist is able to master the manipulation of marionettes, it can be a useful therapeutic aid. The use of marionettes should enhance the fun element of therapy and can thus be helpful in getting therapeutic messages across to the child. It can also aid the therapeutic relationship, when the child admires the therapist's skill in the manipulation of the figures.

Shadow puppets are traditionally two-dimensional figures cut from material such as wood or leather. Stiff cardboard can also be used (Kruger, 1990:43), as cardboard should be available even in the most deprived communities. According to Kruger (1990:43), shadow puppets should have clear outlines without too much detail. Strong emphasis on and even exaggeration of the characteristic form is required.

Paper dolls can be constructed by the child with the help of the therapist. Various situations and stories can be portrayed with these dolls. The child may draw family members, cut them out and use them as paper dolls. Photos may also be used. He may even draw his home or homes, cut them out and use them in his play.

Mills and Crowley (1986:199-203) have developed the **The magic puppet theatre**, which is a technique whereby the child is encouraged to use paper to make a puppet theatre, decor and dolls from paper. When this is completed, he is encouraged to act out scenes. Dolls made by the child as part of the magic puppet theatre can function as metaphors for his environment and perceptions, while they are also a mechanism for carrying metaphorical therapeutic messages directed by the therapist — in actual fact, therefore, a metaphor within a metaphor. The dolls may even serve as symbols of the child's inner world.

Therapists should use their creativity and available material to produce dolls and puppets in one or more of the forms discussed above. It should be beneficial to the therapeutic process and should ultimately help the child client to make sense of his world.

Telephone play

A telephone is a so-called non-toy toy (Spero, 1980:57). Van der Merwe (1991:197) mentions possible problems concerning the use of the office telephone in therapy. It may cause trouble at the switchboard if an office phone is off the hook while being used in dramatic play by the child client, as this can block incoming calls. It is also often possible for people at the switchboard to follow the child's conversation with an imaginary person, which is a breach of confidentiality. Depending on circumstances, a play phone should rather be used.

The use of the telephone in counselling children has various advantages, as cited by Spero (1980:58):

- It is an accepted way of communicating.
- It has potential symbolic value as it combines talking and listening, as well as reactions and gesture of self-assertiveness that are invisible to the person at the other end of the line. When playing, the child can imagine and direct these reactions and the meaning thereof.
- The use of a telephone is often significant as many children see the ability to dial a number and talk to someone as the mastery of adult skills. This can give them a feeling of power, pride and control.
- Telephonic contact can be broken immediately if one of the parties finds it threatening.
- In therapy, the telephone stimulates fantasy when the child is in dialogue with a party that he has chosen.
- The child can pretend to make contact with someone with whom he has no contact owing to death or divorce. This may help him to work through unresolved feelings.
- Trying to convince an imaginary person of something of which child himself is not so certain may help him to develop insight, for example, concerning the value of therapy.
- If he feels anxious in the therapeutic situation, the child can phone or pretend to phone somebody to share his whereabouts and what he is doing there. In this way, the therapist can gain insight into the child's perception of therapy and his expectations. Such telephone contact can also serve to put the child at ease.
- The choice of partner for conversation, the nature of the conversation and the role that the child plays can bring valuable information to the attention of the therapist.

The child may use the telephone as he wishes. Often, he will talk as himself and also pretend to be the person on the other end. He can also talk on his own and pretend to listen to someone else, without telling the therapist what he imagines hearing. The child can request the therapist to play herself or to play some sort of role on the other end of the line. To make the discussions more realistic, the therapist can even go to another office and phone the child from there. Each child's functioning will determine the way in which the telephone is used in therapy (Van der Merwe, 1991:198).

Masks

By putting on a mask, the child can replace himself into a symbolic world. By taking over another character's facial form, he can release his feelings indirectly and bring more information on his situation to the fore. The child client can make masks from all sorts of material, such as paper plates and bags. In this way, dramatic play is again combined with creative play.

Conclusion

Children find dramatic play exciting. Usually, they take part in this form of play with enthusiasm and creativity. In the beginning and final phases of therapy, it is helpful when trying to reduce the intensity of therapy. In the change-oriented phase of therapy, it is an aid when trying to reach deeper therapeutic intensity. It seems that the more guided forms of dramatic play tend to reduce therapeutic intensity, whereas the unstructured forms, such as free play with dolls and a doll's house, tend to bring deeper feelings to the fore.

Bibliography

Cantrell, R.G. 1986. Adjustment to divorce: Three components to assist children. *Elementary School Guidance and Counseling*, 20(3): 163-173.

Dunne, P.B. 1988. Drama therapy techniques in one-to-one treatment with disturbed children and adolescents. *The Arts in Psychotherapy*, 15: 139-149.

Frey, D.E. 1986. Communications boardgames with children. In Schaefer & Reid: 21-41.

Gardner, R.A. 1976. *Psychotherapy with children of divorce*. New York: Jason Aronson.

Gardner, R.A. 1983. The Talking, feeling, doing game. In Schaefer & O'Conner: 259-274.

Gardner, R.A. 1986. The Talking, feeling, doing game. In Schaefer & Reid: 41-72.

Ghiaci, G. & Richardson, J.T.E. 1980. The effects of dramatic play upon cognitive structure and development. *The Journal of Genetic Psychology*, 136: 77-83.

Graver, C.M. & Morse, L.A. 1986. *Helping children of divorce: A group leader's guide*. Illinois: Charles C. Thomas.

James, R.K. & Myer, R. 1987. Puppets: The elementary school counselor's right or left arm. *Elementary School Guidance and Counseling*, 21(4): 292-299.

Kruger, M.S. 1987. Poppespel — 'n Ondersoek na die historiese ontwikkeling, die spelbeginsels, karakter en gebruiksmoontlikhede van die toneelpop met 'n omvattende bronnelys. Unpublished MA thesis. Stellenbosch: University of Stellenbosch.

Kruger, M.S. 1990. *Poppespel: 'n Gids vir beginners*. Cape Town: Delos.

Krüger, A. 1988. "The Talking, feeling and doing game" — 'n Voorlopige ondersoek. Unpublished MA thesis. Stellenbosch: University of Stellenbosch.

Mills, J.C. & Crowley, R.J. 1986. *Therapeutic metaphors for children and the child within*. New York: Brunner Mazel.

Porter, C. 1983. Spelterapie met die sorgbehoewende kind. Unpublished MA thesis. Pretoria: University of Pretoria.

Schaefer, C.E. & Reid, S.E. (Eds.). 1986. *Game play: Therapeutic use of childhood games*. New York: John Wiley.

Spero, M.H. 1980. Use of the telephone in child play therapy. *Social Work*, 25(1): 57-60.

Van der Merwe, M. 1991. Maatskaplikewerk-beraad met jong kinders in egskeidingsituasies met fokus op speeltegnieke. Unpublished MA thesis. Stellenbosch: University of Stellenbosch.

10 Creative play

M VAN DER MERWE

Introduction

The phrase *creative play* is used by Porter (1983:242-271) who also explains it in detail. Creative play is inventive; it can be manifested in various forms of art and handcraft. In a way, it is related to art therapy, but in a broader sense of the word. Various authors are of the opinion that art is an important medium of communication with the young child whose verbal skills have not yet developed properly (Crompton, 1980:156; Jefferies & Gillespie, 1981:9; Allan & Clark, 1984:116; Gillespie, 1986:19).

Art therapy is a specialist area for which therapists are equipped through advanced study. Crompton (1980:158) also regards the interpretation of children's art as a specialist area, but emphasises that all social workers can utilise children's drawings to determine what the child is trying to say and to search for possible meaning.

Before describing some techniques for creative play, such as children's drawings, a few advantages of this form of play need to be spelled out. However, this play form is not suited to all children. In Van der Merwe's (1991:274) research, one specific child loved this play form. Early in the process, he stated that he was his mother's artist. He loved to draw and to work with clay. Often he combined the two. Creative play was a good medium for working with this child. In contrast to this, another respondent clearly stated that he could not colour in. When asked to draw a person, he said that he was unable to do so. Regarding creative play, he only liked playing with clay. On the whole, however, he preferred the other play forms. Clearly, the play form must be suited to the child client.

Advantages of creative play

☐ Drawing and painting can be relaxing and can therefore create the correct atmosphere for further therapy.
☐ Creative play is functional in establishing a rapport between therapist and child and

thus promotes communication (Roosa, 1981:169; Di Leo, 1983:5; Porter, 1983:242-271; Rubin, 1988:185; Van der Merwe, 1991:277).

- It is a way of gaining information concerning the child's world. This may be information that the child cannot verbalise or that is on a subconscious level (Roosa, 1981:269; Klepsch & Logie,1982:6; Porter, 1983:242-271; Van der Merwe, 1991:278).
- Creative play may be used for assessment or for direct counselling (Allan & Clark, 1984:116).
- Creative play offers the child the opportunity for examination and release of feelings; this is often followed by personal growth as it activates change and leads to insight (Klepsch & Logie, 1982:7; Porter, 1983:242-271; Gillespie, 1986:19; Rose, 1988:48).
- When a child is praised for his creativity, his self-image may be enhanced. He may experience a feeling of success (Porter, 1983:242-271; Allan & Clark, 1984:117; Mills & Crowley, 1986:165).
- Situations are relived and adaptations are made during creative play, while acceptance may follow (Jefferies & Gillespie, 1981:11).
- By using creative play, the therapist may reach children who are emotionally frozen and blocked (Gillespie, 1986:19).
- Creative play may serve as therapeutic metaphor (Mills & Crowley, 1986:166).

Media and art forms

Various media and art forms can be utilised for creative play: drawings and clay may be used, while the dolls, puppets and masks that are used in dramatic play can be made as part of creative play.

There is almost no limit to the activities that can be used for creative play. What may well be limiting, though, is the creativity of the therapist and child client. They should therefore continuously be on the look-out for new sources of inspiration.

Children's drawings

There are three approaches to using drawings in therapy, as cited by Allan (1986:105-106), namely, the directive, non-directive and partly directive approaches. Often, a child starts to draw spontaneously. If it is clear that he knows what he is drawing and that it has therapeutic value, the therapist should leave him to do this within the supportive therapeutic environment. This is an example of the non-directive approach.

Withdrawn children who tend to produce stereotypical kinds of drawings need stronger guidance. An aggressive child can also be guided by asking him, for instance, to draw a volcanic eruption. The therapist should continue being directive until the child shows that he can reflect his feelings in drawing. Rose (1988:48) has some suggestions for involving children who are unsure of themselves:

- Let them draw with their eyes closed. This is especially helpful for those children

who are inhibited when drawing as they focus too much on the accuracy of the drawing.
- They can draw with the hand that they do not usually draw with.
- They can scribble with their eyes closed. They can then make drawings out of the random figures that emerge.

The therapist can also be partly directive, for instance, when a child draws certain symbols often. The therapist can then periodically ask the child to draw the same symbols, so that development can be observed.

Rose (1988:49) mentions various possibilities that can be suggested to the child if he does not know what to draw, namely, a wish, specific feelings, fear, a secret, a dream, a self-portrait, an important event, the present, future or past, an important relationship, life-sized shadows of the child's body or a drawing of how he would like to be.

Van der Merwe (1991:275) comes to the cautious conclusion that colouring in is generally not a good therapeutic activity. It takes a lot of time. Furthermore, it tends to make some children tense. It appears that they get all sorts of instructions concerning colouring in at school. They state, for instance, that the teacher instructs them to colour only with strokes in one direction or within the lines. In general, child clients find it difficult to understand their freedom of choice within the therapeutic situation. Conflict may develop when the therapist instructs them to ignore their teacher's rules during therapy. One respondent said that she liked colouring in, but she liked playing more. This indicated that she saw colouring in as work and maybe even associated it with school.

Interpretation of children's drawings

Interpreting children's drawings can be a valuable means of assessing the child and of obtaining information about his situation – that is, if it is used correctly. Therapists should be careful not to make deductions from children's drawings too early in the process and without enough evidence, knowledge and experience. Children's drawings should be interpreted with extreme care. If someone without the necessary theoretical background interprets children's drawings, serious misinterpretation may result. On the other hand, if the interpretation is done with the necessary background and takes into account the guidelines mentioned in the chapter, it can be useful for assessment. Furthermore, therapists should use the interpretation of children's drawings as part of a whole array of assessment techniques and never on its own. A few general guidelines may be offered for the interpretation of children's drawings:

- Discuss the drawings with the child before coming to conclusions.
- Observe a series of drawings by the child over a few weeks before deciding what they mean.
- Be careful not to use the guidelines for evaluating children's drawings rigidly and without the necessary experience.
- Therapists should be careful not to depend solely on sources that prescribe the interpretation of drawings, for instance, stating that mouths with lots of teeth suggest feelings of aggression in the child.

❐ Developmental phase should also be taken into account, as stressed by Mortensen (1975:17), Klepsch and Logie (1982:14) and Di Leo (1983:6). If a child draws in a way typical of earlier developmental stages, it may indicate problems. Mortensen divides the development of children's drawings as follows:

    1 - 3 years — Scribble stage
    4 - 6 years — Pre-schematic stage
    7 - 9 years — Schematic stage

The typical scribbles of children in the **scribble stage** are well known. It is difficult to identify what the child is drawing, as the mere motor activity of drawing satisfies him. He does not look for content or try to portray something in his environment as in the pre-schematic stage (Mortensen, 1975:22-25).

In the **pre-schematic** stage, the drawing typically consists of a round head, with legs joined to the head. Later on, the child usually draws more body parts, for instance, arms, feet and facial features. In this age group, the child does not work according to a scheme when drawing, but experiments with forms. He likes to use various colours, but does not attach specific values to colours, for instance, that blue is used when drawing the sky. Colour is mostly used to depict his emotional attitude towards an object. A person is the most common object drawn at this stage.

In the **schematic stage**, the child's drawing skill is influenced by environmental aspects, such as school education. There may be great differences between children's drawings depending on the factors that have influenced them. The human figure is drawn in all sorts of ways. The body should, however, form part of the drawing; the head has facial features and sometimes hair; legs are drawn with feet; the arms may have fingers on, but seldom hands. Arms and legs are often out of proportion and legs may differ in form and thickness. People are usually depicted from the front. The use of colour is more realistic and according to the real colour of the object (Mortensen, 1975:26-36).

It is commonly accepted that the child's use of colour, space and size contains information, if the child's developmental stage is taken into account and if the drawings are evaluated in context. It is also important to individualise by finding out what each colour means to each specific child. The distance between objects and figures may also give an idea of their emotional relations while the size of people in drawings may indicate their significance in the child's world. The following specific indicators can be used to assess children's drawings:

Colour

The child's use of colour, and specifically excessive use of colour, can be meaningful (Crompton, 1980:158-159; Klepsch & Logie, 1982:35; Porter, 1983:246-248; Rose, 1988:49). Pre-schoolers, in particular, tend to have brown, orange or black phases. This is quite normal.

According to an article in *Beeld* (5 February 1991), children in Iraq were helped to cope with the experience of missile attacks by using play therapy. Therapists noted that red and black were the colours most used in drawings of missile attacks on apartments. The use of colour can hint at the following:

- **Red:** violence and excessive emotion; aggression; cheerfulness; when used by preschool children, red may indicate good adaptation
- **Yellow:** hostility; dependence; infantile behaviour
- **Orange:** good relations with environment; may show areas of discomfort
- **Blue:** controlled reactions; self-control
- **Green:** controlled reactions; when blue and green are often used together, it may indicate that the child feels safe when he is in control
- **Black:** controlled reactions; anxiety; intellectualism; compulsiveness
- **Brown:** bashfulness, shyness; regression; the combined use of brown and black can point to anxiety and depression.

Size

Big drawings can indicate aggression, while small drawings may point to shyness. Overactive children with few inhibitions and little self-control often draw beyond the borders of the paper and find it difficult to fit their drawings onto the page (Klepsch & Logie, 1982:43).

Space

The use of space can also give some indication of the child's functioning. For the purposes of analysis, the page can be divided into four parts, by a horizontal line crossed by a vertical line in the middle of the page.

It is commonly accepted that small figures that are drawn near the foot of the page suggest feelings of depression, inadequacy and insecurity. Similarly, when a baseline of grass (or something else) is drawn, it may show a need for security and support. This is also the case when a figure is drawn with feet touching the foot of the page. However, such drawings may also indicate a good sense of reality. Drawings in the upper part of the page may signify optimism, narcissism, fantasy, or a quest to accomplish something.

There is no clarity regarding the placing of drawings to the left or the right of the page, even though it has been suggested that placement on the left may indicate an emphasis on the past and placement on the right an emphasis on the future. It is also significant to see where the child positions himself in relation to family members in a drawing (Crompton, 1980:159-161; Klepsch & Logie, 1982:46; Di Leo 1983:13-16).

Line quality

Line quality contains certain information. A drawing with light, unsure and broken lines may point to an unsure, unhappy child with low levels of energy and many inhibitions. On the other hand, a clear, unbroken and freely drawn line may indicate self-confidence and a feeling of security. Heavy lines may show aggression, high energy levels, and may even be a sign of excess tension in the muscle tone (Klepsch & Logie, 1982:46; Di Leo, 1983:17; Rose, 1988:49).

Emphasis and omission of body parts

Emphasis, exaggeration and omission of body parts often occur. Over-emphasis and under-emphasis also have specific meanings, according to Klepsch and Logie (1982:43-44) and Rose (1988:49):

- **Heads:** People feeling intellectually inadequate may draw the head too big or too small.
- **Mouths:** Over or under-emphasis of mouths often typifies the drawings of people with language deficiencies, as well as those of very dependent children. When the mouth is omitted completely, problems with socialising may be indicated. The form of the mouth may reflect the facial expression and this may point to the child's emotional state.
- **Eyes:** Empty eyes without pupils are sometimes characteristic of the drawings of children with learning problems owing to visual problems.
- **Arms:** Big or long arms appear in the drawings of those looking for power, as well as in the drawings of physically disabled children who would like to have more power. Small arms or arms with light lines may depict fear of power and feelings of inefficiency and powerlessness. When a child older than six years omits the arms in a drawing, this may show feelings of insufficiency, mistrust and inadequacy. The child may also be withdrawn, anxious and lacking in self-confidence (Mortensen, 1975:95; Di Leo, 1983:80).
- **Legs:** Legs support the body. When these are omitted, it may point to a feeling of powerlessness and lack of strength.
- **Feet:** Children needing security often draw big feet. The omission of feet may suggest feelings of helplessness and lack of security.
- **Noses:** Children with respiratory problems often emphasise the nose in drawings. The omission of the nose may also point to feelings of powerlessness as the nose is often seen as a symbol of the aspiration for power.
- **Ears:** Ears are often accentuated by children with hearing problems. When a child suspects people of talking about him behind his back, he may enlarge the ears in his drawings.
- **Hands:** Excluding the hands in drawings may hint at a lack of security and an inability to handle the demands of the environment.
- **Teeth:** The drawing of teeth represents aggression.
- **Genitals:** Children who see their parents naked often draw genitals when drawing figures. This is usually quite normal, although it may also allude to poor impulse control.

Shadows

Shadows and colouring of drawings may show anxiety. The body part that is coloured is often the source of anxiety. However, this does not include shadows used for artistic reasons (Klepsch & Logie, 1982:46; Di Leo, 1983:22).

Integration of the human figure
Integration of the human figure is usually accepted as normal. When body parts are drawn from the body, especially by children of school-going age, it may hint at behavioural dysfunction, motor learning problems or poor progress at school (Klepsch & Logie, 1982:46; Di Leo, 1983:24).

Erasure
Erasure is quite normal when it is used to improve drawings. Erasure of parts of the drawing without improving them may show anxiety and uncertainty. The part that is erased may point to specific fears regarding that body part (Klepsch & Logie, 1982:46).

Content
- A **smoking chimney** may portray warmth in the family.
- The **sun** may indicate parental love and support. It is a source of warmth, just as caring parents are. When the sun is covered by clouds, it may indicate insufficient parental affection.
- A **tree** with a closed crown may show a reserved nature and a scar on the tree may point to trauma (Di Leo, 1983:80).
- When older children emphasise **buttons**, it may indicate maladjustment, especially when they are overly dependent on the mother (Klepsch & Logie, 1982:45; Di Leo, 1983:8).
- When an older child draws **stick figures**, it may hint at an unwillingness to expose himself.
- Children with poor self-images and negative thoughts often draw **clowns**.
- **Witches and monsters** may also indicate a poor self-image (Klepsch & Logie, 1982:45). Influences from stories, movies and television may, however, also motivate children to draw such figures.

Di Leo (1983:78) has found that it is sometimes difficult to interpret a drawing when it contains a mixed message. A figure can, for instance, have small feet, pointing to lack of security. It can be without hands, portraying passivity or problems with socialising. A dark cloud on the picture can show a threat. Yet the figure, as well as a sun and balloon can be drawn with a laughing face, contradicting the former indicators. Di Leo advises that such drawings be interpreted together with the child's personal history and as part of a series of drawings.

Environment
Influences from the child's environment must be taken into account when interpreting his drawings. Di Leo (1983:199) cites the example of two children drawing Christmas trees, the one on the day before Christmas and the other in the middle of the year. In the

latter case, the tree may have a special meaning.

Another example of environmental influence is violence. Reports frequently state that children growing up in a violent environment seem to become neutral and unfeeling to violence and death, dancing and playing around burning cars and corpses as if they couldn't care. However, the situation certainly does affect them. In *The Citizen* (9 September 1993) it was reported that violence in areas of South Africa, and especially in the Natal Midlands, is leaving lasting scars on the minds of children. This psychological trauma is sometimes expressed in their drawings. Children in Alexandra, for instance, tend to draw pictures of guns, blood and Caspirs. (*Die Burger*, 9 September 1993) This may be a way of handling their feelings towards violence. A psychologist at the University of Natal, Beverly Killian, also describes children's drawings of action figures engaged in violence or the aftermath thereof. She links these drawings to the erosion of family life in townships, owing to high levels of violence. In a further study, carried out in 1992, 148 drawings were obtained from preschoolers. Fifty of these drawings depicted violence in progress, with guns firing, spears, and soldiers or police attacking people; 22 depicted many people running away; 63 contained drawings of soldiers and policemen, and 34 children drew the aftermath of violence in the form of burning houses, putting the injured in ambulances, finding corpses and carrying parcels to a new home.

Stavrou (quoted in *Die Burger*, 9 September 1993) states that stress is common amongst children in black townships. Emotional and behavioural changes brought about by violence are, amongst others, a lack of trust and love. In the long-term, people experiencing problems with trust have difficulty in maintaining relationships, friendship, political alliances and relationships at work. To counter the negative long term results of exposure to violence, it is essential to reach the victims, especially the children, as soon as possible. Therapeutic aid to children affected by violence and displacement is an urgent need in South Africa. Research and the development of programs to address this problem are essential. Fortunately, organisations like Child and Family Welfare are in the process of developing programs to reach this target group, while centres, such as the Centre for the Study of Violence at the University of the Witwatersrand and the Waverley Crisis Centre, are also attending to this problem.

Projection techniques

Rubin (1988:183) is of the opinion that the interpretation of projection-type drawings is often nothing more than educated guesswork on possible meaning and is therefore more positive regarding spontaneous drawings. Child therapists should not use standardised projection techniques unless they are specifically trained to do so.

One well-known projection technique is the **house-tree-person test**. It is valuable in that clear indicators of possible symptoms are given through specific trends in the drawings. Allan and Clark (1984:117-118) describe the technique, whereby the child is asked to draw a house, then a tree and then a person. The therapist then asks four questions, namely:

❐ Is there a story about the drawing?
❐ Has anyone ever hurt the house, tree or person?

❏ What does the house, tree or person need?
❏ Does the house, tree or person have a wish?

It is often possible to make certain deductions when the child spends a lot of time on certain aspects of the drawings, focuses on the symbolic content, or makes his emotions clear in the picture. If the child, for instance, draws a tree that is badly damaged, growth can be measured after a while when he is asked to make a follow-up picture. Symbols of pain are often wounds or damage on the objects that are drawn, for example, a tree with a scar on the trunk. Growth is often depicted by symbols such as new trees, flowers or babies. The therapist can be directive and ask the child to expand on previous drawings.

As early as 1966, Faure (1966:96-98,124) emphasised the tree as an important symbol through which the child reveals something of himself. The size of the tree, its position on the paper, the visual appearance and the quality of the lines can all point to certain characteristics in the child.

The drawing of the person depicts the child's self-image. Analysis of this drawing can bring information to the fore regarding the child's needs, urges, shortcomings, compensations, deviations and conflicts. The drawing of a house also contains information on the child's inner conflicts. Progress can be measured when the child draws a house in the beginning and again at the end of the helping process.

Gabel (1984:187-196) describes another technique that is a combination of drawing and stories, namely the **Draw a story game**. He delineates it as a projection technique. The therapist makes a mark on a piece of paper. The child must then change this into a picture. The therapist asks some questions about the drawing and draws a follow-up drawing on a mark the child has made. She tries to discover the direction of the child's thoughts and constructs her drawing accordingly. Then the child draws again with an accompanying story. The drawings reflect aspects of his thought processes, motor functioning, attitudes and characteristics.

Roosa (1981:270-272) describes the **family drawing storytelling technique**, also a projection technique. It is especially suitable for use in therapy with children younger than ten years. The child is asked to draw his family with the name of everyone next to his or her picture. He should explain what has happened, how each person feels and how the story ends. If the child is too withdrawn to tell a story, the therapist can question him about the figures in the drawing. Then the child can draw significant people who are not depicted on the first drawing on another piece of paper. Photocopies of the drawings are made and the various characters are cut out. The child then places assorted sub-systems on the paper, as requested by the therapist. He tells stories about these sub-systems. It is preferable to begin with sub-systems of positive relationships. This technique enables the therapist to come to certain conclusions regarding the functioning of the child client's family system. It can also evoke a discussion on problem areas.

For further discussion of projection techniques, see chapter 4.

Playing with clay

According to Cass (1972:27), clay is a primitive play material in the same category as water, soil, mud and sand. It offers an acceptable medium for releasing feelings of hostility and aggression. Porter (1983:255-262) regards clay as a creative medium. It can be handled roughly, as the child can throw, knead or form it, according to his feelings at a given time. Jefferies and Gillespie (1981:12), Jewett (1982:67), Porter (1983:256-262) and Rubin (1988:181) cite some advantages of playing with clay:

- The child may use it to change and form his situation as he chooses. When realising that he can form clay as he wants to, he may even be motivated to change his situation.
- Clay can be used to portray relationships between significant people in the child's life. By forming human figures with clay and handling them, he can live through relationships and release his feelings. Various alternative relationships can be played out by moving the soft, clay figures around. The child may gain insight into some aspects of his relationships and this can initiate behavioural change.

  The intricate patterns of tribal family life should come to the fore during clay work with the black child who must form the figures of significant people in his environment and play with them to show the dynamics of the various relationships.
- Children affected by violence and family disruption can be encouraged to make clay models depicting the scenes of violence. They can also make models of the future with the guidance of the therapist. They can look at alternatives and make these from clay.
- Often there is no identifiable end product after playing with clay. It does help the child to relax, though, and it serves as a calming activity during verbal conversation.
- Clay work is especially suitable for stimulating the release of feelings in a quiet child with poorly developed verbal skills.
- By kneading the clay, the child can release feelings of aggression. Even though the source of the aggression is not eliminated, the child should be calmer and ready for further working through of his feelings.
- The use of clay offers the child the opportunity to regress.

Clay can be used in combination with drawings of the child's environment. He can make clay figures of the significant people in his life and move them around on drawings of his house. He can even use them on an ecomap.

Clay is easy and cheap to make from flour, salt and water. In some rural areas, clay can be found readily. It can boost the child's self-confidence to identify areas where clay is to be found, take the therapist there and then use the clay as part of further therapy.

Handicrafts

Various handicrafts can be used in therapy with children, for instance, making masks, dolls, life books and completing pictures.

Children can also be taught to make "warm fuzzies". Graver and Morse (1986:98) use the warm fuzzy symbol and instruct children to make them in a variety of forms: they can make pompons from wool and paste smiling faces on them; they can also paste smiling faces onto pins to wear. Biblio-play can be used in conjunction with the making of warm fuzzies, by relating the well-known story of warm fuzzies and cold pricklies (Stuart, 1980:65-69).

When he is feeling sad, the child can make himself warm fuzzies. He can also be encouraged to make them for someone else. The child can be helped to think about warm fuzzies and to realise that a warm fuzzy can also be a smile or a hug. In relation to this, children can be taught the principle of "caring days" (Stuart, 1980:197-199). In this way, they can learn to relate to people in a positive way without expecting a reward.

Conclusion

Creative play can be one of the most enjoyable forms of play. The following statement by Allan and Clark (1984:117) epitomises the central value of creative play:

> Painting and drawing, especially in the counselling setting, activate growth and change; that is, the images and symbols a child uses are both safe "containers" and "transformers" of emotions and feelings. Once painful images have been expressed in this way, new growth occurs both in the conscious and the unconscious.

This illustrates that creative play liberates vague feelings that are suppressed because they are too painful, too confused or have originated in the pre-verbal years. After working through these feelings, the child may reach a higher level of equilibrium than before as a result of the growth process.

Bibliography

Allan, J. & Clark, M. 1984. Directed art counseling. *Elementary School Guidance and Counseling*, 19(2): 116-124.

Allan, J.A.B. 1986. Serial drawing: A Jungian approach with children. In Schaefer: 98-132.

Cass, J. 1972. *The significance of children's play*. London: Batsford.

Crompton, M. 1980. *Respecting children: Social work with young people*. London: Edward Arnold.

Di Leo, J.H. 1983. *Interpreting children's drawings*. New York: Brunner Mazel.

Faure, J.S.M. 1966. *Die pedagogiese diagnostisering en behandeling van gedragsmoeilike kinders deur middel van spel, met verwysing na bepaalde pedagogiese kriteria.* Pretoria: HAUM.

Gabel, S. 1984. The Draw a story game: An aid in understanding and working with children. *The Arts in Psychotherapy*, 11:187-196.

Gillespie, A. 1986. 'Art therapy' at the familymakers project. *Adoption and Fostering*, 10 (1): 19-23.

Graver, C.M. & Morse, L.A. 1986. *Helping children of divorce: A group leader's guide*. Illinois: Charles C. Thomas.

Jefferies, B. & Gillespie, A. 1981. Art therapy with the emotionally frozen. *Adoption and Fostering*, 106(4):9-15.

Jewett, C.L. 1982. *Helping children cope with separation and loss.* Massachusetts: Harvard Common Press.

Kinderkuns vertel van oorlog-hel. *Beeld*, 5 Februarie 1991: 8.

Klepsch, M. & Logie, L. 1982. *Children draw and tell.* New York: Brunner Mazel.

Mills, J.C. & Crowley, R.J. 1986. *Therapeutic metaphors for children and the child within.* New York: Brunner Mazel.

Mortensen, K.V. 1975. *De kindertekening: Ontwikkeling en uiting.* Rotterdam: Kooyker Wetenschappelijke Uitgeverij.

Porter, C. 1983. Spelterapie met die sorgbehoewende kind. Unpublished D. Phil thesis. Pretoria: University of Pretoria.

Roosa, L.W. 1981. The family drawing/storytelling technique: An approach to assessment of family dynamics. *Elementary School Guidance and Counseling*, 15(3): 269-272.

Rose, E. 1988. Art therapy — a brief guide. *Adoption and Fostering*, 12(1): 48-50.

Rubin, J.A. 1988. Art counseling: an alternative. *Elementary School Guidance and Counseling*, 22(3): 180-185.

SA violence 'scars children's minds.' *The Citizen*, 9 September 1993.

Schaefer, C.E. (Ed.). 1988. *Innovative interventions in child and adolescent therapy.* New York: John Wiley.

So beïnvloed geweld ons kinders. *Die Burger*, 9 September 1993.

Stuart, R.B. 1980. *Helping couples change. A social learning approach to marital therapy.* New York: Guilford Press.

Van der Merwe, M. 1991. Maatskaplikewerk–beraad met jong kinders in egskeidingsituasies met fokus op speeltegnieke. Unpublished MA thesis. Stellenbosch: University of Stellenbosch.

Part 3

Problem solving through play:

Intervention in specific problems

Summary

Introduction
The aim of this book is not to give a detailed account of helping children with specific problems and needs, but rather to provide a broad model that is applicable in various situations. While the emphasis of welfare in therapist in South Africa is shifting to primary social services and more and more social workers are diverting their attention to community development, specialised services to children still remain extremely relevant. The children of today will have to lead the nation into the 21st century. Some of the babies born now, will even live to see the 22nd century. They will have to have well developed coping skills to face challenges that are still unknown.

Post Traumatic Stress Disorder
Our generation cannot let children scarred by violence, community disruption, displacement, divorce and other stressful life events go on into adulthood with scars and unresolved feelings related to the trauma they have been through. It is a fact that people can still suffer from the effects of trauma years after the event if they have not received timely therapeutic inputs. Post Traumatic Stress Disorder is a typical reaction to unusually stressful life events. Thousands of children probably suffer from PTSD after the disruption and violence characteristic of South African society in the past years. While basic needs are met with primary social services, it is also essential to help these children, possibly in groups, to work through unresolved feelings.

Exposure to trauma metaphorically opens files in the ego part of the child's brain. He can either suppress these files by throwing them throwing into the id where they boil away to a pulp, creating general, unidentifiable discomfort, or he can be helped with therapy to work through these files and master them. He can then store the files in the archives of the ego where they will be reactivated from time to time when other stress is encountered. He can be prepared for possible reactivation and helped with general skills in problem solving and coping.

In therapy with children, a general aim is to help them to explore and use their own strength and to gain confidence in their own ability to cope with their problems. If a child can be helped to function on a higher level than before a crisis, a major contribution has been made towards putting the child's feet steadily on the road to the future. It is also important to ensure that they are able to carry over the coping skills from one problematic situation to another.

Lapses in development
When experiencing difficulty such as divorce, children tend to divert energy that should have been used for normal development, to struggling with the problematic situation.

Children should be helped in therapy to distinguish between constructive and destructive use of energy. When anger is used constructively, for instance by sorting out problems regarding visitation, it should be encouraged. General anger focused on the divorce, combined with prolonged hope for reconciliation, is unproductive. It can detract the attention from normal development, resulting in developmental delays.

Often, children will recuperate through natural processes in time and be able to put bad experiences behind them. There are, however, two particular risks when leaving them and hoping that time will heal. In the first place, Post Traumatic Stress Disorder may develop. Cumulative stress can lower their defences and make them more vulnerable, if timely therapeutic inputs are not made. The second risk is that children may use valuable energy that should have been employed for normal development for prolonged grief or other stress related reactions. The author often uses the following example to sensitise children of divorce to this danger. She tells them that they run the risk of falling behind in maths completely if they tend to daydream about parental reconciliation in maths class. If they do this for a week or two, it should not damage their long-term maths skills too badly. If they, however, have problems with concentrating on maths for six months or even for the two year period that is usually seen as an average period of adaptation after a divorce, they will probably have some gaps in their maths skills forever. Therapy can help children to move through a traumatic period constructively and without allowing long lapses in normal development.

Focus of part 3

Because the focus of this book is to give general information and models applicable to a variety of problems and needs of children, the aim of part 3 is not to give a comprehensive overview of applications to various needs and problems. Therefore, only three problem areas are touched on.

The phenomenon of street children has been researched widely in the past years, especially in combined efforts by the HSRC and the Department of Welfare. Research has focused especially on causes and incidence of street children in South Africa with the aim of developing treatment models, rehabilitation and prevention programs. Working conferences have been held to determine policy guidelines and to combine the efforts of role players concerned with street children countrywide. At this stage, the problem has been described clearly by, amongst others, Maphatane (1993), Schurink, Maphatane, Rip, Schurink, Smith and Tiba (1993), Swart (1988) and Ross (1991). The chapter on street children in this section gives an overview of the street child phenomenon, looking at therapeutic inputs without losing perspective of community factors impacting on the problem.

Chapter 12 focuses on handling aggression in children. According to Gardner (1976: 180-181), anger is an inborn protection mechanism often activated by danger. Encountering violence, divorce, death and poverty spells danger to children. Everything that touches their security such as constant conflict between parents and even more minor events, such as moving to a new community and school, may be experienced by them as a threat and may lead to aggression. Children should be encouraged to release their feelings of aggression in acceptable ways. Without such opportunity, they may turn the anger and aggression to the inside and develop neurotic reactions and depression. Children should be helped to determine whether anger is productive and constructive. They should establish whether anger contributes positively to changing their situation. They should be motived to let go of counterproductive anger that is a pointless way of utilising valuable energy.

In chapter 13, the five forms of play described in part 2 are applied to a specific problem, namely children of divorce. It should show the reader how the model described in this book can work in practice.

Conclusion

Child therapists should be able to cope with the diverse problems and needs that children bring into therapy if they have sound knowledge of normal development, basic play therapy and specific forms of play supported by a wide range of techniques. They should also build knowledge and skills regarding specific problems and needs. For instance, building resources to use in bibliotherapy should be an ongoing task. There are books available on heterogeneous problems and needs, for instance the old, but still valuable "It's O.K. to say no to drugs" (Garner, 1987) and "Sometimes it's O.K. to tell secrets" (Lenett & Barthelme, 1986).

Core professionals in the area of direct work with children should look for new approaches and ideas with creativity and enthusiasm. One of the best sources of new ideas is the children themselves. They tend to help with the refinement of simple techniques, building into them multi-purpose, workable tools.

Working with children is satisfying and rewarding. It can also be emotionally draining, especially when a specific child client does not cooperate on account of somatic obstacles such as hunger, thirst, tiredness or feeling sick. Therapists should tune in finely to catch the child client's rhythm. That will also dictate the pace and the focus of the interview. A tired child that is extremely upset, for whom the problem is not clearly defined, will probably find an unstructured approach more acceptable whereas an energetic child with a specific problem such as coping with remarriage will probably benefit from a structured, more directive approach. The child and his problems should be the barometer for determining the best approach. Child therapists should be careful not to build their inputs around their knowledge and fall into the trap of hammering everything because of the availability of the hammer. The problems and needs of the children should dictate the nature of the therapy.

Bibliography

Garner, A. 1987. *It's O.K. to say no to drugs! – A parent-child manual for the protection of children*. New York: RGA Publishing Group.

Lenett, R. & Barthelme, D. 1986. *Sometimes it's O.K. to tell secrets! – A parent/child manual for the protection of children*. New York: RGA Publishing Group.

Maphatane, M.T. 1993. Black street children and their families: Towards the development of basic support services. Unpublished MA thesis. Johannesburg: Rand Afrikaans University.

Schurink, W.J., Maphatane, M., Rip, S., Schurink, E., Smith, L. & Tiba, M. 1993. Street children: An investigation into the causes and incidence of the problem of street children in the RSA with the aim to develop a model for treatment, rehabilitation and prevention programmes. Working document. Pretoria: HSRC.

Swart, J. 1988. *An anthropological study of street children in Hillbrow, Johannesburg, with special reference to their moral values*. Unpublished MA thesis. Pretoria: Unisa.

Ross, C. 1991. Street children: Survival strategies. *Indicator South Africa*, 8(4): 69-72.

11 Street children

S MATSEMELA & M VAN DER MERWE

Introduction

The phenomenon of street children is highly visible. Especially in winter, street children can be seen lying on pavements, huddled close together to benefit from each other's body heat. Their attempts to get money are just as visible. They can be seen in the streets waving pieces of rags to direct motorists to empty parking spaces, selling fruit or newspapers, or begging for food or money. Even though they are visible, not everyone observes them in the same light. Shop owners may view them as a nuisance ruining their business, the police may see them as part of their daily work, whereas the passers-by may perceive them as part of the city scene. Taking into account the history of South Africa, plagued by unemployment, poverty, poor housing, migratory laws and poor education, coupled with the violence and displacement of the past years, it is not surprising that such a large group of children lives on the streets.

According to Schurink and Burger (1994:3), there are an estimated 10 000 street children in South Africa. Peacock and Theron (1992:27) estimate the number of street children in South Africa as being between 5 000 and 9 000. Given the population increase, swelling amongst other factors by growing numbers of illegal immigrants, unemployment, poverty and housing shortages, it can be foreseen that the number of children taking to the streets will grow.

Street children are not unique to South Africa (Gebers, 1990:11). Jarvis (1992:8) says of the street children of Brazil that: "On the streets of Brazil there is no such thing as childhood." Janus (1987:17) cites the research findings of Garbarino, which indicate that about 12% of American youth run away from their homes. According to Tyler, Tyler, Echeverri and Zia (1991:398), most street children in India are boys. Seemingly, the proportion of girls on the streets is higher in the United States than in Third World countries. Research in South Africa (Schurink, Maphatane, Rip, Schurink, Smith & Tiba, 1993) indicates that only about 10% of street children in this country are girls.

Even though much can be learnt from other countries regarding their programs for street children, it is important to heed the warning of Cockburn (1993:8) that American programs are not for us. She supports the concept of an effective indigenous model evolving right here in South Africa. She also warns against providing expensive services reaching only a few street children. The South African situation is unique. Cockburn (1993:8) states further that: "Huge capital expenditure on plant, personnel and therapy is a very Eurocentric notion." She argues that it is not feasible to use elaborate settings to prepare children for the realities of life in the disadvantaged communities to which they must return.

In this chapter, the definition of street children is debated, followed by a profile of street children and a discussion of causal factors. Looking at push and pull factors, the advantages and disadvantages of street life are discussed. Some ideas on intervention are shared. Maphatane's (1994: 22) conviction that intervention should be from an ecological perspective is supported. It is no use to work with the street child in isolation from his environment.

Defining street children

When defining street children, it is important to keep in mind the distinction made by UNICEF and cited by Konanc (1989:13) between children *on* the street and children *of* the street. Children on the street are those children who still sleep at home often or occasionally. They venture out to the streets to make some money and are in danger of becoming more and more engrossed in the street culture. They have not abandoned their families or been abandoned by their families. They are working children. Home circumstances may be extremely difficult. They may, however, also come from families where there is enough cohesion and/or positive feelings urging them to work in order to prevent the family from disintegrating. They may end up as fully-fledged street children if not reached timeously and effectively by prevention programs. Children of the street are those children who have abandoned their homes. They live on the street permanently. The Children's Foundation Report on Street Children (1990:3) defines street children as follows: "Children living on the streets due to unsatisfactory home conditions, i.e. in need of care but on the streets." Gebers (1990:11) quotes the UNICEF definition: "a street child is one who has made the street his real home." Schurink, et al. (1993:5) define a street child as

> a boy or a girl who is under the age of eighteen and who left his/her home environment part-time or permanently (because of problems at home and/or in school, or to try to alleviate those problems) and who spends most of his/her time unsupervised on the streets as a part of a subculture of children who live an unprotected communal life and who depend on themselves and each other, and not on an adult for the provision of physical and emotional needs such as food, clothing, nurturance, direction and socialization.

It is important to assess every street child as an individual and not just to fit him/her into the categories of existing definitions. When planning intervention, one can easily fall into the trap of fitting the child into the program, instead of using programs flexibly to suit every child's specific needs and circumstances.

Profile of street children

Street children typically have poor physical hygiene, want independence and adventure, and hate a structural environment. They tend to abscond from formal structures such as Places of Safety. They call themselves names such as "stroller", "homestead boys" and "drifter" (Cockburn, 1993:8). In Johannesburg, they label themselves "malunde", meaning those not sleeping at home and "malalapipe", meaning those sleeping in stormwater pipes (Swart, 1988:33-41). Keen (1988:12) distinguishes between bush children (of homeless families living in the bush surrounding urban areas); real street children (in the inner city) and dump children (scavenging daily for food or actually living on the rubbish dumps).

According to Cemane (1990:2), street children comprise a group of poorly socialised children, who fail to develop commitment and attachment within society. Cemane further points out that they commonly have no incentive for conformity and social sanctions that inhibit antisocial behaviour. Usually, they do not hesitate to engage in unacceptable behaviour. Gebers (1990:12-14) indicates that most of the daily activities of street children, whether aimed at survival or for leisure, put their health at risk. A large number of them are knocked down by cars, often on account of being intoxicated. Their abuse of solvents and drugs changes their perceptions and reflexes, making them particularly vulnerable to medical trauma. Swart (1988:11) notes that squabbling and fighting are often a result of substance abuse.

Carr (1995:40) mentions the existence of a street culture, stating further that children in the street form communities. They sleep and move together. Within this system of survival, they gain knowledge on avoiding conflict with other groups and generally learn ground rules of existence on the street. Younger boys sometimes have to pay for their protection, giving money or food to the group leader. These children often become involved in undesirable activities such as petty theft, prostitution and the sniffing of glue. According to Schurink et al (1993:197), the majority of street children interviewed came into contact with the law due to them being in need of care, or being juvenile delinquents. They listed crimes street children commonly get involved in. These crimes are confirmed by Peacock and Theron (1992:28):

- prostitution
- drug and alcohol abuse
- theft
- robbery
- shop-lifting
- assault.

Mini-research by Matsemela partly verifies these findings, even though the six children interviewed pointed out that the "other boys" engaged in prostitution, drugs, theft and shop-lifting. They probably felt ashamed to admit that they were also involved. Only two of the six admitted that they used to sniff glue. Jansen, Richter and Griesel (1991:13-15) address the complex problem of glue sniffing and warn that it can lead to a lifetime of chemical dependency. According to Richter (1988:13), street life is very dangerous for children. Glue sniffing may lead to death or permanent organ damage. This danger is even more acute because of the children's limited access to medical help.

Maphatane (1994:25-26) found in research that children on the street mostly had regular contact with their families. They did sleep at home from time to time and the majority of children in her study operated only in one turf. According to her study, children on the street are still in the process of drifting further towards street life, and of becoming children of the street.

Mangwana (1992:14) mentions personality dynamics of street children that will have to be taken into account when designing programs. A short attention span is common, resulting in street children being easily bored. Therapeutic inputs should therefore be short and offer variety. Street children often have a good sense of humour and should respond positively to the fun part of therapy. Their high sense of adventure should also be taken into account when planning programs.

Causal factors

There are various internal and external variables influencing a child's decision to move to the streets. Internal factors such as personality, temperament, developmental stage and resilience to trauma may play a role, as well as external variables such as conflict in the home, peer pressure, severeness of problems experienced at home and extent of emotional and physical deprivation will influence whether or not a child will take to the street.

Personal maladjustment

According to Garbarino, et al. (1986:44), runaway behaviour has been associated with various types and degrees of personal maladjustment. They refer to a study by Edelbrock who matched samples of children referred to mental health services and others not referred. The outcome of this study was that more of the children previously referred to mental health agencies engaged in runaway behaviour than those not referred. Garbarino, et al. (1986:45) further point out that in the same study by Edelbrock, running away was associated with five problem behaviours: truancy, use of alcohol and drugs, delinquency, incorrigible misbehaviour at home, and attempted suicide. However, Edelbrock, cited by Garbarino, et al. (1986:45), warns that these behaviours are not necessarily predictive of running away since the study did not assess the child systematically before this occurred. Garbarino, et al. (1986:45) further cite Jenkins and Boyer who indicate that runaway delinquents seemed to have the least well-organised personalities of three delinquent groups studied.

Schurink, et al. (1993:108) mention the following factors, which contributed to children's decision to live on the streets: a feeling of inferiority because parents can't afford books or uniforms; a need for personal attention which is impossible in large families; poor school performance; a feeling of uselessness; and a desire to survive.

Family disorganisation

According to Schurink, et al. (1993:108), the respondents in their study pointed out that the following factors within the family could give rise to the street child phenomenon:

- parents who move to cities without making adequate provision for the maintenance and care of their children
- poverty within the family
- irresponsible procreation
- single parenthood
- absence of parents due to long working hours
- children being sent to cities to beg, or look for a missing family member without a fixed place of abode.

Swart (1988:12) states that some street children have been abandoned or orphaned. She mentions destitution, abuse and neglect as other factors pushing children towards the street, as well as eviction from farms where parents were employed and unrest in black townships, especially schools.

Maphatane (1994:26) has established that structural characteristics of the family, such as single parenthood with families headed by grandmothers, female headed households and extended families living in crowded circumstances were factors determining children's decisions to leave for the street. Richter (1991:8) points out that in her work in urban South African townships, about 20% of households are female headed and that the father is absent from about 40-50% of the homes in which the mother and children live. She further states that in rural areas, due to migratory labour, fathers (and sometimes mothers) may be absent from most homes.

Where two or more generations share a dwelling, many adults have an influence on the children, each responding individually to the child and creating confusion as to what should be internalised. While several authority figures in the home can affect the child's socialisation patterns adversely, Maphatane (1994:27) also found that children learn to manipulate such a set-up to their own benefit.

Cemane (1990:3) cites the following factors within the family which contribute to the street children syndrome:

- lack of communication between family members
- in-fighting
- physical and emotional neglect
- chronic illness of one of the family members which subjects other members to stress
- imprisonment of a key family member
- orphanhood
- stepparenthood
- divorce.

Garbarino, et al. (1986:46) point out that there is adequate evidence documenting the role of parental mistreatment, including physical abuse, neglect and incest in producing runaway behaviour. They further indicate that for youth exposed to chronic mistreatment at the hands of parents or guardians, running away from home may constitute a "healthy and adaptive response to an impossible situation".

Peer group influence

Cemane (1990:3) is of the opinion that the peer group has a marked influence on the social development of a child. He points out that the child's decision to leave home is usually the culmination of a series of events leading to his disengagement from the family. This period of uncertainty and anxiety leaves an emotional vacuum most easily filled by his peer group or friends, and he turns to them for support. The vulnerable child lacking in self-confidence and needing acceptance and appreciation is almost bound to become a victim of group pressure.

Interviews by Matsemela with six children confirmed the abovementioned causal factors. Two of the six blamed their parents for ill-treating them by severely punishing them for the slightest mistakes. Another two pointed out that they had to leave school because their parents were unable to pay for their schooling. As a result, they resorted to the streets. One of these two, who has been institutionalised for about four months, stated that he had no intention of absconding because of his attending school. The remaining two children blamed their friends for influencing them to leave home.

Push and pull factors

The respondents in the research of Schurink, et al. (1993:116) mentioned the following advantages of street life:

- The peer group on the streets provides empathy and security.
- It is a way of escaping maltreatment by parents.
- It is an escape from unbearable home circumstances.
- Children earn money.
- In their effort to survive on the streets, they develop their creative skills.
- Street life fulfils their need for adventure.

The following disadvantages facing street children have been mentioned by Schurink, et al. (1993:116-117):

- On an emotional level, there was the fear of being unloved and alone, coupled with low self-esteem.
- Their health suffered on account of unhygienic living conditions, contagious diseases, malnutrition and sexually transmitted diseases.
- Lack of schooling led to educational backlogs.
- Antisocial and exploitative practices such as assault, rape and prostitution take place.

- Harassment by rightwing radicals and the police has been mentioned as a danger on the streets by children admitted to the Jabulani Welfare Complex.

In a true behaviour therapeutic fashion, the above can be used therapeutically by enhancing the children's aversion to the disadvantages of street life. Programs for street children should strive to encompass some of the advantages of street life, such as providing peer group support and developing creative skills.

Intervention

Rothman (1991:106), in talking about intervention, describes runaway behaviour as a complex, multifaceted phenomenon. He further points out that individual and family aspects are highly interrelated and are intertwined with community and societal influences. Maphatane (1994:22) rightly maintains that intervention should encompass the totality of the person and the environment.

Prevention

It is important to reach out to street children as soon as possible, preferably when they can still be regarded as children on the street. By then, they are usually not so involved in the street culture, and negative behaviour, such as sniffing of glue, may not have started. Gebers (1990:13-14) emphasises that the longer children are on the street, the more distanced they become from rehabilitation resources as they become more and more engrossed in the street culture. Street children can be seen as a hard-to-reach population. Baizerman (1988:13) observes that the number of children on and of the street is relatively low when compared to the numbers at risk of living there. This points to the extreme importance of prevention programs aimed at families at risk of losing children to the streets. It also stresses the importance of looking at the street child in the context of family, poor housing and poverty (Baizerman, 1988:14).

In the South African situation, broader societal issues such as violence, disrupted education and unemployment will also play a role in the street child phenomenon. Baizerman (1988:14-15) suggests that focused, consistent, culturally sensitive services to children and families in a community context can be effective as clinical prevention.

Shelters

There are different views on shelters for street children with some professionals feeling that shelters are not the answer to the street child problem. Swart (1988:11-12) notes the criticism that shelters actually attract more children to the streets, but is of the opinion that such instances are minimal. The general opinion is that street children should be reintegrated into their families of origin. This is, however, often the ideal and not the practical solution. Richter (1988:13) states that only in some cases can family life be rehabilitated. Working with the family system is certainly necessary whenever they can be located. It will possibly be a timely process to eliminate the circumstances which made the child leave home in the first place. In the meantime, the child will need some sort of structure. Part of rehabilitation is to teach the children to cope with routine and to set specific goals and tasks. According to Swart (1988:13), the most effective projects address the problem on the spot and not by taking children away to structures in other areas.

Street workers

Street workers have been employed successfully in various communities as reported by, amongst others, Levin (1992:3-4) and Cockburn (1993:9). These workers literally walk the streets and build relationships with the children. They have roles such as monitoring, advocacy, referral, counselling, education and health care. They share information with the children on pertinent topics such as Aids, monitor their legal status and find alternative accommodation for them. Street workers serve as an important resource on the street.

Five-level program

Before intervening therapeutically, it is important to attend to the street children's somatic needs. When they are hungry, tired, cold or thirsty, therapeutic inputs will have less effect than when they feel comfortable and other somatic needs have been met. This view is supported by Baizerman (1988:15) who views the meeting of basic needs as the first step in a five-level model program:

- **Level 1:** Basic needs
- **Level 2:** Basic services (such as medical care, basic literacy, recreation and spiritual support)
- **Level 3:** Pathways from the street (services to prepare youth for life, such as mastery of work skills)
- **Level 4:** Inter-organisation (linkages between and among programs)
- **Level 5:** Clinical prevention (to keep children off the streets)

These five levels are a guide to a comprehensive service to street children. Current programs can measure their effectiveness by evaluating whether the five elements are represented in their programs. MacCurtain (1988:8) also views meeting of the street children's dependency needs as a prerequisite before growth needs can be met.

Therapeutic programs

Therapeutic programs for street children should have elements of fun to motivate children to enter and keep the children motivated to stay involved in the program. Music therapy can be especially effective in creating a productive therapeutic climate, as well as serving as a starting point for more intense therapeutic inputs.

The therapeutic process can be structured into a beginning, change-oriented and final phase, using the five forms of play described in this book, namely relaxation play and assessment play in the beginning and final phases, and biblio-play, dramatic play and creative play in the change-oriented phase. With street children, therapy will be on a long-term basis, with inputs made to change their environment. Within this therapeutic process, it is possible to include significant subsystems, such as parents, whenever necessary and possible. Individual counselling, group counselling, family counselling, peer group counselling and teaching basic problem-solving skills can be utilised in the street child helping program.

An important part of programs for street children should be Aids education, as they often use sex for survival, or are exploited sexually. When receiving the correct knowledge regarding Aids, their attitude regarding sexual behaviour should also be influenced positively. There are puppet shows such as "Puppets against AIDS" that can be used in street theatre and should keep the attention of the street children. Literacy programs are also extremely important, as literacy may prevent children from continuing a life of crime and begging as adults.

Therapeutic inputs should also be directed to help the street child to learn new adaptive social skills. Therapeutic inputs on a long-term basis will probably be necessary as life style education will have to supplement other therapeutic inputs. Life style education in a group context will ensure that peer inputs support the education and reinforce it. Other therapeutic inputs regarding the reasons the child took to the streets and assessing the extent of each child's problems will have to be done on an individual basis. An individualised treatment plan should be developed for each child. Programs to educate and aid children in their communities of origin seem to be the answer.

Intervention should be focused on the main problems experienced by street children, as identified by Rothman (1991:107), namely:
- low self-esteem
- lack of control
- poor problem-solving skills
- being emotionally depressed
- running away from reality by running away from home, abusing drugs and attempting suicide.

Gestalt therapy is applied through a treatment plan suggested by Rothman (1991:108). This program, to be used with street children, includes the following actions:
- **Help client identify how his problems are shared by others, to develop a "critical consciousness" from which to act:** The Gestalt therapy objective of creating awareness in the client should be applied. Perls (cited by Louw, 1992:639) is of the opinion that awareness on its own is curative. Through awareness, the street child will come into contact with his own needs and feelings, and learn how to take responsibility for what he is and what he does.

  Thompson and Rudolph (1992:121) suggest involving the child in creative activities such as finger painting, creating with clay and drawing to express themselves and to enhance awareness, whereafter the child can be encouraged to verbalise his feelings. Oaklander's (1988:53-56) model consisting of 14 steps (see chapter 4) can be used to help the child express himself through creative play.
- **Have client participate as much as possible in decisions that impact on his life:** According to the Gestalt approach, it is important to give the child control. By decid-

ing with the child on the treatment plan and giving him choices, the therapist will actually be giving the child control. With information and guidance from the therapist, the child will be able to make an informed choice as to whether he wants to return home, be admitted to a shelter for street children, or be placed in an institution.

- **Demystify information so that client can understand what you are doing and give client as many tools and skills as possible to work on his own problems:** The client should be empowered and enabled to work on his problems with adequate guidance and support from the therapist and his family. The street child should be equipped to handle his problems instead of running away from them. In other words, the therapist must help to build the child's inner strength.

  A useful metaphor is to compare problems and needs with greedy worms eating life apples (Van der Merwe, 1994:30). This technique helps the child to assess all his problems and needs by writing each problem on a separate worm and indicating the size of bite that each worm takes from the life apple. When the nature and impact of each worm is understood, the plan of action for every worm can be planned, using the metaphor of "Doom" or poison for creeping, crawling or flying insects. This aid can also be used in group therapy with street children. An advantage of this technique is that the street children tend to feel that they have more control over their problems and needs when they are depicted visually. It is easier to visualise victory over a worm than over the problem of addiction to glue. As soon as the addiction problem is seen as a worm eating away quality of life, the child can develop a more objective and concrete plan of action focusing on the addiction.

- **Help client expose the role that oppression has played in his life:** This brings to mind a client who has many introjections (uncritical acceptance of negative messages from society and living according to those negative labels). Development can be restricted by such introjections. In such a case, the child will have to be led to the insight that those introjections might hamper the treatment process. He should be helped to question and confront situations.

  Thompson and Rudolph (1992:115) suggest the use of the topdog/underdog technique to confront such introjections. They describe the topdog as a bully working with "you should" and "you should not", whilst the underdog works with "I want." According to Thompson and Rudolph (1992:115), two chairs can be used to help the children resolve "I want" versus "I should" debates. The one chair is labelled the topdog and the other is labelled the underdog. While sitting on the topdog chair, the child is asked to present his best "I should" argument. He does this facing the underdog chair. The child then moves over to the underdog chair and facing the topdog chair, presents his best "I want" argument. The debate then goes on back and forth until the child exhausts all arguments from both points of view. Processing the activity often reveals on which side of the argument the child feels that the greatest integration of shoulds and wants occurs, thus allowing the child to have the best of both sides. (This technique is further discussed in chapter 4 on projection techniques.) According to Thompson and Rudolph (1992:116), the best outcome from the topdog/underdog debate occurs when the client can identify areas in which the "I shoulds" and "I wants" are the same. Street children, for example, should be able to say: "I love to go to school, I want to go to school and I should go to school."

- **Help client find peer support in his environment:** Here the therapist has to help the child identify people and structures within his environment which can serve as support systems. The strong support system formed by the peer group on the street has been mentioned. The peer group compensates for the rejection and feelings of not being loved that street children have often experienced at home.

- **Make client independent and make yourself eventually unnecessary:** The Gestalt therapy objective of self-support can be applied here. According to Perls (cited by Louw, 1991:639), real development in the client will not take place as long as the client regards the therapist as his main support. Real development only takes place once the client starts taking responsibility for his own life and becomes self-supportive.

Through the use of semantic clarifications such as "I message" and substituting "won't" for "can't", the child will be helped to take responsibility for his thoughts, feelings and behaviour. An example of an "I message" is a child saying "You know how it is when you can't understand maths and the teacher gets on your back." When "you" is substituted with "I", the message becomes "I know how it is when I can't understand maths and the teacher gets on my back" (Thompson & Rudolph, 1991:114).

To refine the complicated intervention process regarding street children within their environments, child therapists have the responsibility to do continual research. Developmental research is, for instance, aimed at developing and revising social technology. It is also easy to integrate into the therapeutic plan of action (Van Rooyen, 1994:16-17).

Obstacles in the helping process

Resistance

A lot of resistance can be anticipated when dealing with the street child. Mangwana (1992:14) states that initial contact with the street child may be characterised by defensiveness, suspicion and mistrust. As their response to adults is often reactive, they should respond positively when treated with respect. It would be difficult to convince the street child that it would be better for him to be off the streets, when he regards the streets as a refuge from maltreatment by parents, as well as a way of exercising independence. Oaklander (1988:198) points out that children are resistant and defensive for good reasons, as they see it as a way to survive and a means of self-protection. The therapist can win the child's trust by showing unconditional love and acceptance, patience, and consistency within a warm therapeutic relationship. This can serve to overcome the child's resistance. Swart (1988:13) and Mangwana (1992:14) emphasise the importance of the engage them in the process and to get some sort of commitment from them to stick to the helping process.

Conclusion

Much as the street child phenomenon is a fast-growing reality, no clear-cut solutions to the problem have yet been found. At first, South African society tried to turn a blind eye to the problem, hoping that it would disappear overnight, only to be faced with it again the next day. Judging by the increasing number of non-governmental organisations giving attention to the plight of the street children, research done by the Human Sciences Research Council and the Department of Welfare, and working conferences held involving role players working with street children, it is hoped that in the not too distant future appropriate programs will be developed. These programs should be based on the constructive groundwork done by organisations such as Streetwise, Twilight Children's Organisation, the Homestead and PROSCESS. Programs should be aimed at equipping street children to be reintegrated into their families and communities with dignity.

Bibliography

Baizerman, M. 1988. Street kids: Notes for designing a programme for youth of and on the streets. *The Child Care Worker*, 6(11): 13-15.
Carr, R. 1995. Knysna takes the initiative regarding their street children: Without you its back to glue. *Social Work Practice*, 1.95: 39-41.
Cemane, K.B. 1990. The Street Child Phenomenon. *Social Work Practice*, 1. 90: 2.
Cockburn, A. 1993. Services for street children. *The Child Care Worker*, 11(1): 8.
Cockburn, A. 1993. What's in a name? *The Child Care Worker*, 11(1) : 8.
Garbarino, J., Schellenbach, C.J & Sebes, J.M. 1986. *Troubled Youth, Troubled Family*. New York: Aldine De Gruyter.
Gebers, P.E. 1990. Health of street children in Cape Town. *The Child Care Worker*, 8 (9): 11-14.
Jansen, R., Richter, L.M. & Griesel, R.D. 1991. Glue sniffing: A community problem. *The Child Care Worker*, 9(11): 13-15.
Janus, M. 1987. *Adolescent runaways: Causes and consequences*. Lexington, Massachusetts: Lexington Books. D.C. Health and Company.
Jarvis, M. 1992. No way home. *The Child Care Worker*. 10(7): 8-9. (First published in *Image*, June 1991.)
Keen, J. 1988. Street children, bush children and children working in the street: Preliminary results of a field study in Turkey. *The Child Care Worker*, 7(11): 13-15.
Konanc, E. 1989. Street children and children working in the street: Preliminary results of a field study in Turkey. *The Child Care Worker*, 7(11): 13-15
Levin, J. 1992. Street worker. *The Child Care Worker*, 10(3): 3-4.
Louw, D.A. 1992. *Suid Afrikaanse handboek van abnormale gedrag*. Johannesburg: Southern Boekuitgewers (Edms) Bpk.

MacCurtain, B. 1988. Education: The lost property of our people. *The Child Care Worker*, 6(4): 8-10.

Mangwana, T.C. 1992. Working with street children: Hints for child care workers. *The Child Care Worker*, 10(5): 14-15.

Maphatane, M. 1994. Understanding support systems for Black street children and their families: An ecological perspective. *Social Work Practice*, 1. 94: 22-30

Oaklander, V. 1988. *Windows to our children: A Gestalt therapy approach to children and adolescents.* (2nd ed.). New York: The Gestalt Journal Press. Inc.

Peacock, R. & Theron, A. 1992. Die verband tussen swart straatkinders se biologiese en emosionele behoeftes en die tipe misdaad wat deur hulle gepleeg word. *Suid Afrikaanse Tydskrif. Sosiologie*, 1992, 23(1).

Richter, L.M. 1988. Street children: The nature and scope of the problem in Southern Africa. *The Child Care Worker*, 6(7): 11-14.

Richter, L.M. 1991. Street children in South Africa — General theoretical introduction: Society, family and childhood. *The Child Care Worker*, 9(8): 7-9.

Rothman, J. 1991. *Runaway and homeless youth — Strengthening services to families and children.* The Centre for Child & Family Policy Studies. School of Social Welfare. Los Angeles: University of California.

Schurink, W., Maphatane, M., Rip, S., Schurink, E., Smith, L. & Tiba, M. 1993. *Street Children.* Pretoria: Human Sciences Research Council.

Schurink, E. & Burger, M. 1994. Addressing the street child phenomenon in the South African society. *Social Work Practice*, 3. 94: 2-8.

Swart, J. 1988. Community perceptions of street children in Hillbrow. *The Child Care Worker*, 6(6): 11-13.

The Children's Foundation. 1990. The National Status of Street Children Organizations.

Thompson, C.L. & Rudolph, L.B. 1992. *Counseling children.* Pacific Grove, California: Brooks/Cole Publishing Company.

Tyler, F.B., Tyler, S.L., Echeverri, J.J. & Zia, M.C. 1991. Making it on the streets in Bogota: A psychosocial study of street youth. *Genetic, Social and General Psychology Monographs*, 117(4).

Van der Merwe, M. 1994. Assessment of problems and needs: Greedy worms eating life apple. *Social Work Practice*, 3. 94: 30.

Van Rooyen, C.A.J. 1994. Developmental research — A practical approach to social work research. *Social Work Practice*, 2. 94: 16-21.

following principles when working with street children:
- acceptance of and respect for the child
- faith in his potential
- recognition of his dignity
- giving understanding and security within a healthy environment
- individualisation
- redirecting self-responsibility to the right channels
- confidentiality and privacy.

Polarities

Oaklander (1988:157) stresses the importance of working with polarities. She points out that children become confused when they find themselves feeling angry and hateful towards someone they actually love. Street children may experience polarities such as:
- love and hate towards parents
- running away from home but the desire to be reunited with the family.

Oaklander (1988:281) suggests creative play techniques such as art, clay, collages and stories to enable the child to deal with polarities in his life.

Building self-image

Rebuilding the damaged self-image of the street child can be a long and time-consuming process. MacCurtain (1988:9) cautions that the lower the street child's self-esteem, the more he will fantasise. His ambitions will tend to be unrealistic and therefore also impossible to fulfil. As dignity and self-esteem are restored, the child should be encouraged to strive for attainable goals. According to Oaklander (1988:281), a baby is not born with bad feelings about himself. She further points out that a child's feelings about himself after some time depends to a great extent on the early messages he receives about himself from his parents. Oaklander (1988:282-283) suggests basic guidelines for parents to enhance a child's self-esteem. These guidelines can also be used therapeutically:
- Listen to, acknowledge and accept the child's feelings.
- Be honest with the child.
- Be specific in criticism.
- Remember the uniqueness principle — the child is wonderful and amazing in his own way, even though it may be a far different uniqueness from yours.
- Avoid being judgemental; avoid giving a lot of "shoulds" and needless advice.

Even though possibly hardened by their circumstances, street children remain children. The components of therapy described in this book also apply to street children. An approach that is goal-directed and structured, employing techniques that bring fun into therapy, should enhance the street children's motivation. Above all, it is important to

12 Handling aggression in children

J P SCHOEMAN

Introduction

The Reader's Digest Oxford Complete Wordfinder (1992) describes anger as extreme or passionate displeasure, hostility, indignation, resentment or exasperation toward someone or something, rage, wrath. The word *anger* comes from the old Norse word *angr*. Anger, to the Vikings, referred to someone who was tightly or painfully constricted by pain and grief; anger also denoted a painful spike (in the flesh).

Oaklander (1988:221) is of the opinion that anger is the ". . . most feared, resisted, suppressed, threatening emotion — because it is so often the most important and the deepest hidden block to one's sense of wholeness and wellbeing."

Anger may also imply a sense of "being wronged". The child thus suffers a lot of pain. A feeling of unfairness towards the wrongdoer exists. This anger may then be experienced as the urge to "get back at" the wrongdoer or to demand repayment or restitution.

The child cannot sit still with the "painful spike in the flesh". Anger results in activity, in doing something about the cause. The child, however, with a lack of experience and diplomacy, may often express himself in an unacceptable way. For example, a child may say: "I hate you. I will kill you". If adults hear this, they are shocked and forbid such self-expression. The child then represses or internalises these feelings. The child is thus made to feel that he cannot effectively manage or control his anger. He learns to keep such feelings to himself. He often then starts with physical problems, like stomachaches and headaches; enkopresis, enuresis and stealing also occur. All of these problems appear because the child turns his negative energy inside his body. He may not own it, therefore he represses it.

The child who owns his anger can feel his emotions and is more in contact with himself than the child who continually tries to suppress the anger and assumes that no negative feelings exist. It is the task of the therapist to guide the child towards handling this aggression and anger. This can be achieved through play therapy.

Anger seen developmentally

The social learning hypothesis is based on the viewpoint that anger is a learned condition. The learned condition is a response to role models. If the role model has a high status, or is in a position to reward the child for "good" behaviour (that is, not being angry), the behaviour is internalised. The child relates to this role model and expects the same results from other people. Unfortunately, this does not always happen. For example, children often react with anger in a play session according to what is happening in their home situation. Children will react as they believe right. If a child is not allowed to show any form of anger, he will be cautious and avoid doing so. It is of great importance to such a child to please the therapist and not to offend her with undesirable attitudes.

This hypothesis can be combined with the social cognition approach. According to this approach, one might argue that it is not the behaviour that is deviant, but how children see and understand behaviour, which can be attributed to a developmental delay or lag.

Needs of the aggressive child

Anger is a primitive, ancient feeling that lives deep within us. Babies are born with anger. Visit the neonatal ward at the local maternity hospital and see how newborns express their extreme displeasure with hunger, thirst and physical discomfort. Crying out their anger can be seen as a basic survival skill for newborns.

A child's behaviour is always an attempt to satisfy his basic psychological needs. Therefore, it is important to realise that no child will act without a reason. A child will act to get what he wants. Sometimes, he will use angry behaviour to gain what he wants. This is a natural way of getting the message through, of making a point.

A child thus functions according to psychological needs. Some of these needs are often in imbalance. This forms an unfinished gestalt in the child's perceptions. Some of these needs will be discussed below.

Freedom

Although a child cannot always make the correct decisions, he has the drive to make his own choices. He wants to be free and not have limitations. A child wants to take charge of his own life. On the other hand, the child who has no boundaries feels unsafe. He wants to know what is good for him and what is acceptable. It is also important for a child to experience the satisfaction of his parents with him. Therefore, a child must be given the room to make decisions within the boundaries needed for security.

Fun

For a child, it is very important to enjoy life. If there is no fun in doing activities, children will not be amused or prepared to act voluntarily. If a child is forced to do something, he is robbed of freedom of choice. However, if a child is allowed to combine duty with fun, he learns to enjoy life and learns a healthy work ethic.

...ger seen developmentally

The social learning hypothesis is based on the viewpoint that anger is a learned condition. The learned condition is a response to role models. If the role model has a high status, or is in a position to reward the child for "good" behaviour (that is, not being angry), the behaviour is internalised. The child relates to this role model and expects the same results from other people. Unfortunately, this does not always happen. For example, children often react with anger in a play session according to what is happening in their home situation. Children will react as they believe right. If a child is not allowed to show any form of anger, he will be cautious and avoid doing so. It is of great importance to such a child to please the therapist and not to offend her with undesirable attitudes.

This hypothesis can be combined with the social cognition approach. According to this approach, one might argue that it is not the behaviour that is deviant, but how children see and understand behaviour, which can be attributed to a developmental delay or lag.

Needs of the aggressive child

Anger is a primitive, ancient feeling that lives deep within us. Babies are born with anger. Visit the neonatal ward at the local maternity hospital and see how newborns express their extreme displeasure with hunger, thirst and physical discomfort. Crying out their anger can be seen as a basic survival skill for newborns.

A child's behaviour is always an attempt to satisfy his basic psychological needs. Therefore, it is important to realise that no child will act without a reason. A child will act to get what he wants. Sometimes, he will use angry behaviour to gain what he wants. This is a natural way of getting the message through, of making a point.

A child thus functions according to psychological needs. Some of these needs are often in imbalance. This forms an unfinished gestalt in the child's perceptions. Some of these needs will be discussed below.

Freedom

Although a child cannot always make the correct decisions, he has the drive to make his own choices. He wants to be free and not have limitations. A child wants to take charge of his own life. On the other hand, the child who has no boundaries feels unsafe. He wants to know what is good for him and what is acceptable. It is also important for a child to experience the satisfaction of his parents with him. Therefore, a child must be given the room to make decisions within the boundaries needed for security.

Fun

For a child, it is very important to enjoy life. If there is no fun in doing activities, children will not be amused or prepared to act voluntarily. If a child is forced to do something, he is robbed of freedom of choice. However, if a child is allowed to combine duty with fun, he learns to enjoy life and learns a healthy work ethic.

Power

A child has the basic need for power. He wants to be heard. He also wants to say or do something that makes a difference. For most people, it is very important to be recognised as an individual. Similarly, children want adults to pay attention to them and to respect them. If he has no power, the child feels that he loses control. For some reason, adults often feel that children must be subordinated, otherwise they cannot discipline them. In reality, power means that a child is allowed to take responsibility for his own life, to make decisions concerning his own functioning, without harming himself or any one else. Power also means that a child is allowed to negotiate about his situation and to take action after properly thinking things through.

Belonging

A need to belong drives the child to join other children. Children will do things to make themselves acceptable to others. They dress alike, talk alike, play alike, do every thing like their friends just to be accepted and to get into a group where they can belong.

Associated with the need to belong is the need to be loved. Love is one of a child's most wanted emotions. He wants to love somebody or something and he wants to be loved by something or somebody. That is why children always choose "best friends". They also adore pets and, for this reason, must have a pet, if possible. A pet fulfils the need to give love without reservation. The child can be himself, be nasty to the pet, ignore the pet or fight with it, but the pet will be patient, loveable and humble.

Reasons for aggression in children

If a child is denied one of these above-mentioned needs, he has reason to be angry. He becomes angry in the hope that his needs will be met. Just like an adult, a child also tries to bring his organism into balance. Because he lacks the experience to do that, he often chooses the wrong attitudes and mechanisms to get his needs met. Children often express anger for the following reasons:

- ❏ Children quickly learn that anger gets other people's attention. A little baby learns that when he cries and fusses, his mother feeds him, changes his nappy and gives him attention. The next time, he will do the same to get the required attention of his mother. If it has worked once, it will work again.
- ❏ Children seek reasons for why they do not want to change or improve negative behaviour. They want to stay angry because it gives them a weapon. An example for this can be the following: "I was so angry when my father hit me, that I could not think straight." (The child tries to give the reason why he broke the window.)
- ❏ Children often try to gain powerful control in a temper outburst. They have to generate negative energy to make their point. If adults want to calm the child down, they often give him attention for the first time. The child might have asked before, but with no results. However, parents will do anything to please the child and not to upset him. Therefore, the child takes advantage of the situation. He thus uses his anger to manipulate.

- Anger can empower a child. A child who feels powerless thinks of himself as being vulnerable. In order to take control, the child tries to scare the other person by acting angrily. The child feels that his actual fear and powerlessness are camouflaged and that he can be safe.
- Anger may be used as an excuse for the child's unwillingness to do something. A child shall sometimes say: "I am so angry with my parents, I will not do my homework."
- Sometimes, the child aims his anger at himself. Such a child is unable to say what he means and does not mean what he says because he is not in contact with himself. The child has not mastered the ability to verbalise his experience. The child is thus in a dilemma: he acts aggressively because of an inability to verbalise, but is then required to verbalise the reasons for his aggressive behaviour which is unacceptable to adults. Children will then tend to search for solutions or explanations, avoiding expressing their anger. The danger then exists of the child turning the aggression inward, retroflexively. Yontef (1993:183) believes that similar behaviour is manifested by adults who have not learned to utilise aggression in an adult way. Yontef (1993:186) adds: "These patients maintain this lack of clarity by two related processes: thinking without integrating the sensory and affective and using their aggression more against themselves than for contact and assimilation."

The child who does not respect himself is not in a position to defend himself. He denies himself any negative feelings, even healthy feelings of rage, by distorting himself. Such a child fails to develop the ability to nurture and always subordinates himself in conflict situations. Oaklander (1991:4) is of the opinion that when children are unable to escape their anger, they are diminishing the self, cutting themselves off.

Handling aggression in children

Violent actions have little value and are, in any case, to nobody's advantage. To direct feelings of antipathy and aggression towards someone or something has no point and may even result in a condition of dysphoria. It is thus negative for a child to remain in a state of anger. On the other hand, it is important to allow a child to experience negative feelings and to contain these. This can be achieved through verbal expression or through play.

Unfortunately, children may sometimes be angry, but unable to express what they are feeling. Fighting children are sometimes hiding the real reason or source of their anger.

A child who remains angry makes himself sick. He closes down his senses, constricts his body and closes his mind. Children cannot explore problems with their schoolwork, relationships and with parents and friends because they are unable to express the part of the self that is angry.

The aggressive child may show hostility towards almost everyone and every object he crosses. The reasons for this hostility are various. Children are confronted with many difficulties today, not only from the environment, but also when they lack the ability to cope with demands that make them angry and fearful. A child does not have the mechanisms to handle the feelings that are often generated by the environment. It has to be stressed that a child does not become aggressive over night; it takes time to build such aggression. The process is usually gradual because the child gets tired of expressing his needs in a subtle way. He, as discussed previously, has to exaggerate his behaviour and it is at this point that conflict is caused. However, a child who is aggressive and acting out this anger is easier to work with than children who are inhibited and who repress their anger.

In containing the aggressive energy, it is necessary to first work generally with the child. It will only serve to aggravate an aggressive child if the therapist begins with accusations like: "I hear you tried to set your stepfather's car on fire." Start with things the child likes to do and then gradually move to more direct feelings. The pain, anger and hurt will emerge spontaneously. Unfortunately, a child is often taught to suppress his feelings. He often learns that to be angry is bad and guilt feelings start to emerge instead of the child acting out what he feels. Oaklander (1988:209) is of the opinion that: "It is no wonder that anger is like some awful lurking monster continually having to be pushed down, suppressed, deflected and avoided."

Oaklander (1988) mentions four phases in working with children's anger:

- Give children practical methods of expressing their angry feelings.
- Help children move towards the actual feeling of anger they may be holding and encourage them to give emotional expression to this anger right there with the therapist in her office.
- Give children the experience of being verbally direct with their angry feelings: saying what they need to say to the person they need to say it to.
- Talk with them about anger: what it is, what makes them angry, how they show it, what they do when they feel it.

A working model for handling aggression

To address aggression and anger, the author has developed the following steps which form a working model in addressing anger and aggression in a therapeutic process.

Awareness

Get the child to talk about the anger. If the negative energy level is very high, it will be necessary to support the child to act the anger out. Make him aware of what he is feeling and thinking, smelling and hearing. Give him direct clues by asking questions like the following:

- Can you name the anger?
- Where does it come from?
- What do you feel right now?
- How does it feel in your body?
- How do you want to express it?

It will sometimes be necessary to do some exercises and creative dramatics with the child. This can help the child to be more aware of his body. Sensory work's purpose is for the child to feel more in touch with the self. Touching wet clay or sand, finger painting, looking at objects, listening to music, smelling, and tasting open up the senses.

Listening

The play therapist will have to listen very carefully. The therapist will have to keep in mind that the child is very angry for a reason. He is trying to get his needs met. Look at the child's body image and listen to the message behind the words. If the child is given the opportunity to reason about his anger, the emotional energy level is automatically lowered. Give the child enough time to say what he is feeling, even if you disagree with him. If the child gets the feeling that you are trying to understand what he is saying and that you are patient and open to his point of view, the anger diminishes. As the child gets the opportunity to come into contact with what he is feeling, the emotional energy level is automatically lowered.

Expressing and containing the negative energy

When this happens, the child must be equipped with self-support. In the process of expressing the anger, the child comes to terms with his own feelings. He is given the opportunity to acknowledge his feelings.

It is necessary to evaluate the child's need for balance. Sometimes, in a session, the feelings of anger emerge so hectically that the need to experience it right then and there is big. Children must be supported to own feelings and contain the negative energy so that it can be dealt with.

To contain a child's aggressive energy, it is sometimes helpful to make use of items to let the child express his feelings. Useful ideas to help children express angry feelings during a therapy session are:

- Wet newspapers and then hold them up in front of the child so that he can hit through them with his fists.
- The child can draw his frustration or the person that frustrates him; afterwards he can tear it up.
- He can punch pillows.
- He can run around the block.
- He can make a clay model and destroy it afterwards.
- Oaklander (1988:214) also mentions the following items with can be used to express anger: the bataca (a foam-covered batlike object with a handle); a rubber knife; a dart gun, and an inflated doll for punching.

Acknowledging the anger

This can be done by summarising and paraphrasing what is heard. The therapist can demonstrate her understanding by using words like: "I can understand your anger", or "No one likes the feeling that he is seen as young and irresponsible."

If the therapist can succeed in containing the anger and exaggerating it a little, the negative energy will automatically be reduced. Some therapists use the technique of inciting the child to try and intensify the negative energy to such an extent that the child gets uneasy with the situation. He then moves onto a level where he starts finding reasons for his anger.

Apologising for the anger

A very interesting approach is followed by Confer (1987:12) where he suggests that the therapist apologises for the pain and suffering the child may be experiencing: "I am so sorry that you are not satisfied with what is going on in your school." Many African cultures have a similar way of expressing their empathy. When you get hurt or become very cross, they apologise for your unpleasant feelings or hurt.

An honest and genuine apology is very fruitful. It demonstrates the other person's confluence and honest empathy and means a lot more than when you just mention your understanding. When you apologise for the person's anger, you mention it by name and do not offer only an empty set of polite words.

However, if the therapist does not experience a genuine sense of empathy or feeling for the angry child, it will do more harm than good if she pretends that she is feeling that way. A child knows when adults are sincere and genuine. If he finds any insincerity or false emotions in the therapist, it will only serve to increase his anger.

Agreeing with the anger

The reason for this is to give the child the encouragement to feel and experience his anger. At this stage, the therapist can say to the child that he has all the reason in the world to feel this way. The therapist literally gives the child the opportunity and the permission to show his anger, motivating him to let go. The therapist agrees with the facts of the situation: "Yes, your father did promise to buy you a bicycle." The next point is to argue in principle: "I agree a promise must be kept." The third point is to agree with the right of the child to have his own opinion: "Yes, I can fully understand your anger towards your father for promising and not keeping his promise. I do not blame you for being angry."

Giving the child permission to criticise

This permission serves as an invitation to the child to verbalise all his ill feelings. The child can be invited to identify what he really would like to have happen. At this stage, the child makes contact with his own feelings, which helps him to move from a critical and blaming stance to bringing his unfinished business to the fore.

Oaklander (1992:20) stresses that the child must be given the reassurance that there is no right or wrong to his behaviour. The child must come to his own conclusion after being given the reassurance that it is acceptable to be angry. Children are often given the hidden message that only a bad child is angry. Feelings of guilt are thus often nurtured in children. These become introjections and, if a child is not therapeutically led to handle them, the angry feelings will become a bigger problem.

Choosing how to express anger

Children can be helped to express their feelings and verbalise what they need to say to the person with whom they are angry. Enactment is a valuable technique to motivate the child to put his feelings or thoughts into action. There are many ways of helping the child to express his feelings. He can do it through creative play, namely sandwork, clay work or drawings. He can do it through metaphor and he can do it through chair work.

Chair work

In handling anger, there are always polarities concerning the balance of the child's functioning. To bring out the polarities and handle them successfully is quite an extreme exercise. In chair work, this can be done, bringing the two sides out into the open at the same time so that they may confront one another, thus opening the way toward resolving the split.

The "hot seat" is where the child himself sits, while the "empty chair" is placed a few feet away, facing the hot seat.

What helps a lot in chair work is that the work that is done with the child is not goal-oriented. The therapist must be content with whatever happens. The child therefore has the choice to bring to the fore whatever he wants to say and discuss at the present. The role of the therapist is to help the child to "let go". When the therapist starts with chair work, the child must have completed the steps above. If the child does not own his anger, the possibility of resistance and denial can jeopardise this technique.

In the **first stage of chair work**, both sides of the conflict are brought into awareness. Friedman (1993:105) stresses the following in the first stage: if the child plays the victim, it necessarily follows that he has internalised the victimiser already. What is interesting is that there cannot be a victim without a victimiser. The possibility can be that the child has externalised the victimiser and is projecting it onto someone or something else. The first step, then, is to take the child back to that stage and let him own the projection. (See chapter 4 on projection techniques.) For example, the child can actually speak directly to the projection in the other chair and then change chairs. The value of this exercise is that the child can immediately feel and experience the impact.

The first stage of chair work aims to enable the polarity to come into awareness and to enable the child to take responsibility for both sides. The following serves as an example:

The conflict is between a father and a twelve-year-old boy. The father gave the boy a hiding because he failed his tests.

Child: My father never liked anything I did.
Therapist: What does that feel like?
Child: It feels like s____
Therapist: Could you tell him that now?
Child: (*Speaks to empty chair.*) Dad, you are always criticising me; you never approve of my marks. I feel like a failure.
Therapist: (*Asks the child to switch over as dad. Child refuses.*) (*As dad*) It is because

	I want the best for you and I want you to work hard. (*The therapist says this and asks the child to repeat it as dad.*)
Child:	(*Repeats what the therapist has just said.*)
Therapist:	(*Asks the child to switch back to himself and comment on it.*)
Child:	(*Sometimes the child cannot perform to this stage because of his introjections.*)
Therapist:	(*As child*) I do not believe it. If you loved me, you would listen to my reasons why I failed my tests.
Child:	(*Repeats*)
Therapist:	(*As dad*) Well, it is my responsibility to look after you. It is my duty to help you shape up. (*Ask the child to repeat.*)
Child:	(*Repeats*)
Therapist:	What do you feel as dad?
Child:	That he is evading his responsibilities.
Therapist:	Could you tell him that some more? Do it more openly.

The reason for stressing the conflict here is to bring it out as much as possible so that the child can come into contact with his real feelings.

This leads to the **second stage**. The two sides confront one another and the conflict is intensified. Greenberg (1984:143) mentions three aspects in the second stage: flat disagreement between the two sides, followed by actual dialogue, followed in turn by resolution. The last phase in the second stage begins when the so-called topdog lets go of the oppositional role and tries to listen to the under dog. It is interesting to note that the child, because he is so natural and without pretensions, shifts very quickly at the outset into the actual self where he can experience himself in his real world. The topdog thus becomes the other chair.

During the second stage, conflict must be joined and suffered through. There is no sense in trying to remove the conflict. If the conflict is suppressed or even interpreted away, the child never gets the opportunity to develop a self-regulating system. When a child learns how to accept the conflict, the solution comes easily and he experiences the wholeness of a truly resolved conflict. As Goodman (cited in Friedman, 1993:108) explains, the conflict must be suffered through rather than "removed". When the topdog and the underdog have said the worst to each other, the third stage may evolve.

The real reason why the conflict developed and the needs that are involved come to the fore. The chairwork can be continued as follows in **the third stage**:

Therapist:	(*To dad*) What do you need from your son?
Child:	(*As dad*) To make me feel that I am not a failure.
Therapist:	How?
Child:	I need him to give me something to be proud of.
Therapist:	(*Reaching for the feeling*) To make up for your own failure?
Child:	I have messed up everything.
Therapist:	Could you tell your son what you feel about him now?
Child:	No. It is too painful. *Or* Yes. I understand your feelings and obsessions more now.

Therapist: (*Switch over and be the child. To dad.*) Dad, I want you to be proud of me. But I don't want to have to buy it. I just want you to tell me that you love me as I am.
Child: (*Repeats and adds more if desired.*)

At this stage, the chair work can be regarded as complete. A peaceful climate and a nurturing situation must be achieved to help the child to cope with his pain. The child may be given a teddy bear to hold, or, if the child is older, a cushion from the couch.

Empowering the child

Part of the "cure" involves empowering the child. This can only happen when the relationship between the therapist and the child is so supportive that the child can take responsibility for himself. This must take place in an atmosphere where the child can feel that he can trust his friend (the therapist) with confidential information.

To facilitate this, the therapist can use "mad sessions" where the child can talk about the things that anger him. Encourage the child to talk to his parents and ask for sessions where both the parties can talk about their frustrations.

Oaklander (1983:282) gives basic guidelines for enhancing a child's feelings of self and thus empowering him:

- Listen to, acknowledge, and respect the child's feelings.
- Treat him with respect.
- Accept the child's feelings.
- Give him specific praise, to the point.
- Be honest with him.
- Use "I" messages, rather than "you" messages.
- Be specific in criticism.
- Consistency with rules and controls is essential. Give the child the space to organise his own things.
- Give him responsibilities.
- Give the child independence.
- Give him the freedom to make choices.
- Involve him in decision making and problem solving.
- Respect his feelings, needs, wants, suggestions and wisdom.
- Allow him to experiment.
- Remember the unique principle: each child is wonderful and amazing.
- Be a good role model.
- Avoid judgemental attitudes.
- Take the child seriously.

Children are sometimes so diminished that they cannot make choices. By making a choice, a child is saying who he is. There are sometimes self-induced boundaries that block a child from taking action or making choices.

Through empowerment, a child must get a feeling of power: he must get the feeling that he is in control of his anger.

Self-nurturing

In order for the child to maintain this power, he must learn to nurture himself. He must be able to forgive himself for what he has done and must even be able to spoil himself a little. The aggressive child often has a mental block about himself. Therefore, it is essential that polarities in this regard are made clear to the child. In other words, not everything the child experiences is negative — there are also positive aspects present in his life. The child must thus be helped to bring the negative to the fore and to accept the caring parts of his being. When this happens, the child will experience the integration of his total being.

Pitfalls in handling aggression

There are certain actions that should be avoided while addressing a child's anger.

Never debate the facts

An adolescent often draws the therapist into this pitfall. An angry person is unable to deal logically with the problem while there is anger within his body. Emotional energy is very high at this stage and rational energy low. Debating facts will increase the child's emotional energy and he will react defensively.

Never ever ask "why?"

Children usually answer a "why" question with "because". However, if a child knew the reason for his behaviour, his coping mechanisms would have been better implemented to address his aggression. A "why" question will make him disheartened as the child will be unable to answer.

Never jump to conclusions

The child who is filled with negative energy cannot handle a logical interpretation. The therapist must therefore be patient. Do not analyse the angry child's motives or reasons for being angry. This is *not* the role of the therapist.

Never hurry or rush

Take time and go with the angry child's continuum. Be in confluence and be with him. Stay with him all the time.

Never be sarcastic

There is no place for sarcasm. Whether conveyed by your words, tone of voice or the expression on your face, sarcasm causes a child to feel put down, insulted and treated without respect. Sarcasm will increase emotional energy, not lower it.

Never blame or criticise
Criticism, even so-called constructive criticism, has no place in working with children. No therapist has to play the role of the parent or the teacher. Blame, similarly, always implies "you are bad or wrong." If you want to maintain a good relationship with the child, blame and criticism will only serve as a stumbling block.

Never judge
The therapist must keep her ideas and opinions to herself. Value judgements can hinder the therapeutic process. Once the negative energy has been resolved, there will be enough time to put your point across.

Never nag or preach
A child who is in the process of containing anger does not want to hear words like should, must and have to. These words can serve to provoke even more angry emotions. A higher value must be placed on the autonomy and self-determination of the child than on other values.

Never put the child down
Although a child has a great sense of fearlessness, it weakens him when he is in a subordinate position. If the therapist says something like: "I cannot trust you because you promised to phone me and then did not", the child may feel guilty, weak and put down.

Never take the child at face value
The angry child often overstates his position. He sometimes even fantasises around certain situations, just to make the situation more forceful. The angry person also says things that are not really meant.

Conclusion
Anger is the most negative emotion. Children learn at an early age of their lives that anger and aggression are bad. Because the child does not have the language to express himself and because he learns that such expression is dangerous, he represses his feelings. It is important to remember that a child does not choose certain emotions: he feels them inside. The more a child absorbs negative messages, the more his self-image takes the blame. The child that starts to build a wall around him is in a process of protecting himself. He often blocks out the sensory stimulation and generates unhealthy muscle tone. The child then starts to lose contact with himself. The unexpressed emotions stay in the child like a stone. It is the task of the therapist to help the child to handle anger positively.

To feel angry is a function of the child's organism, leading him to satisfy needs. When a situation generates stress for the child, contact, in the form of anger, can be used to provide a release of tension of the unfinished gestalt.

Anger can thus be seen as serving the function of maintaining the child's health and growth in his best interest.

Bibliography

Confer, C. 1987. *Managing anger: yours and mine.* Jacob R. Sprouse Jr.

Friedman, N. 1993. Fritz Perl's "Layers" and the Empty Chair. A reconsideration. *The Gestalt Journal*, (XVI) 2: 95-119.

Greenberg, L.S. 1980. The intensive analysis of recurring events from the practice of Gestalt therapy. *Psychotherapy, Theory, Research and Practice*, 17: 143-152.

Oaklander, V. 1988. *Windows to our children. A Gestalt therapy approach to children and adolescents.* (2nd ed.). New York: The Gestalt Journal Press. Inc.

Oaklander, V. 1991. Anger. *Family Times*, Sept/Oct.: 4-5

The Reader's Digest Oxford Complete Wordfinder, 1991. London: The Reader's Digest Association Ltd.

Yontef, G.M. 1993. *Awareness, dialogue and process. Essays on Gestalt therapy.* New York: The Gestalt Journal Press. Inc.

13 The use of play techniques when counselling young children in a divorce situation

M VAN DER MERWE

Introduction

A divorce is a traumatic event in the life of a child, often with negative results that may be carried into adulthood. Children in a divorce situation should be involved in timely and effective therapy. When such children are left to their own devices, valuable energy that should have been used for the handling of normal growth related tasks may be used instead for adapting to the divorce. If this happens over a period of time the children's development may stagnate or regress, with long-term negative repercussions.

Children react in different ways to parental divorce. Various possible effects are discussed in the literature on this subject. The effect on each individual is largely determined by internal and external variables. Individualisation is therefore important when determining a helping program for a specific child. When keeping in mind the target group, namely, children of single parent families where financial problems are common, it is clear why counselling should be goal-directed and cost-effective.

Theoretical basis

Van der Merwe (1991:133-136; 1994:10-15) describes the person-directed, goal-directed nature of counselling children in a divorce situation. This is related to goal-play, as discussed by Smith (1982:129-139): goal-play is the purposeful utilisation, refocusing and directing of the child's play to a clear and specific goal. The viewpoints mentioned above are connected to the model developed by Dennison and Glassman (1987) which is based on the premise that the formulation of goals is central to the helping process. The focus of this shifts between content and process goals according to the needs of the client and the phase in the helping process.

Van der Merwe (1991:133) views goal-directed, person-directed play as eclectic because a single theory is not used. Goal-directed play is based on various approaches to social work and play therapy, for instance, the psychoanalytic approach of the founders of play therapy, Sigmund and Anna Freud, Helmuth and Klein. The relationship approach also forms a part of the theoretical basis. This approach is an umbrella for the relationship therapy of Rank, Taft and Allen; the client-centred approaches of Rogers and Moustakas, and client-centred play therapy, as described by Axline. Various structured approaches, such as Hambidge's active play therapy, Jernberg's theraplay, and fair play therapy, as described by Peoples, have much to offer to those with a goal-directed, person-directed approach (Van der Merwe, 1991:112).

The goal-directed, individualised approach that forms the basis of the work with young children in a divorce situation, as described in this chapter, is based strongly on the viewpoints of Schaefer and O'Connor (1983:1,89). They also oppose the point of view that one approach is the only possibility for treatment. They argue that this places the child within a rigid framework and instead recommend that a prescription is worked out for each specific child client. They refer to this as a *prescriptive approach*. As this reminds one of the medical model, the term is not recommended for social workers. It seems, though, that child therapists should take the responsibility for choosing the most appropriate therapeutic techniques for each client, based on that individual's unique personality and problem. The therapist must have a broad knowledge base to be able to do this.

Working in a goal-directed and individualised way and making use of a broad theoretical base does not imply that techniques and approaches may be used haphazardly. Sound theoretical knowledge and skills should direct the therapist's planning and helping.

On the basis of the above, it is clear why one refers to play techniques in working with children in a divorce situation and not to play therapy. The goal-directed, individualised approach does not exclude spontaneous, unstructured play, but where it does occur, it is usually a planned part of the helping program. Furthermore, while traditional play therapy often omits the use of the role of educator, education and building of the client's knowledge are integral parts of goal-directed, individualised therapy. Moreover, this form of therapy is limited by time and structured to suit the target group. Play techniques are divided into five play forms, namely, relaxation play, assessment play, dramatic play, creative play and biblio-play. These play forms are broadly divided into a process made up of a beginning, change-oriented and final phase.

Factors influencing the child's reaction to divorce

Internal variables are the intrapsychic factors that differ from person to person. These are, for instance, temperament, cumulative stress, age, developmental stage and ethnic group.

Each factor will influence the child's reaction in different ways. For example, according to Hetherington (1979:852) and Nichols (1984:29), children that parents view as difficult are less adaptable and more vulnerable in problematic situations than children with easier temperaments.

These writers also refer to the effect of multiple traumatic events or **cumulative stress** as a determining factor. A person who has had to handle the death of a loved one or a pet, a car accident, subsequent moving between towns and houses and hospitalisation will possibly find it more difficult to work through the additional trauma of a divorce than a person who can direct all his or her emotional energy to the working through of a single stressful event. Those people who have had to handle cumulative stress, though, may have the advantage of having developed certain coping strategies.

Kelly and Wallerstein (1976:20-32) have found that children's adaptation to the divorce crisis differs according to their **age group** and **developmental phase**. Young children have an egocentric perspective that may lead them to believe that the divorce is their fault. Research findings on this variable are contradictory, but Feldman (1981:332-355) and Kelly and Wallerstein (1976:20-32) give full accounts of the possible reactions of children in different age groups to divorce.

Various researchers discuss the **gender** variable. It seems that boys have more problems when adapting to a divorce than girls, especially in the younger age group (Hess & Camara, 1979:87; Hetherington, 1979:853; Goldman & King, 1985:281). There are some explanations for this, for instance, that discipline towards boys is often stricter. They may get less nurturing and positive support than girls (Wallerstein & Kelly, 1980:165-166).

Even though leading research (Hetherington, Cox & Cox, 1979; Wallerstein & Kelly, 1980) has focused on Caucasian, middle class families, Wallerstein and Kelly are of the opinion that children from mixed ethnic marriages will probably find a divorce more difficult. This may be owing to the fact that they may be isolated already on account of the mixed marriage of the parents. Felner, Farber and Primavera stated in 1980 that there is a dearth of literature on the effect of **ethnicity** on children's adaptation to divorce. It seems that this is still the case and that it is an urgent research need.

Another variable is **birth order**. It may happen that the eldest child is overburdened with more roles after the divorce, whereas the youngest child is overprotected.

External variables that influence the child's experience of divorce are the family circumstances before the divorce, the nature of the divorce process, the life changes and the changes in relationships after the divorce (Van der Merwe, 1991:25). In cases where there has been much conflict and change before and during the divorce, children usually experience more problems with adaptation afterwards.

A checklist of variables is a valuable aid in assessment. This will be discussed when examining the beginning phase of therapy with young children in a divorce situation.

Typical reactions of young children to divorce

Each child's specific circumstances, including the external and internal variables mentioned above, will lead to his unique experience of and reactions to the crisis. Graver and Morse (1986:82) have adapted the following diagram depicting the process of grief and recovery after parental divorce:

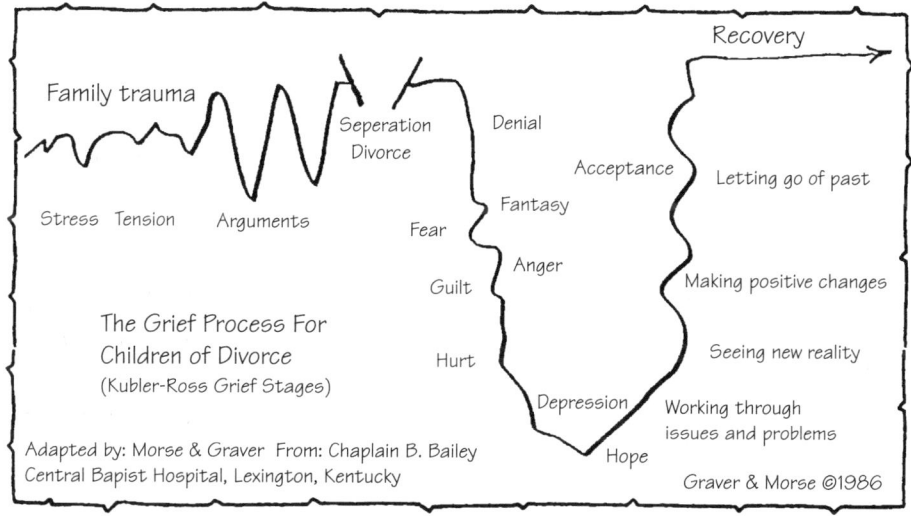

Figure 13.1: **Grief stages**
(From Graver & Morse, 1986:82)

The diagram depicts the period of family trauma prior to the divorce and the separation or divorce. Young children do not really understand the legal processes surrounding. When separation takes place, they experience it as divorce. It is a final step showing them that things have changed. Their process of grief and recovery therefore may start long before the legal divorce of the parents. The aspects mentioned on the diagram as essential to the process of recovery can form part of the problem-directed goals for treatment, namely, working through issues and problems, seeing new reality, making positive changes and, ultimately, letting go of the past.

Certain typical reactions to divorce have been isolated. As the focus of this chapter is on the helping process, the reactions will only be discussed briefly:

- **Grief** is the emotional reaction to loss. It is important that children work through the process of grief, as divorce brings about a number of losses.
- **Denial** is a primitive human defence mechanism that blocks trauma from the consciousness. This reaction inhibits the child's adaption and acceptance of the divorce.
- **Depression** manifests itself in a number of ways, for instance, concentration problems, problems connected to eating, boredom, apathy and a tendency to self-criticism. According to Wallerstein and Kelly (1979:469), childhood depression is often reactive. Owing to the natural recuperative ability of children, depression is less common than in grown-ups. Where it does occur, it is important to give timely help to the child, to prevent him from carrying this reaction into adulthood.
- The expression of **anger** should be encouraged. However, too much or too little anger may be counterproductive. Anger leading to constructive action is positive, whereas destructive anger uses emotional energy unnecessarily.

- The **fear of abandonment** is realistic when one takes into account that one parent has left the home. It is quite logical for the child to wonder when the other parent is going to desert him as well. To prevent this fear, it is particularly necessary to explain the difference between parent-child love and the love between adults.
- Feelings of **conflicting loyalty** can hinder the child's adaptation after the divorce, especially when there is unresolved conflict between the parents. In the interests of their children, it is important that parents learn to act neutrally towards each other after the divorce. It is also helpful if they can move through their own adaptation phases as quickly as possible. The development of a healthy coparental relationship is critical.
- A child may feel **guilty** and blame himself for the divorce, owing to a child's natural tendency to be egocentric. Sometimes parents do blame their children, or children may remember incidents where parents threatened to leave on account of children's bad behaviour. Gardner (1976:150-158) describes this reaction in full. He argues that the child feels safer when he can see the parent as perfect. Therefore he rather blames himself so that the parent's image stays intact. When he feels responsible for the situation, he probably also feels that he has more control over it, including the possibility of changing it back to what it was.
- **Regression** and **hyper-maturity** lie on the ends of a continuum. When confronted with a parental divorce, most children move to one of the two extremes. Regression is an energy-saving relapse in development. When a child relapses into a previous developmental stage that he has already mastered, he has more energy available for working through his feelings regarding the divorce.

   Often in the process of or soon after the divorce, the parents experience problems in their social functioning. This may lead to the development of maturity in the child, when he has to accept responsibilities for which he is still too young. He becomes the comforter and caretaker of the parent. When these reactions occur over a short period, it is quite normal. If they continue indefinitely, however, the child's development may be negatively influenced.
- Children recurrently **hope for reconciliation** between parents, even when everything suggests that this is improbable. To enable the child to adapt to the divorce and to reorganise his life, he must be helped to let go of this unrealistic hope of parental reconciliation. Planning reconciliation impedes his adaptation.
- The **gender identification** of children can be influenced negatively after a divorce. Even when there is a lot of contact with the absent parent, there is still a lack of a constant role model in the family home.
- In some instance, a divorce may also have **positive influences**. Where there was serious conflict between parents before the divorce, the atmosphere often changes for the better thereafter. The child is more at peace. The handling of the trauma can also lead to insight into human emotions, personal growth, realism, a sense of responsibility, as well as the development of skills in problem solving and the resolving of a crisis.

Counselling

The counselling process broadly consists of a beginning, a change-oriented and a final phase. In the beginning and final phases, the main forms of play are relaxation play and assessment play. In the change-oriented phase that is directed to treatment, the main forms of play are biblio-play, dramatic play and creative play.

The techniques as described in the chapters on the five forms of play can be used. Only a few will be elaborated on here to illustrate their use with the specific target group. These will be discussed under the specific phases in the helping process.

Beginning phase – exploring, assessment and planning

Usually, it is necessary to see either one or preferably both of the parents for a thorough assessment before the child is involved in therapy. During this interview, an interview schedule can be used. This usually focuses briefly on identifying details, making it possible to identify certain trends and conflicts early on. When it becomes clear that the parents have big age differences, belong to different churches and have different educational histories, some deductions can already be made.

There is a short focus on the family background when the period of desertion before the divorce is discussed; the family relationships in the past and present, as well as the specifics concerning the divorce, such as date and basic reasons are mentioned. The consequences of the divorce are discussed, especially concerning the legal aspects such as custody and visitation rights. The changes in the family after the divorce are examined. It is important to ask if either of the parents experienced a parental divorce in their childhood. If they did have such an experience and still have unresolved feelings, there may be transference and counter-transference in their transactions with their children. They may perceive their own divorce as an extremely bad experience. The adverse effect on their social functioning may also be detrimental to the child.

In this phase, the external variables are looked at thoroughly, as seen above. This is important for determining the effect of the divorce on the child. However, unnecessary time must not be spent dwelling on the past. If parents tend to discuss this for too long, they are usually referred to FAMSA or somewhere else for individual counselling. Even though good relationships are usually built with the parents during therapy with their children and some support is given to them regarding their own adaptation, this is not the focus of the counselling. From the beginning, it is made clear to the parents that the child is the main focus of concern. The parents are partners in the helping process.

The rest of the assessment focuses on the specific child. Aspects that are examined are the antenatal history and birth, the child's development, serious illnesses and behaviour problems before the divorce. It is important to know if and how the child was told about the divorce. His reactions are looked at thoroughly with the use of a checklist of possible reactions. General personality traits are looked at by asking parents to state if the child is aggressive or passive, an introvert or extrovert and by discussing a few more general traits. The influence of internal and external variables can be assessed by looking at the extent of the input of each variable.

The child's history of therapeutic help is documented. It is also important to look at his preferences regarding forms of play to determine which techniques can be used. Parents are usually able to identify these quite easily.

After completing the basic assessment, the parents are informed of the nature of the helping process. They also receive guidelines for their handling of the child to aid the process. Practical aspects are discussed. They are asked to bring along an exercise book. All relevant drawings and written work are done in this book. After completion of therapy, the child takes the book home. It serves as a reference book. It is also helpful during family meetings or further therapy.

The first interview with the child usually consists of relaxation and assessment play. Simple icebreakers are used, for instance, brainstorming regarding fifteen ways to use a witch's broom. One child was so creative as to say that the straw of the broom could be used as toothpicks! The drawing below depicts another icebreaker: the child is to think of things the tree can say to avoid being chopped down!

Figure 13.2: **Example of an icebreaker**
(Adapted from: Muncy, 1985:128)

In the beginning phase, finger puppets may also be used to put the child at ease, but to set the tone for the rest of the therapy as well. The puppets often start the discussion of divorce related material.

As regards assessment, various techniques are used. Depending on the child's gender and age, a picture is used with specific questions written on it. Through this, the child's preferences regarding taste, smell, colour, sound and touch are determined. At the same time, the therapist can disclose her preferences.

In the first interview, the child's knowledge of feeling language is assessed. There are many ways of doing this. For older primary school children, paging through a magazine looking for pictures expressing different facial expressions works well. These can then be drawn in their exercise book using the simple therapeutic aid developed by Dennison and Glassman (1987:232):

(Figure 13.3: **Feelings completion**
(Adapted from: Dennison & Glassman ,1987:232)

The child can try to imitate the different facial expressions while the therapist draws them in the exercise book. The therapist and child client can work out how the different expressions will look by thinking of the eyebrows, eyes and mouth. Just by drawing these three features in a circle, various feelings can be expressed. The following guide depicts about 82 different facial expressions of feelings ranging from bored, horrified, or puzzled, to surprised, lovestruck or satisfied, and is a valuable aid when working on feeling language:

Figure 13.4: **Facial expressions**

The concept of the **emotional barometer** can be explained in this interview and the child can "take his fever" by drawing a line on the barometer (see example in chapter 8, page 125). If there is time, a joint exploration of big life events, both happy and sad ones, is completed.

A symbol of a camel is often used to assess the child's problems and needs, with the following drawings as visual aids:

Figure 13.5: **Visual aid: Camel with large hump**

Figure 13.6: **Visual aid: Camel with small hump**

The child's problems and needs are compared with the hump on the first camel's back. The long-term goal of therapy is to make this hump smaller, as shown in the second picture. Problems and needs can be written on the camel's hump. The actions that will be taken in the various interviews to address the problems and needs can be written underneath. This is an easy and non-threatening way of formulating goals.

The child is also prepared for the process that will follow. Without misleading him, the play element is stressed. Children frequently express their enjoyment of therapy even in the first interview.

Change-oriented phase

This phase may already start during the first interview. Usually by the second interview, the work has really begun.

Bibliotherapy works particularly well during this phase. Children's stories are used with success; for example, the book, *Dinosaurs Divorce — A guide for changing families* (Brown & Brown, 1986) is a valuable aid. Children in the age group of four to nine years are often very interested in dinosaurs. This tendency is further encouraged by a few television programs that are currently running. The book addresses misconceptions that children may have concerning divorce and offers the correct information. The feelings that children experience are portrayed in such a way that children can easily identify with them. Aspects such as parents' new friends and reconstituted families are addressed.

The book *Daddy doesn't live here anymore* (Boegehold, 1985) appeals to younger children (more or less four to six years). This book can be used successfully in combination with a doll's house and dolls because these are also portrayed in the story. Various divorce related reactions are touched on, for instance, hope of parental reconciliation, fear of abandonment and anger. These reactions can be worked through using the book. In the course of the story, various incorrect ways of handling the divorce are demonstrated. The children can thus learn what to avoid by observing the protagonist of the story.

A life line can be used in a unique way with children in a divorce situation. The author uses it in combination with a spider's web and washing line idea. When the life line technique is used, the parents must be present. This can be motivated as follows:

- Parents are expected to help with the restructuring of the child's life history.
- Parents' own history can be depicted.
- This technique usually brings all sorts of feelings to the fore in the child. When the parents are involved, they have more understanding of the short-term disturbance that the child may experience.
- As partners in the helping process, the parents are an important part of the therapeutic process, as becomes very clear when using this technique.
- It often happens that parents take over the interview and the therapist stays in the background, giving guidance and support.
- During this interview, the parents and children discuss their feelings. Often it is the first time that they have discussed the whole process surrounding the divorce, including the adaptation process thereafter.

- ❏ They can develop a special family language that can serve as a sort of a coded message to use when certain situations arise.
- ❏ When using this technique, parents are needed to support the child, while the therapist remains an objective outsider, helping the family to discuss its past and future.
- ❏ This technique has been used successfully when families plan to join through a marriage. Both families are helped separately to constitute their life lines. Then they are joined together, depicting the complications of living in stepfamilies very clearly.

The life line technique basically works as follows: a piece of string or wool is hung up within the child's reach. Photos, drawings or cuttings of relevant people and events are hung on the "washing line" with washing pegs. Usually, the story starts with the parents' relationship and marriage. The child's antenatal period is discussed, followed by annual photos (for instance of birthday parties).

Usual and everyday incidents are discussed and depicted until the family is ready for discussion of difficult times. Then, all the different houses that they have lived in are identified. Drawings of houses are pinned where the moves took place. Focusing on moves helps everyone involved to assess the effect of change on a family. This is followed by putting faces depicting feelings on the washing line.

Various happy life events, for instance, when the child was born, and the different birthdays are indicated by cards depicting smiling faces. The unhappy times are also depicted with unhappy faces on the line. These are then discussed. Where the divorce takes place, the line is cut, and it splits in two.

The non-custodial parent's new house and relevant information regarding his/her new life are portrayed on the one line. If the parent becomes absent and uninvolved, the line is kept very short. Usually, this is worked through with the children. They are led to understand that the lack of parental involvement is not the children's fault. Alternative ways of handling this are discussed. The children also understand that it is difficult to predict what will happen to the absent parent's life line in future. This parent may choose to become involved again, in which case his/her life line will grow into the child's life line again. If not, it may be a short, seemingly insignificant line crossing the child's line somewhere in the past. It will always be there and the child cannot ignore it. One child kept saying that she wanted nothing more to do with the absent parent, after many disappointments regarding broken promises. She said that she wanted to cut him out of her life. By using this technique, it could be conveyed to her that ignoring and denying her feelings will not keep the father's actions from influencing her. This could be demonstrated practically by pulling on the father's line and showing her how her own line moved.

Another child understood very clearly that she could not be blamed for the father's lack of interest. She stated that he had to sort himself out first, before coming back into her life.

All new parental relationships can be portrayed by tying further pieces of string to the child's life line. Again, these new lines can be pulled to show the child that they do affect him. In the end, there is a complicated cobweb of life lines showing the child's life situation in a concrete and visual way. At this stage, dolls are usually fastened to the line, using string. A doll is used for each significant family member, as well as for people with whom parents have formed new relationships. Various situations can then be played out. To illustrate how children can get caught up in conflict between parents, the dolls can be manipulated so that the rope of the child doll gets mixed up with those of the parents. In some interviews, a whole new language develops that symbolises the problems. Clients tend to talk of knots instead of problems and usually understand that where the knots are uncomplicated, they can sort them out on their own. Sometimes, however, they need the help of a "knot-doctor" (the therapist) to help them to straighten things out.

To give the child perspective on the future, the empty washing line, portraying the future, is discussed. The child gains the insight that the future will also hold disruption in the form of changes, such as moving house. There will also be sad times, but the experience of compiling the life line has shown that sadness does not persist for ever. According to the example of the life line, it is clear that sad times and happy times fluctuate. The child should be led to understand that he should not be paralysed by the divorce, but that he should work actively to adapt.

Usually, this is a good time to discuss the child's future relationships. He should realise that marital relationships cannot be broken at random, just because his parents got divorced. Through this technique, the child usually acknowledges the complexity of relationships and sees that it takes a great deal of emotional energy to keep them going.

The diagram by Graver and Morse (1986:82) as seen in figure 13.1 may be used therapeutically. During counselling, children can draw feeling faces on this chart. It can also be used in the beginning and final phases of counselling to formulate goals and to discuss progress. It is necessary to inform the child that he can proceed from one step to the next within a few hours. The working out of grief is therefore not necessarily a long process. Discussing this should prevent the complexity of the chart from discouraging the child.

There are several effective techniques that are part of dramatic play and that are especially suitable for use in the change-oriented phase. **The Talking, feeling and doing game** (Gardner, 1986:41-72) has dramatic elements, especially in the doing part. The questions in this game can be adapted for use with young children in a divorce situation.

The **Could this happen? game** was designed by Epstein (1986:173-176) especially for group therapy with children in a divorce situation. It can be adapted for individual counselling, however. Hypothetical situations regarding divorce are put to the child. He has to choose between four possible alternatives.

Finger puppets are used with success with this target group. The therapist uses them to dramatise situations similar to those the child is experiencing.

Creative play also offers many possibilities. The pain-pain better technique (Mills & Crowley, 1986:174-180) was initially used for children experiencing physical pain. From there, it was adapted for use in therapy with children with a variety of other problems. This technique comprises the child being asked to draw his pain concerning the divorce. Then he must express in drawing what would help to make the pain better. Although this seems like an abstract instruction, experience has shown that children do not find it difficult to do this. One child expressed his pain in the form of a drawing of his absent father who lived far away. He drew the father surrounded by empty wine bottles. Then he drew himself on an aeroplane on his way to his father. He said that this portrayed the action that would make his pain better. Another child drew her pain in the form of a face with tears streaming into a big river. She drew the mother's new friend as the object that made her pain better.

In this way, children are given the opportunity to bring their feelings out into the open. They start to think about alternative ways of handling their pain. Misconceptions can also be discussed. In the latter example mentioned above, the therapist and the child discussed that it was a big risk to pin her hopes on a person who was possibly only a temporary part of her life.

When the child sees his pain in a concrete form on a piece of paper, he seems to distance himself from his problems and may even feel more in control. By asking him to draw something that can make the pain better, the therapist implies that the pain can become better. Metaphorically, a bridge is then built from discomfort to a more comfortable situation (Van der Merwe, 1991:211).

The **Draw a family/story technique** (Roosa, 1981:270-272) entails the child drawing each family member, identifiable by their names. He is then asked to tell a story about each family member's action in the drawing. Then he can cut them out, rearrange them and tell other stories about them.

Another way of discussing the child's feelings concerning family members is to ask him to draw his family in symbols (Oaklander, 1988:26-30). He can then discuss his choices. A child once drew her father, with whom she had a stressful relationship, as a lemon because he was always angry and irritable.

Playing with clay gives the child the opportunity to use primitive play material to work through his feelings. It can be used in combination with drawings of the child's environment. He can make clay figures of significant people and then move these around on one or more drawings of houses, for instance, the houses of his two parents. One child covered dolls depicting himself, his parents and the father's new friend with a thick clay blanket. Very subtly, he then moved the friend out. This reflected his strong wish for reconciliation and his problems regarding acceptance of his father's new relationship. It seemed as if he wanted his family as it used to be.

Final phase

In the final phase of therapy, the focus is, to a great extent, on process goals. Assessment play and relaxation play are used mostly at this stage. It is necessary to prepare the child to cope with his problems without the help of the therapist. He should be able to use and identify relevant support systems. The child in a divorce situation may experience loss negatively, making it especially important to handle the losses involved in the termination of therapy with care.

Hepworth and Larsen (1982:510) have identified several tasks that must be accomplished to help the child with the transition from being a client to being on his own, namely:

- ❏ A decision must be taken when to implement termination.
- ❏ Emotions commonly experienced during the process of separation should be mutually resolved.
- ❏ The therapy and the extent to which goals were attained should be evaluated.
- ❏ Plan should be made to consolidate the gains of therapy, while change maintenance strategies should be planned.

The last interview must be used effectively. Therapy is expensive and it is important to use time constructively. It is important to have an open door policy regarding follow-up therapy.

Conclusion

Children in a divorce situation are expected to work through the divorce, handling the tasks that Wallerstein (1983:230-243) has identified, namely:

- ❏ **Task 1:** Accept the reality of the marital disintegration.
- ❏ **Task 2:** Learn to stand objectively regarding parental conflict and to resume own concerns.
- ❏ **Task 3:** Handle the losses that divorce brings about.
- ❏ **Task 4:** Handle anger and feelings of guilt and self-reproach.
- ❏ **Task 5:** Accept the permanence of the divorce.
- ❏ **Task 6:** Develop realistic hope regarding future relationships.

These tasks must be mastered together with the usual developmental tasks. This is a tall order for children. Person-directed, goal-directed help will enable them to work through these tasks as soon as possible. They can then resume their usual development. As divorce brings about feelings that recur at different developmental stages, the counselling should also help the child to develop coping skills to enable him to handle future problems.

The forms of play discussed offer the child the opportunity to vent his feelings and to understand the changes in his life situation by playing in a safe, non-threatening way in a sheltered environment. This enables him to reorganise his life. The techniques mentioned offer a practical way of helping the child to bridge his problems at his own level and at his own pace.

Bibliography

Dennison, S.T. & Glassman, C.K. 1987. *Activities for children in therapy: A guide for planning and facilitating therapy with troubled children.* Illinois: Charles C. Thomas.

Epstein, Y.M. 1986. Feedback and Could this happen: Two therapeutic games for children of divorce. In Schaefer & O'Connor: 159-186.

Feldman, J. 1981. Divorce and the children. In Getty & Humphreys: 332-355.

Felner, R.D., Farber, S.S. & Primavera, J. 1980. Children of divorce, stressful life events and transitions: A framework for preventive efforts. In Price, Monahan, Bader & Ketterer: 91-99.

Gardner, R.A. 1986. The Talking, feeling, doing game. In Schaefer & Reid: 41-72.

Getty, C. & Humphreys, W. (Eds.). 1981. *Understanding the family: Stress and change in American family life.* New York: Appleton Century.

Goldman, R.K. & King, M.J. 1985. Counselling children of divorce. *School Psychology Review*, 14(3): 280-290.

Graver, C.M. & Morse, L.A. 1986. *Helping children of divorce: A group leader's guide.* Illinois: Charles C. Thomas

Hepworth, D.H. & Larsen, J.A. 1982. *Direct social work practice: Theory and skills.* Illinois: Dorsey Press.

Hess, R.D. & Camara, K.A. 1979. Post-divorce family relationships as mediating factors in the consequences of divorce for children. *Journal of Social Issues*, 35(4): 79-96.

Hetherington, E.M. 1979. Divorce: A child's perspective. *American psychologist*, 34(10): 851-858.

Hetherington, E.M., Cox, M. & Cox, R. 1979. Play and social interaction in children following divorce. *Journal of Social Issues*, 35(4): 26-47.

Kelly, J.B. & Wallerstein, J.S. 1976. The effects of parental divorce: Experience of the child in early latency. *American Journal of Orthopsychiatry*, 46(1): 20-32.

Mills, J.C. & Crowley, R.J. 1986. *Therapeutic metaphors for children and the child within.* New York: Brunner Mazel.

Muncy, P.T. 1985. *Springboards to creative thinking.* New York: Centre for Applied Research in Education.

Nichols, W.C. 1984. Therapeutic needs of children in family system reorganization. *Journal of Divorce*, 7(4): 23-44.

Oaklander, V. 1988. *Windows to our children: A gestalt therapy approach to children and adolescents.* (2nd ed.). New York: The Gestalt Journal Press. Inc.

Price, R.H., Monahan, J., Bader, B.C. & Ketterer, R.F. (Eds.). 1980. *Prevention in community mental health: Research, policy and practice.* Beverley Hills: Sage Publications.

Roosa, L.W. 1981. The family drawing/storytelling technique: An approach to assessment of family dynamics. *Elementary School Guidance and Counseling*, 15(3): 269-272.

Schaefer, C.E. & O'Connor, K.J. (Eds.). 1983. *Handbook of play therapy.* New York: John Wiley.

Schaefer, C.E. & Reid, S.E. (Eds.). 1986. *Game play: Therapeutic use of childhood games.* New York: John Wiley.

Smith, C.M. 1981. *Leer die kind ken: Riglyne vir die maatskaplike werker.* Pretoria: Academica.

Van der Merwe, M. 1991. Maatskaplikewerk-beraad met jong kinders in egskeidingsituasies met fokus op speeltegnieke. Unpublished MA thesis. Stellenbosch: University of Stellenbosch.

Van der Merwe, M. 1994. A social work moderl for short-term intervention with young children of divorce. *Social Work Practice*, 2(94): 10-15.

Wallerstein, J.S. & Kelly, J.B. 1979. Children and divorce: A review. *Social Work*, 24(6): 468-475.

Wallerstein, J.S. & Kelly, J.B. 1980. *Surviving the breakup: How children and parents cope with divorce*. New York: Basic Books.

Wallerstein, J.S. 1983. Children of divorce: The psychological tasks of the child. *American Journal of Orthopsychiatry*, 53(2): 230-243.

Index

A
active play therapy, 185
adopted children, 113, 117
aggression, 38, 154, **171–183**
   acknowledging, 176–177
   agreeing with, 177
   and creative play, 51, 147
   apologising for, 177
   dealing with, 174–181
   expressing and containing, 176, 178
   in children's drawings, 141, 142, 143
   needs regarding, 172–174
   pitfalls in handling, 181–182
   reasons for, 173–174
   working model, 175–181
AIDS, 160, 165
alcohol abuse, 99, 155, 156
anger, *see aggression*
animals
   in fantasy, 93
   see also pets
anti-social behaviour, 102
anxiety, 75
   in children's drawings, 74, 138
approaches
   client-centred, 185
   cognitive, 43
   goal-directed, 13, 61, 126, 169, 184, 185, 198
   person-directed, 184, 185, 198
   prescriptive, 185
   psychoanalytic, 89, 185
   relationship, 185
   social cognition, 172
   structured, 13, 61, 169
   see also Gestalt approach
aroma therapy, 46
artistic development, 75
art therapy, 138

assessment, 11, 93
   forms for use in, 105
   in biblio-play, 111, 126
   in creative play, 36, 139, 140
   of projections, 71–72
   phase of therapy, 189–194
   play, **98–107**, 197
assimilation, 55
audio-visual therapy, 108
awareness, 29, 35, 38, 45, 46, 54, 57
   as aim of therapy, 30–31
   exercises to enhance, 30
   in chairwork, 178
   of anger, 175–176
   on sensory awareness continuum, 52, 55

B
bataca, 176
belonging
   child's need for, 173
biblio-play, **108–127**, 148
   advantages of, 109–110
   limitations of, 110–111
   techniques and materials, 111–126
biblio-therapy, 108, 109, 194
breathing, 52, 75
bubble mixture
   recipe for, 50

C
caring days, 148
cartoon characters, 123
chair work, 69, 166, **178–180**
child client
   characteristics of, 3, **6–9**
   communication with, *see communiction*
children's drawings, 139–146
   and projection, 66, 72–75, 145–146

colour in, 141–142
content of, 72, 144
emphasis and omission of body parts in, 72, 73, 74, 143
environmental influences on, 144–145
erasure in, 144
gender as influence on, 72–73
genitalia in, 73, 143
integration of human figure in, 72, 144
interpretation of, 72, 140–146
  by child, 74–75
line quality in, 72, 142–143
shadows in, 72, 144
size of, 74, 142
space in, 142
transparency in, 72
children's homes, 117, 122, 131
children's stories, 86-94, 109, **111–116**, 123
  as songs, 45
  criteria for choice of, 90–94, 111–114
  fables, 72, 85, 86
  fairy tales, 85, 86
  folktales, 86
  forms and applications of, 115–116
  parables, 86
  phases in use of, 114–115
child therapist, *see therapist*
child within, 4, 9
Christianity, 93–94
clay work, 50–51, 69, 72, 138, 147, 176, 178, 197
clichés, 31–32
client role, 8
comic strips, 123
communication, 16, 19, 78
  conversation openers, 21
  improving, 20, 46, 81, 82
  neutral zone, 21
  non-verbal, 7, 19, 45, 52, 87, 93, 98
  resistance to, 32
  stumbling blocks in, 20
  symbolic, 86

  through body language, 21, 57
  through dramatising, 130
compulsive
  children who are, 102
computers, 108
computer games, 125–126
concentration, 54
concretisation, 89–90
confidentiality, 135, 180
confluence, 31–32, 72, 177
contact, 34, 54–57, 177
  see also sensory contact
contract, 62–63
corporeality, **48–51**, 53, 57
  exercise on, 49
counselling, *see therapy*
counter-transference, 4
creative movement, 129
creative play, 85, **138–149**, 168, 196
  advantages of, 138–139
  and biblio-play, 120
  media and art forms, 139–148
  to express anger, 178
criticism
  by child, 177–178
  role of therapist, 36, 180, 181
cultural groups, 113

D

death
  and telephone play, 135
  and time graphics, 120
dependency, 102
depression
  in children's drawings, 142
developmental phases, **65–67**, 98, 102, 153, 154
  and anger, 172
  and projection, 65–67
  artistic development, 75
  embodiment, 65
  exploration phase, 65

in symbolic play, 94–95
dialogue, 32, 179
diaries, 127
displacement
    as environmental influence, 141
    in life books, 117
divorce, 155, **184–200**
    and biblio-play, 117, 118, 120, 122
    and dramatic play, 128, 129, 132, 133, 135
    and street children, 161
    children's reactions to, **186–188**, 194
    factors influencing children's reactions to, 185–186
dolls, 132
dough
    recipe for, 50
dramatic play, 128–137
    advantages of, 128–129
    sequence of, 129–130
    techniques of, 130–136
Draw a family/story technique, 71, 146, 197
    see also games
Draw a person (DAP) test, 72
dreams, 38
    as fantasy, 96
    as projection, 70–71
    nightmares, 88
drug abuse, 99
    by street children, 159, 160, 163, 165, 166

E

ecomaps, 105, 147
ego, 89
egocentric
    children who are, 102
emotional barometer, **125**, 193
empathy, 11, 87-88, 177
empowerment
    guidelines for, 180–181
enactment, 178
    see also chair work

environmental influence, 141, 156, 163, 193, 198, 199
equilibrium, 33
external variables, *see environmental influence*

F

fables, 72
fair play therapy, 185
family disruption
    and creative play, 147
    and street children, 161
family drawing storytelling technique, 147
    see also Draw a family/story technique
fantasy, 7, 38, **85–97**, 99, 182
    and biblioplay, 123
    and dramatic play, 129, 132, 133, 134, 135
    and dreams, 94–95
    and gender, 95
    and music, 95
    and projection, 64–65, 70, 85
    and the secondary world, 85
    and the supernatural, 93–94
    play, 94–95
fears, 88–89
feeling faces, 52, 104, 191, 192
feeling language, 104, 106, 191–192
feelings, 52–53
finger paint, 176
    recipe for, 51
foster care, 117
freedom
    as need of a child, 172, 180
fun
    as aim of therapeutic relationship, 34
    as characteristic of therapist, 7
    as need of child, 172
    importance of in therapy, 23, 26, 78, 81, 106, 124, 129, 134, 160, 164, 169
    with parents, 25

G

games
  bag games, 100-101
    Bag of Things game, 100
    Bag of Toys game, 100
    Bag of Words game, 100–101
  board games, 98–100
    Board of Objects game, 95 98–99
    Don't talk to strangers, 99–100
    Ungame, 99
  Checkers, 101–102
  Could this happen? game, 196
  Draw a story game, 81
    for relaxation, 81
  Giant's treasure, 44
  musical hats ormats, 45
  musical chairs, 45
  Talking, feeling, doing game **130–132**, 196
  to enhance sensitivy to sound, 44
  True-false exercise, 51
  Yes-no exercise, 51
genograms, 119
gestalt, 37
  unity of, 36–37, 57, 70, 172, 173, 183
Gestalt approach, 4, **29–40**, 42, 52, 165
Gestalt therapy, 29, 38, 165, 167
  and relationships, 33
goals
  content, 61–62
  formulation of, 8, 61, 194
  process, 61–62, 77, 78
  see also approaches, goal-directed
group therapy, *see therapy group*
guardianship, 33

H

handicrafts, 147–148
healing, 29
hearing, 43–45
  problems, 143
helping network, *see support systems*
homeostasis, 55

cycle, 56
house-tree-person test, 71, 145–146
humility, 33
humour, 92
hyperactivity, 54

I

icebreakers, 102, 106, 190
imagination, 85–97
inclusion, 32
incomplete sentences, 119, 124
individualisation, 62, 78, 91–92, 129, 180, 184
information
  supplying child with, 33–34
introjection, 37, 166
intuitive perceptions, 51–52

L

laughter
  as therapeutic tool, 34
learning problems
  as indicated in children's drawings, 74
letters, 124
life books, **117–120**, 120, 122, 148
life lines, 194–196
life–stories, 109
  dramatisation of, 132
limits, *see therapy, limits in*
line drawings, 102–104
listening, 11, 20
  to anger of child, 176, 180
literacy programs, 165
live silhouette, 67

M

mad sessions, 180
magazines, 52, 71, 122–123
masks, **136**, 148
metaphor
  as therapeutic medium 87, 178
  fantasy as, 85–97
  for street children, 166

in biblioplay, 134
in creative play, 139
in dramatic play, 134
in games, 100
in music, 78
in puzzles, 83, 84
reactions to, 94
mime, 53
monsters, 52, 66, 68–69
morality, 90
music, **44–45**, 122
and aggression, 176
and fantasy, 95
and street children, 164
for relaxation play, 77–79
mutual storytelling technique, 116–117

O

open-door policy, 198
organismic indigestion, 38, 68
organismic self-regulation, 67, 68, 179

P

pain, 48
pain ladder, 48, 49
pain-pain better technique, 196
paranoid
  children who are, 102
passive
  children who are, 102
peer group pressure, 100
  on street children, 161
permissiveness, 8
pets, 13, 82, 173
phototherapy, 120
physical abuse
  assault, 162
  incest, 161
  neglect, 161
  rape, 162
  sexual molestation, 76, 99
physical contact, 21, **47–48**
picture completion, 102–104

pictures, 122–123
play
  forms of, 12, 61, 63, 129, 164, 185, 189
  materials, 12
    choice of, 14, 50–51
    controversial, 13
play therapy, *see therapy*
poetry, 53, 121
polarities, 35–36, 168, 178
poles of distinction, 35
  see also polarities
Post Traumatic Stress Disorder, 153, 154
posture, 52, 75
poverty, 161, 163
power
  child's need for, 173
presence, 32
present
  as focal point of therapy, 34–35
  in projection, 67
projection
  aids, 71–72
  and normal development, 65–67
  and unfinished business, 68–69, 70, 71–72, 73, 75
  assessment of, 71–72
  definition of, 64
  goals and objectives of, 67–70
  in biblioplay, 110, 114, 115, 123, 124
  in chair work, 178
  in creative play, 141–143
  nature of, 64–65
  reasons for, 70
  techniques, 61, **64–76**, 145–146
projective play, 65
projective tests, 71
prostitution
  by street children, 159, 162
puppets, **132–134**, 165, 190, 196
puzzles
  for relaxation, 80–81
  used metaphorically, 81

R

relaxation
  definition of, 53
relaxation play, **77–84**, 197
  techniques of
    aromatherapy, 46
    breathing exercises, 54
    games, 80, 81, 125–126
    progressive muscle relaxation, 77, **79–80**
    systematic desensitisation, 77, 80
reserved
  children who are, 102
resistance, 24, **167–168**
  in communication process, 32
road maps, 122
role-playing, 37, 130

S

self
  sensory experience of, 53
self-acceptance, 68
self-descriptions, 121
self-growth, 67
self-hood, 36
self-image
  in children's drawings, 74
  problems with, 31, 102, 183
  rebuilding, 35, 36, 168–169
self-knowledge, 89, 92
self-nurturing, 180
self-regulation, *see organismic self-regulation*
self-statements, 67
self-support, 67, 167, 176
senses, 42–51
sensory contact, 4, **41–57**
sensory level
  assessment of, 53
sensory modalities, 4
sensory tactile stimulation, **49–51**, 71, 176
sexual abuse, *see physical abuse*

shoplifting
  by street children, 159
sight, 42–43
significant others, 23, 25
smell, **45–46**, 47, 71, 176
social learning hypothesis, 172
street children, 154, **157–170**
  causal factors regarding, 160–162
  definition of, 158
  prevention of, **163**, 164
  push and pull factors regarding, 162–163
  shelters for, 163–164
  street workers for, 164
  therapeutic programs for, 164–167
suicide
  attempts by street children, 160–165
support systems, 82, 104, 165
  peer group as, 167
  self-support, 67, 167, 176
suspicious
  children who are, 102
symbolic play, 65, 85, **94–96**

T

taste, 46–47, 176
telephone play, 135
temperature, 47–48
therapeutic milieu, 4, 14, 88
therapeutic relationship
  building of, 125
  continuity of, 23
  objectives of, 29, **30–39**
  objectivity in, 22
  responsibility in, 36
  stablising, 30
  trust in, 83, 109
therapist
  aims of, 29–30, 34
  characteristics required by, **9–11**, 38, 39
  role of, 9, 11, 17, 24, 33, 36, 171, 181–182, 183

theraplay, 185
therapy
   components of, 3, **6–28**, 168
   group, 3, 61, 120, 130, 133, 196
   limits in, 7, 15, 17
   obstacles in, 23, 31, 37, 38, **167–169**
   process of, 189–198
   termination of, 8
third–object techniques, 20, 108, 124
time, 31, 181
time graphics, 120–121
topdog/underdog technique, *see chair work*
transference, 24, 37
   see also counter-transference
trips and outings, 81–82

U

unemployment, 163
unfinished business, 37–38
   expressed as violence, 38
   expressed through projections, 68–69, 70, 71–72, 73, 75

V

violence, 38
   and creative play, 147
   as environmental influence, 141, 163
   in children's drawings, 142
   in life books, 117

W

warm fuzzies, 148